College Financial Aid

College

Financial Aid

Highlighting the Small Print of Student Loans

Carol Jensen

ACE Continuing Education

Copyright © 2014 by Carol A. Jensen

Published by ACE Continuing Education

Printed in the United States of America

ISBN 978-0-9889171-0-1

Cover art: Dreamstime.com

Cover design, interior design, and typesetting by Leigh McLellan Design

Preliminary editing by Marcy Protteau

Copyediting by Elissa Rabellino

*For my grandchildren,
whom I envision will someday be college students.*

Contents

Acknowledgments		ix
Introduction		xi
1	Subtle Changes	1
2	Simplifying Financial Aid and Student Loans	27
3	The Undercurrent	65
4	Cost of Attendance and Free Application for Federal Student Aid	87
5	Comparing Federal and Private Student Loan Options	123
6	Federal Student Loans	147
7	The Credit Report: A Report Card for Life	171
8	Private Student Loans	183
9	Hypothetically Speaking	207

Appendix A	Financial Aid Shopping Sheet	213
Appendix B	FAFSA Form—English Version	215
Appendix C	FAFSA Form—Spanish Version	225
Appendix D	Private Education Loan Applicant Self-Certification Form	235

Glossary	237
Select Bibliography	249
About the Author	265

Acknowledgments

I AM FOREVER grateful to the college financial aid counselors who agreed to be interviewed anonymously in 2008. Their candid responses and the details of their student loan counseling practices are invaluable. Their front-line experiences ignited the beginning thoughts for this book.

As luck would have it, or some may call it fate, I received royalties from a book publishing company at a time when I had never written a book. After searching online, I was able to find the author and the rightful owner of that royalty check, another Carol A. Jensen. I accepted that whole experience as one more sign that I should give some serious thought to writing a book. To mutual acquaintances, she is Carol SF and I am Carol IA. Because of that publisher's confusion, I gained a mentor who has gone above and beyond to help me in this process.

I thank all of the students and families who have shared their financial aid challenges and their college loan experiences along the way. Their real-life stories gradually led me toward this book. The graduate student who took my finance course in 2012, and is quoted in this book's introduction, is the one who finally sealed the deal. The passion in that message convinced me that it was time.

Carol SF introduced me to the book's designer, Leigh McLellan, and they were the ones who recommended my copy editors, Marcy

Protteau and Elissa Rabellino. They have all patiently guided me through the details of writing a book, and I sincerely thank them.

I thank Dr. Dana L. Miller from Doane College for her guidance in preparing me to conduct meaningful research, and I thank Dr. Donald L. Uerling, the chairman of my doctoral committee at the University of Nebraska–Lincoln. The results of my study on private student loan counseling were much more than I ever imagined and nothing like what I expected.

Introduction

We do advise students in our orientation session and when we meet with families that they should really review loans, the small print, and encourage them to look at all their options and compare their options before making a decision. —Financial aid counselor, 2008

STUDENT LOANS play a very large role in higher education. The combination of rising college costs, the shrinking purchasing power of federal and state grant aid, and difficult economic times continues to make loans a prominent feature of financial aid packages and college award letters. In the United States, much of higher education is funded through loans, obtained by students and their families and viewed as an investment rather than a basic right. As a result, college students and their families can incur high debt levels. According to the Consumer Financial Protection Bureau (CFPB), student loan debt has reached an excess of $1.2 trillion and continues to increase, making it the largest consumer debt class in the United States, after home mortgages (Nelson 2013).

There are no guarantees of college students earning a college degree even when they and their parents have borrowed money to invest in college and are eventually faced with repaying those loan amounts, with interest. A report issued in 2011 by the nonprofit group

Complete College America shows that many college students never earn their college degree (Lewin 2011). *The American Dream 2.0*, a 2012 report funded by the Bill & Melinda Gates Foundation, identified that today's financial aid structure and delivery is based on enrollment, and it is not based on obtaining a college degree (HCM Strategists 2012). Most students attend college for at least six years, and even then only 55 percent get their degree. The national trend in American higher education has some 400,000 students dropping out of college every year, incurring debt, and having no degree to show for it (Selingo 2013).

I began a career in banking in the early 1980s and have been able to maintain a front-row seat while watching the financial crises shift from agriculture to housing to college student loans. In the past five years in banking, in particular, I have seen steady increases in the sheer number of student loans and in the total amount of college debt. There are more consumers with negative-net-worth statements, due mainly to their total student loan debt.

The bank I work for is not a direct student loan lender, in either federal or private student loans. It is likely to encounter student and parent loans when consumers are applying for other types of loans, such as car or house loans, and their college loans are verified on a credit report and included in a repayment ratio analysis. In addition, bankers who do not offer unsecured student loans can become involved in both federal and private student loans when they are asked to help applicants navigate through the current financial aid process and when searching for college financing alternatives. Whenever that situation occurs, I often ask general financial questions about their existing college loans, such as loan amounts, interest rates, whether the interest rates are fixed or variable, and the maturity dates. Very few borrowers know the answers to those basic loan questions. They typically know a monthly payment amount, but only if the loan is already in repayment mode. There are also people who do not know that they have college debt until it is verified on a credit report under their Social Security number; they do not realize that their financial aid awards were actually neatly packaged loans and do not remember signing or accepting any loan offers.

The lack of basic understanding and the overall confusion that students have regarding their own college debt is discouraging, especially considering that paying for a college degree could be the second-largest investment they will make in their lifetime, after their house. This, along with the fact that Iowa was the state ranked first in the nation in 2007 for having the highest average student debt (The Project on Student Debt 2008), led me to conduct a study, while attending the University of Nebraska–Lincoln, to identify the loan counseling practices of college financial aid counselors. Congress mandates exit counseling for federal loan borrowers and entrance counseling for first-time college students obtaining federal Perkins, Stafford, and Graduate PLUS Loans; colleges help in the process (Jensen 2008). Parents (and their creditworthy cosigners) can borrow up to 100 percent of college costs with a federal Parent PLUS Loan; however, they are not required to attend any loan counseling. Federal student loan counseling is mandated only for college students, and it is offered both in person and online.

> *You know, the Internet's their life. It's not unusual for them to do everything online. But, online it is very easy not to read any of it and just click: Yes, I agree. Yes, I've read it, and go on.* —Financial aid counselor, 2008

The 2008 study targeted private student loans and involved interviews with college financial aid counselors in 12 Midwestern states to determine how they counseled undergraduate students on private student loans at four-year public and four-year nonprofit private colleges and universities (for-profits were not included in the study). Few researchers have interviewed front-line financial aid counselors prior to this study. Their insights provide us with a view of college financial aid counseling that has been seen by few others. Their candid responses are printed verbatim and are quoted in **_bold italic_** throughout this book.

The Department of Education has no jurisdiction over private student loans, and no private loan counseling is required for students and their creditworthy cosigners (typically the parents, and more recently the grandparents) to be able to obtain up to 100 percent financing for college costs through private student loans. According to the results of the 2008 study, any private loan counseling that is provided by college financial aid counselors could be considered voluntary and a value-added service. While I had envisioned many ways in which college students were possibly being counseled by financial aid counselors on private loans, it never occurred to me that colleges would not be responsible to provide any type of private student loan counseling for the private loans that they package or certify.

> **_Our students who are borrowing only private loans, who have not even elected to fill out a FAFSA form and seek federal loans, really aren't getting any counseling whatsoever._**
> —Financial aid counselor, 2008

A 2012 survey, conducted by National Economic Research Associates (NERA) and Young Invincibles (YI), found that more than 40 percent of students with federal loans believed that they had not received any kind of financial counseling, either online or in person (Whitsett and O'Sullivan 2012; Lorin 2012; Owens 2012). How could that be possible, since Congress mandates entrance and exit counseling for students obtaining federal loans? Did students just click "Yes, I've read it" and forget that they attended online?

Just prior to the publication of the 2012 NERA and YI survey results, I finished teaching a finance course for graduate students. The following testimony is from a college student who took the course and who also happened to work in a college financial aid office. It was a "light bulb" moment that explains why 40 percent of college students may not have received federally mandated loan counseling, why many people may never fully understand their college loan obligations under the current financial aid structure, and the immediate need for college students (along with their parents, grandparents, and any other creditworthy cosigners) to educate themselves about student loans and the long-term consequences of repaying that debt, even if they do not want to. At the time, this quote was simply a posting within a weekly online course discussion. For our benefit, the financial aid employee agreed to share this on an anonymous basis.

> One would think with so many entities and individuals (Department of Education, lenders, guarantors, high school counselors, financial aid counselors, parents, students themselves) assisting students with applying to and choosing a college, program of study, completing scholarship applications and the FAFSA application, all parties could work together on educating students on student loans and debt. Students should not have to seek out this information. It should be readily available and be part of the senior year, applying for college, attending college, paying for college, the graduating college experience. No one wants to take on this responsibility, including the student. A 30-minute entrance counseling interview is not working, and neither is the exit counseling interview, which is regulatory, but only for the schools.
>
> The Department of Education requires financial aid departments to notify a student that they must complete an exit counseling interview when they drop below half-time, stop attending, or apply for graduation. The exit [interview] is to counsel the student on their loan debt, repayment options, etc. Schools have 30 days to notify students. If students have not completed

> the counseling, schools are required to notify the student again. However, the student is not required to complete the counseling. The Department of Education requires this of schools, and if not in compliance, schools can receive negative findings during an audit. This seems a bit backwards to me. Why not require students to actually complete it? Isn't something better than nothing at this point? We used to require students here to complete an exit [interview] prior to receiving their second loan disbursement. If not completed, we would not release their funds. We received a negative audit finding, as we were advised we could not hold up their funds for not completing the exit requirement.
> —College graduate student and financial aid employee, 2012

Along with identifying many of the disjointed players in the current financial aid structure, this testimony supports the idea that colleges are able to satisfy a federal mandate requiring federal student loan exit counseling by simply notifying students that they must attend. According to this financial aid employee, federal loan counseling is ineffective, and even if it were effective, college students cannot be required to complete an exit counseling interview that includes information on their federal student loan repayment terms, the consolidation options, and the consequences of defaulting on payments.

A *bit* backward? Federal student loan debt currently exceeds $1 trillion, and that amount does not include parent borrowing or credit card debt used for college costs (Denhart 2013). The Federal Reserve Bank of New York estimates that more than 30 percent of borrowers who have begun repaying their loans are at least 90 days behind. The U.S. Department of Education reported that the 2012 combined default rate on federal loans for public colleges, private nonprofit schools, and for-profit colleges during the first three years that students are required to make payments was 13.4 percent (Hechinger and Lorin 2012). To be included in the default tally, a federal student loan payment has to be over 270 days (nine months) past due. The

13.4 percent default rate on student loans is higher than default rates for credit cards, auto loans, first-mortgage loans, second-mortgage loans, and payday loans (Coy 2012).

In August 2012, the CFPB reported that the federal government eventually collects over 90 percent of the federal student loan dollars that have gone into default. After adjustment for the time and costs involved in collecting these loans, however, the U.S. Department of Education expects the total cost of default to be about $38 billion for federal student loans issued in 2012–2013. U.S. taxpayers are paying those bills.

Students are encouraged by teachers, peers, high school counselors, lenders, guarantors, coworkers, admissions counselors, financial aid counselors, the Department of Education, their parents, their grandparents, and many other family members to attend college. This is when all entities are working in sync, leading students to enroll in college. Some lenders are willing to loan 100 percent of college costs on an unsecured basis; few of those same lenders would loan 100 percent for a secured house purchase. Colleges are packaging and *awarding* students and their parents up to 100 percent in loans so that students can pay a college's cost of attendance (COA); no cash down payment is required.

Federal Student Aid, a part of the U.S. Department of Education, is the largest provider of federal financial aid in the nation. They provide more than $150 billion in federal grants, federal student loans, and federal work-study funds each year to more than 15 million students paying for college or career school. Private (alternative) student loans are nonfederal loans, made by a lender such as a bank, credit union, state agency, or school. Total annual student borrowing has more than doubled over the last 10 years (HCM Strategists 2012). Of the $1.2 trillion in total student loan debt, an estimated $1.035 trillion is in federal student loans (Chopra 2013b). Regardless of whether or not college students graduate, private lenders and the federal government lend money for college to students and to their creditworthy parents and cosigners. When students fail to complete a college degree or borrowers default on their federal student loans, taxpayers owe money on the failed investment.

College students are encouraged to get a degree in order to gain the skills necessary to survive in a competitive job market and to be able to gain financial independence. In reality, some college students are borrowing too much money, losing their financial independence, and taking their parents and other creditworthy cosigners right along with them. In a 2003 interview, Mark Oleson, then director of Iowa State University's financial counseling clinic, said, "Free financial counseling clinics available on college campuses are typically used by students who are already in trouble" (Jerousek 2003).

Subtle changes in the college financial aid process have added to the overall confusion that is perceived by many college students and their families. Student debt has become an anxiety issue for students and families. According to a CNN Money report that included a Fidelity survey of 750 college graduates, members of the class of 2013 are graduating with an average $35,200 in college-related debt (Ellis 2013). More than 10 million people under 30 years old have student loans, and many of them are so overwhelmed by their debt that they choose to ignore it (Golden 2013).

There is currently no one-stop shop where students and families can obtain all college financial aid information and then decipher the differences between available options. This book offers financial guidance to college students, parents, grandparents, cosigners, and anyone investing in college (either directly or indirectly); provides borrowing limits and financial literacy tips to help students and parents protect their financial independence while paying for college; and highlights many of the differences in the small print of federal and private student loans.

1 Subtle Changes

I'm finding so many of the parents don't want to take out a parent loan for the students. They don't want their name on the loan for the student. They don't want to be, I don't know if it's that they don't want to be bothered, or saddled or, you know, whatever, but a lot of our families have indicated that the kid can go to school, but they're going to do it on their own. They're not going to get help from the parents. Now many of our parents are not like that, but a lot of them are. So the student really has no recourse but to go the alternative [private] loan route. And then they run into obstacles because they generally have to have a cosigner. And the parent doesn't want to cosign. So a lot of our students are really caught. I feel sorry for them, I truly do. —Financial aid counselor, 2008

CURRENTLY, almost 9 in 10 young adults graduate from high school, and about 6 in 10 high school seniors go on to college the following year (Longley 2010). Some 50 million Americans now have a student loan, slightly more than the number of people on Medicare and almost as many as receive Social Security benefits; $110 billion in student loans was borrowed in 2011 alone (Selingo 2013). There was an additional $20 billion in new student loan debt in the first quarter of 2013 (Gongloff 2013). The student loan debt tally does not include the balances on home equity loans and credit cards used for college costs. Student loan debt is growing at a much faster rate than other forms of consumer credit—up 20 percent between the end of 2011 and May 2013 (O'Shaughnessy 2013).

The cost of a college degree in the United States has increased 12-fold over the past 30 years. The escalation of college costs has outpaced the price inflation of consumer goods, medical expenses, and food. Medical expenses climbed 601 percent while the price of food increased 244 percent over the same period. According to *Bloomberg*, college tuition and fees have increased 1,120 percent since records began in 1978 (*Huffington Post* 2012). Throughout the past three decades, the average cost of tuition (without room and board) at public four-year colleges has increased by more than 250 percent, while incomes for typical families grew by 16 percent, according to College Board and Census data. Private universities had significant price increases during this same time period (Jaschik 2013).

Students and parents apply for federal financial aid by completing the Free Application for Federal Student Aid (FAFSA) form (Federal Student Aid n.d.-a). Schools must be accredited to be eligible to participate in federal student aid programs. There are nonaccredited colleges that compete for students right along with accredited colleges and universities. Accreditation confirms that the college or career school meets certain minimum academic standards, as defined by an accrediting body recognized by the U.S. Department of Education.

Students are turning to private loans because government programs, which typically have more favorable terms, do not always provide enough money to pay for the cost of college. Federal student loan limits have also remained relatively stable in the past five years and have not kept pace with increasing college costs. The available options for both federal and private student loans have changed over time, and the reasons for the changes are numerous—among them, market changes, loan risk reassessments, and changes in laws and compliance. Here are some of the subtle changes that have happened with college financial aid and student loans since the time when parents of today's college students were their age:

1. More loans than grants are being obtained by students and their families to cover college costs.

   > *We do see an ever-growing population of our students whose parents come in with them as a freshman and say, "I went to college on the Pell Grant, and they'll have to do the same." Well, parents make too much money and students don't qualify for a Pell Grant. Even if they did, it won't pay their tuition. Tuition here is $6,700 for the year, and a full Pell is $4,700.* —Financial aid counselor, 2008

   > *Our cost of school this year is $25,864 for tuition, fees, room, and board. When parents went to school in 1986, for example, tuition, fees, room, and board at that time was $8,200. A whole lot more was covered with grants than loans in those days.* —Financial aid counselor, 2008

2. The ability for college students to qualify for private student loans on their own has virtually disappeared. Very few private lenders will finance 100 percent of a college's COA based on the student's signature alone. Now parents, creditworthy cosigners, and even some grandparents are sought out by college students to sign private loans to help them stay in school.

   > *Counseling is going to take up a whole new meaning compared to what it has in the past, and that's going to be,*

> "Mom and Dad, you're either going to have to cosign for this private loan or Johnny's not going to school."
> —Financial aid counselor, 2008

3. Financial aid counselors no longer recommend a specific private lender for students to obtain private loans. Many college counselors direct students to find their own private loans: search online; do their homework; read the small print; and compare interest rates, repayment terms, application fees, front-end fees, back-end fees, disbursement fees, prepayment penalties, and consolidation fees on their own.

> They just have to do their research and find the lenders that don't charge fees if they don't want to pay it.
> —Financial aid counselor, 2008

4. More college students now have monthly student loan payment amounts near those of home mortgages, but there is no house. The costs to attend college have increased, and students and their families have become comfortable in borrowing 100 percent or more of the costs in order to stay in school.

> The cost of education is so great that now you are talking about your student loan payments not equaling, say, a car payment but a house payment. So if you're going to attend a private university and have private loans filling the gaps for four years, you are going to have a payment, seriously, that is going to be equivalent to a house payment in many parts of the country. —Financial aid counselor, 2008

5. The current financial aid structure and competitive marketing strategies have made it difficult for college students and families

to identify loans and the differences between a federal student loan, a federal parent loan, and various private loans.

> *Deciphering student loan differences was just very difficult, and it was somewhat like trying to compare cell phone plans.* —Financial aid counselor, 2008

Many consumer loan borrowers do not fully understand the differences among their loan options, including the differences between federal and private (alternative) student loans, and this can result in unnecessary debt. In 2012, NERA reported on the results of a survey designed and conducted by YI that involved 27,000 high-debt borrowers, and two-thirds of the 13,000 respondents expressed misunderstanding or surprise about their student loans, particularly relating to repayment terms, monthly payments, and interest rates (Whitsett 2012). *Bloomberg Businessweek* notes that among high-debt borrowers who responded to a survey, recent undergraduate degree recipients had debt over $61,000, and debtors who completed a graduate program within five years owed about $161,000 (Owens 2012).

> *A big part of school loans these days is confusion. You know, what do I have, where do I have it, how much do I have, what's going on?* —Financial aid counselor, 2008

Variable-interest-rate loans were the norm during the 1980s, and few lenders offered fixed-interest-rate loan options at that time. There is currently a generation of college students, and some of their parents, who are too young to have experienced what it is like to manage monthly payments on loans having variable interest rates that increase when the market increases; however, college students and their parents are now handed variable interest rates as the main option for their federal student loans under Public Law 113-28—the

Bipartisan Student Loan Certainty Act of 2013. Fixed interest rates for federal Direct Stafford Loans for undergraduate, graduate, and professional students and Direct PLUS Loans for graduate students, professional students, and parents of dependent students are no longer offered on federal student loans since July 1, 2013, with the exception of the federal Perkins Loan that is available to undergraduate and graduate students with extreme financial need.

With the recent changes in federal student lending options, there is potential for more college students and parents to misunderstand the terms and conditions of their loans, especially when they have larger monthly loan payments because of a market increase in variable interest rates. Under Public Law 113-28—the Bipartisan Student Loan Certainty Act of 2013, new federal student loans now have variable interest rates calculated by adding a predetermined amount (an interest rate spread) to the 10-year Treasury rate index. Under the new law, the variable interest rates can change annually, and the maximum loan rates are capped at 8.25 percent for undergraduate students on subsidized and unsubsidized loans, 9.50 percent for graduate and professional students on unsubsidized loans, and 10.50 percent on PLUS loans for graduate students, professional students, and parents of dependent undergraduate students. Each variable cap rate is now greater than the fixed-rate category it replaced (Congressional Budget Office 2013).

Students and parents typically apply to consolidate their loans after the student leaves school (graduates, attends less than half-time, or drops out, for example). Loan consolidation allows students and parents with several federal student loans to obtain one loan with one interest rate and one monthly payment. For new Direct Consolidation Loan applications on or after July 1, 2013, the interest rate remains the weighted average of the interest rates (rounded up to the nearest ⅛ of 1 percent) on the federal loans that are being consolidated; however, the interest-rate cap protection has been eliminated under Public Law 113-28. The new law sets the foundation to allow federal Stafford and PLUS loans to be consolidated at an interest rate greater than the previous cap rate of 8.25 percent (Federal Student Aid n.d.-d).

Student loans are funded by a variety of sources, including federal and state government, and private lenders such as banks and credit unions. Various interest-rate options and loan fees are offered to consumers on student and parent loans obtained for college. While the majority of college students have federal student loans, private student loans are obtained by students and families when federal financial aid is not enough for the student to be able to stay in school, when they do not apply for federal financial aid, or when they decline federal financial aid.

According to the College Board, private student loan volume grew by 989 percent between 2000 and 2010 (Bissonnette 2010). There was $13.8 billion in private student loan volume as of 2005 (Lederman 2006), and private student loans were considered an essential tool for undergraduates to finance college (Burd 2006). During the interviews conducted in early 2008 with college financial aid counselors, private student loan volume was still increasing.

> *Our volume for private loans the past five years has gone up over 500 percent.* —Financial aid counselor, 2008

Due to the continued decline in the U.S. economy throughout 2008, the loss of jobs, and the increase in private student loan defaults, many private lenders reassessed their loan portfolio and loan approval criteria. This was a significant change that made it much more difficult for students to borrow money from private lenders on their own. Some private lenders left the private student loan business, which resulted in fewer lenders being willing to take the risk of making unsecured student loans. The remaining lenders started tightening their credit underwriting standards and began requiring creditworthy cosigners, lending primarily to students at schools having strong graduation and job placement rates, collecting interest while students were in school to limit debt upon graduation, and requiring collateral in some instances. Due to the heightened risks in these unsecured loans, students found themselves agreeing to some high-interest variable-rate loans to help pay their college costs; some students failed to read the small print.

> *We find that some of the loans are extremely high interest. I had a young man, oh golly, about two months ago, came in and asked me for help, and I said, "What's the problem?" and he said he took out an alternative loan, not knowing what he was doing, of course. Evidently, either his credit or his cosigner's credit was not very good because he ended up paying 24 percent on that loan. He said he received nothing in the mail that told him before, and he did not even know what the interest rate was. So that's something we really have tried to hit home on our website and so forth. You should never sign anything without first knowing how much interest you're going to be paying.* —Financial aid counselor, 2008

> *It's really hard to give a lot of information out to the student because a lot of times they don't know what the interest rate is going to be for them specifically until they are in the process of applying. So that's where we try to educate them to make sure you know what the interest rate is before you sign the master promissory note electronically.*
> —Financial aid counselor, 2008

The Ensuring Continued Access to Student Loans Act of 2008 increased the annual aggregate loan limits on federal Stafford Loans on July 1, 2008 (FinAid n.d.-d), shortly after the interviews were completed with college financial aid counselors. This shifted significant loan volume from private student loan programs back to federal student loans. Private student loan volume dropped in half in 2008–2009, according to the College Board's *Trends in Student Aid 2009* (College Board Advocacy & Policy Center 2009). However, private student loan volume is expected to return to a 25 percent annual growth rate unless there is another increase in federal loan limits or an expansion in federal student loan availability. As long as federal loan limits remain stagnant and many parents do not accept or do not qualify for the federal Parent PLUS Loans, private student loan volume is expected to continue to grow. If current trends continue, annual private education loan volume is expected to surpass federal student loan volume by around 2030 (Sourmaidis 2013).

Sallie Mae, the largest U.S. education-finance company and officially known as SLM Corporation, is preparing for the increase in private student loans. The market demand for securities backed by private student loans was 15 times greater than the supply in March 2013 (Simon, Ensign, and Yoon 2013). Sallie Mae announced in May 2013 that it would separate into two publicly traded companies, with completion expected by May 2014. The education loan management business would focus on serving federal student loans; the consumer banking business, named Sallie Mae Bank, would concentrate on the fast-growing business of making private loans (Agrawal 2013). Students are continuing to turn to private loans because government programs, which typically have more favorable terms, often do not provide enough money to pay for the increasing costs of college. Just as subprime mortgages led to the real-estate collapse, pre-2008 private student loans were easy to get and featured high rates that borrowers often could not afford, according to a 2012 report by the federal CFPB (Hechinger and Lorin 2013). By July 2013, private student loan debt was estimated at $165 billion and growing (Chopra 2013b).

What interest rate should private lenders charge to compensate their risk in offering unsecured private student loans? Most people would not feel confident lending any money to a typical college student, who only has to enroll in college, is not required to earn a degree, can major in almost anything, has no guarantee of future employment, and does not begin repaying the loan until about five years after starting college. The current default rate also suggests that about one-third of the borrowers will be late with their loan payments. According to the counselors in 2008, the interest rates on private student loans were tiered based on credit-risk formulas and the availability of cosigners; rates varied from 8.9 percent to 24 percent. Counselors did not identify whether the interest rates were fixed or variable, although many private student loans have variable rates for their lowest stated interest rates.

> *If a student has a good cosigner for the alternative loan, they might be able to get it for about 8.9 percent. And, if they have a poor cosigner or are trying to get in on their own, I've seen them as high as 15 percent.*
> —Financial aid counselor, 2008

> *I had a borrower who came in and said, "Send it back; I have a 12.5 percent interest rate." You know, so that's double what he would have been paying with a federal loan.*
> —Financial aid counselor, 2008

> *The repayment terms are generally the same, but the interest rates are, for lack of a better word, worse than the federal government interest rate. There are some students who had to pay a 21 percent loan back.* —Financial aid counselor, 2008

Many private lenders break their interest rates and fees into five tiers, based on the borrower's credit score. About 20 percent of the borrowers get the best rate, followed by 35 percent, 20 percent, 10 percent, and 15 percent in each of the lower tiers, respectively. Each tier of successively lower credit scores has an interest rate that is 1 percent to 2 percent higher than the previous tier. This results in borrowers with the worst credit scores having interest rates that are 5 percent to 6 percent higher than the interest rates charged to borrowers with excellent credit. The loan fees are also higher by as much as 9 percent, although some lenders roll higher fees into the interest rates. This means that borrowers with bad credit scores may have monthly payments that are 20 percent to 40 percent higher and may pay two-thirds to 100 percent more interest over the life of a comparable loan than borrowers with excellent credit scores (FinAid n.d.-a).

> *We had one the other day that was 19 percent. I just don't know what's going on. Most of the banks will tell us if they're in the first tier, you know, the good credit tier where the interest rates are reasonable. But it's when you get to the other ones, you know, when they're not so creditworthy—that's when they run into trouble.* —Financial aid counselor, 2008

Private lenders advanced their underwriting standards to include credit scoring and income ratios when assessing the loan repayment risk, fees, and interest rates for loans to applicants. While college students continued to look for private loans on their own, very few college students could qualify. This change alone is what required students to seek help from creditworthy parents or other cosigners.

> *It's going to be difficult for students to secure these loans, because most students who are going after private loans are going after them without cosigners.* —Financial aid counselor, 2008

> *The private lending community gained some additional sophistication in terms of their ability to assess credit risk.*

> *They can price the loan in such a way to offset the risk of loss. They began to operate more like other, more traditional consumer credit, like credit cards and other unsecured kinds of credit instruments.* —Financial aid counselor, 2008

> *The availability of a private loan without a cosigner for a student is next to impossible. They now have to find cosigners in order to even apply for a private loan.* —Financial aid counselor, 2008

Parents had mixed reactions when the loan underwriting change by private lenders resulted in the need for them to cosign loans and become more financially involved in their child's education. According to the counselors, there were still those students who really did not want to involve their parents because they thought they could still handle all of it on their own, and they wanted to maintain their lifestyle.

> *They're clueless…when you're 18 years old and you have no credit history, haven't borrowed any money, and don't know even how the world works, so to speak.* —Financial aid counselor, 2008

> *You know, there may also be some of the parents who are paying the bills, but the student could still borrow through the private loan program, all the way up to the total cost of attendance, including the entire family contribution. That is enabling them to live a higher lifestyle, a lifestyle that they see as being desirable. That's where we're trying to target a lot of our financial literacy efforts, to help them realize that every penny that they borrow while they're in school now is going to detract from what they're able to do once they*

graduate. Students feel it is just more convenient to not involve their parents in the process. —Financial aid counselor, 2008

The results of the 2008 financial aid counseling study support the idea that parents and college students are on their own when it comes to protecting their financial independence through the financial aid process. According to the financial aid counselors, there are also more college students who have no financial support from their parents.

1. College financial aid counselors hesitate to provide any counseling for students and families on their private student loans.

    This reaction by counselors stems from the results of the investigation completed in 2007 by New York Attorney General Andrew Cuomo concerning preferred (private) lenders bribing college employees and private lenders giving donations to schools in exchange for those colleges directing students toward their private loans. The findings resulted in New York's Student Lending Accountability Transparency and Enforcement (SLATE) Act. In April 2007, New York Assembly Speaker Sheldon Silver held a press conference to introduce the SLATE Act. Speaker Silver made it clear that he intended to "ensure that our SLATE legislation is thoughtful and tough without creating any unintended consequences.... No one can deny that this State needs well-educated workers in order to keep our economy growing and competitive. Therefore, our students should have access to the full range of education-funding options and not be steered, like cattle, to a handpicked collection of highly priced preferred lenders" (Assembly Speaker Sheldon Silver 2007). The SLATE Act led to the 2008 Higher Education Opportunity Act (HEOA), which increased federal regulations and heightened compliance requirements for colleges to operate under, including a strict code of conduct. As a result, financial aid counselors basically stopped recommending a particular private lender and hesitated to counsel students and families on private student loans (U.S. Department of Education 2008).

> *Now with Cuomo coming out, geez, you don't even want to recommend a lender. Five years ago I probably would have only been doing Partnership Loans. Not that I was not willing to do loans with other people, and not because they gave me a free pen, or not because, you know, at a conference I got a spaghetti dinner from them or anything like that. Quite honestly, I recommended the Partnership Loans five, six, seven years ago because they were just plain, the best damn loan out there, compared to private loans. Since Cuomo, we did create a sheet of paper. I don't like to call it a preferred lender list, because I don't really see it as a preferred lender list. We just say at the top, here are about 10 lenders we've had our students use in the past. And, hey, if students use other lenders, we'll add to them. We really only have about 10. That's what we've done.* —Financial aid counselor, 2008

2. When directly asked by students and families, college financial aid counselors may provide only general and very limited amounts of private loan information in an effort to avoid compliance violations and fines.

> *Because of changes in legislation, we can't direct them to a specific lender that we have found provides a lot of incentives for students. So, we're much more general in the information that we provide. Also some alternative loan lenders are not doing them as they have in the past. So that changes who we direct students to look for information from.* —Financial aid counselor, 2008

3. There are more parents who are unwilling to help pay their children's college costs.

> *Parents are unwilling to supply, unbelievable as it may seem, a dime to their student's education.* —Financial aid counselor, 2008

> *Parents tell children, "You're 18 and you're on your own; you're independent; you made your decision; we're not going to support you in that."* —Financial aid counselor, 2008

4. Colleges do not provide in-depth training for their financial aid counselors to be able to counsel students and families specifically on private student loans.

> *We need deeper training for our counselors so that we can speak more intelligently about all the different aspects of [private] lending rather than right now we're dealing with surface aspects when we explain interest rates and things like that.* —Financial aid counselor, 2008

5. College students do not bother to read all of the loan information that is provided online by colleges and lenders.

> *So much of it...they apply online. They're supposed to read all the terms and conditions, but how many 18-year-olds are really going to sit and read page after page of all that information? So they get into this [private] loan not realizing that they're going to pay 15 percent interest, that the interest starts day one.* —Financial aid counselor, 2008

The majority of information pertaining to college financial aid is available to students and families online: federal student loan entrance and exit counseling, private lender information and private student loans, state financial aid options, a college's COA, college financial aid award letters, the FAFSA, and a student's college account, just to name a few. Online access is the delivery method of choice for both lenders and colleges in order for them to supply compliant information. This also provides a consistent form of delivery with quick access for timely updates while working with limited resources. Online delivery gives students access to unlimited amounts of education-funding options, as the SLATE Act and HEOA intended, and holds students accountable for accessing their own information. The financial results after making college students find their own financing options, with limited or no guidance, could be considered an unintended consequence.

> *Let's say we've done business with 100 different lenders for [private] alternative loans. We can have those 100 different lenders available on this website, and then our students can just go in and select any different lenders from this list that they feel they may want to go with, and they can do their own comparisons.* —Financial aid counselor, 2008

> *I would argue the most effective private loan counseling is encouraging students to do their own research into the loan that they think is going to be best for them. I can equip them with key factors to look for when they're researching, like interest rate and fees, deferment options. But, by them researching their own loans, they have more of an understanding of what they're getting into and, I think, are more likely to stray from defaulting.* —Financial aid counselor, 2008

In August 2012, the CFPB reported specifically on college student loans. Here are some highlights on the results of the *Private Student Loans Report* (Consumer Financial Protection Bureau 2012):

1. Lenders of private student loans increased their share of loans that required signatures from both the college student and cosigners from 67 percent in 2008 to over 85 percent in 2009. In 2011, over 90 percent of private student loans were cosigned. Cumulative defaults on private student loans exceed $8 billion. Cosigners are equally responsible to repay private student loans that many students are no longer able to obtain on their own.
2. Many college students borrowed more than they needed to finance their education.
3. Ten percent of recent graduates of four-year colleges have monthly payments for all education loans in excess of 25 percent of their income.
4. By September 30, 2011, 9.1 percent of borrowers who entered repayment in 2009–2010 defaulted within those first two years of repayment on their student loans.
5. The federal government eventually collects over 90 percent of the federal student loan dollars that have gone into default. There is no statute of limitations on the collection of federal student loans.

Collecting Federal and Private Student Loans

Between 1982 and 2007, college tuition and fees rose three times as fast as median family income. In 2003, almost 70 percent of awarded federal student aid was student loans. Loan default rates have been increasing since 2007, in connection with the struggling U.S. economy. When the economy collapsed during 2008–2011, student loan defaults increased and additional loan repayment risks were identified.

Private lenders offer fewer options for loan deferments and repayment flexibility than the government offers through federal student loans. This makes it more difficult for students to change their private loan repayment terms during times of financial difficulty. Consumers who have private student loans may find that they have variable rates without an interest rate cap.

> *The [variable] interest rate was low; you could do interest only, or you could do that, or you could do whatever, and the payment was $1,200 a month. And they were like, WOW, I can afford this. Great! [Variable] rates go up and now it's $2,200 a month. I'm defaulting.* —Financial aid counselor, 2008

Federal student loans either have fixed interest rates or they have variable rates with interest rate caps. Federal student loan repayment plans include income-sensitive, income-contingent, pay-as-you-earn, extended, graduated, and standard repayment options. Federal student loans also offer deferment, cancellation, and forgiveness options. However, any loan balance that is forgiven or canceled is considered taxable income during the year the debt was discharged and is based on Internal Revenue Service (IRS) loan forgiveness rules (there are few exceptions). The creditor reports the amount they have forgiven on IRS tax form 1099c. The differences in repayment plans can be found online at http://studentaid.ed.gov/repay-loans/understand/plans#direct-and-ffel.

> *The federal loan programs protect the family to a greater extent.* —Financial aid counselor, 2008

In 1998, Congress changed the law to make it all but impossible to discharge federal student loans in bankruptcy court (Weston 2012). Then, in 2005, the bankruptcy reform law extended the protection to private student loans, which made it next to impossible for any federal and nonfederal (private) student loans to be discharged in bankruptcy (Consumer Reports 2013). The law requires proof of undue hardship, which usually means the borrower cannot maintain a minimal standard of living even without cable, Internet, or a cell phone. Debts such as credit card charges and medical bills can often be discharged in bankruptcy, but very seldom can federal or private student loans be discharged.

The *Chronicle of Higher Education* reported that 13.4 percent of borrowers who entered into student loan repayment during the 2009 fiscal year, or 489,040 people, defaulted within three years (Stratford 2012). In 2012, the Federal Reserve Bank of New York reported that more than a quarter of borrowers had past-due balances. In 2013, the Federal Reserve Bank of New York estimated that more than 30 percent of borrowers who had begun repaying their loans were at least 90 days behind.

In 2012, the U.S. Secretary of Education, Arne Duncan, showed concern about increasing default rates: "In addition to helping borrowers, we will also hold schools accountable for ensuring their students are not saddled with unmanageable student loan debt." Under the measurement of defaults during the first three years that students are required to make payments, colleges must have their loan default rates under 30 percent or risk losing eligibility for federal financial aid. Schools can also be barred from the program if the default rate balloons to 40 percent in a single year. Government data show that roughly 15 percent of students who attended for-profit schools defaulted on their loans in 2009 (Mui 2012). Three-year default rates for for-profit colleges were reported in 2012 at 22.7 percent. For-profit colleges could encourage students to defer payments in their early years, in an effort to reduce the default rates that might eventually jeopardize their federal funding, according to a July 2012 report by the Senate Committee on Health, Education, Labor and Pensions. For-profit colleges cater to working adults and first-generation college students (Hechinger and Lorin 2012).

Lenders of unsecured student loans have nothing to repossess when a student defaults on their loan(s). This poses a problem for debt collectors and affects the loan rates and terms that are offered to consumers. Lenders cannot repossess the knowledge that students gain from attending college. They cannot repossess the future earning power that is possible for students obtaining a college degree. College graduates earn 50 percent more than young adults who only complete high school (American Student Assistance n.d.).

Private lenders have fewer collection resources than the federal government has. Private student loans are part of consumer debt collection, much like unsecured credit cards. With the recent loan underwriting change requiring creditworthy cosigners, private lenders have a better chance of collecting on those private student loans because they can try to get payments from both the student and the cosigner. It could be more difficult for lenders to collect those remaining private loans that are signed by just the individual student. If private loan borrowers do not make any attempt to repay their debt, lenders may try to collect through the garnishment of wages. Some employers may then elect to dismiss people from their jobs if their wages are being garnished. Any collection effort could also negatively affect the credit ratings of all parties who signed the loan(s).

The Department of Education can do any one of the following to collect federal student loan debt: intercept a tax refund, garnish wages (up to 15 percent of the debtor's disposable income), take federal benefits such as Social Security and Social Security disability benefits up to $9,000 per year (supplemental security income is off-limits), revoke professional licenses within the state laws that allow it, and sue for the defaulted amounts plus collection fees.

One of the most effective methods that the Department of Education and loan guaranty agencies use to collect on defaulted federal student loan debt is to intercept a borrower's income tax refund. The IRS receives an annual report from the Department of Education with a list of federal student loans in default. Before a tax offset is taken from a tax refund, the borrower will receive a notification with an option of paying the debt or appealing the offset. The borrower must then file an appeal to the tax offset. If the borrower does not file an appeal, the IRS takes the borrower's tax refund and applies it toward the federal loan payment. Possible reasons for an appeal include (FindLaw n.d.):

- The loan has been repaid.
- The loan is being paid under negotiated repayment terms.
- The loan is in deferment, is in forbearance, or has been canceled.
- The borrower is deceased or suffers from permanent or total disability.
- The loan does not belong to the borrower.
- The loan is unenforceable because of fraud (example: forged signature).
- The school owes the borrower a refund.
- The borrower's school closed.
- The borrower was falsely certified to be eligible for a federal loan.
- The borrower has filed for bankruptcy and the case is still pending.
- In an extreme case, the loan was discharged in bankruptcy.

According to the Federal Reserve Bank of New York, nearly 17 percent of outstanding student loan debt is held by borrowers age 50 or older. Since 2005, debt levels have more than tripled among those ages 50 to 59 and more than quintupled for borrowers ages 60 and up. Data from the Treasury Department show that the number of retirees who had their Social Security benefits reduced because of delinquent student loans increased from 6 cases in 2000 to 122,056 cases in 2012. Recipients of Social Security retirement and disability benefits are sent notices and given numerous opportunities to work out a repayment plan or dispute the debt before their checks are reduced (Couch n.d.).

Loan repayment obligations change when a federal student loan is in default. Here is an example of what has been included in the small print on the promissory note, under the acceleration and default category: "I will immediately notify the U.S. Department of Education of a change of address. At the option of the U.S. Department of Education, the entire unpaid balance will become immediately due and payable upon the occurrence of any one of the following events: (a) I fail to enroll as at least a half-time student at the school that certified the loan; (b) I fail to use the proceeds of the loan solely for education expenses; (c) I make a false representation that results in my receiving a loan for which I am ineligible; or (d) I default on the loan. If I default, the U.S. Department of Education may capitalize all the outstanding interest into a new principal balance. If I default on this loan, the default will be reported to national credit bureaus. I understand that the resulting credit reports will have a significant negative affect on my credit rating. If I default on the loan, my federal income tax refund may be withheld to pay the debt, my wages may be garnished or offset, and legal action may be brought against me to enforce the terms of this note. I will be ineligible for additional federal student financial aid and for assistance under most federal benefit programs."

A number of states allow professional and vocational boards to refuse to certify, certify with restrictions, suspend or revoke a member's professional or vocational license, and, in some cases, impose a fine when a member defaults on student loans. The state laws apply to members of the various professions working in that state. Some of these states' provisions apply to particular professions or vocations such as attorneys, health care professionals, insurance professionals, state officers, and teachers.

> *How in the heck are you going to pay over $100,000 being a $30,000-a-year teacher and try and have a house? I mean, that's tough.* —Financial aid counselor, 2008

Other state provisions apply more generally to anyone whose profession or vocation requires licensing. Below is a list of states with these types of licensing laws. Borrowers should check with their state education departments or other authorities for more information. Other states not on this list may have similar laws (Student Loan Borrower Assistance n.d.).

- Alaska
- California
- Florida
- Georgia
- Hawaii
- Illinois
- Iowa
- Kentucky
- Louisiana
- Massachusetts
- Minnesota
- New Jersey
- New Mexico
- North Dakota
- Oklahoma
- Tennessee
- Texas
- Virginia
- Washington

College Costs Can Involve Parents and Grandparents

Much attention has been focused on students burdened with loans. The recent growth in the federal Parent PLUS Loan program highlights another way in which the financial responsibility has shifted more to families as the costs of college have become too much for most students to handle alone. Mark Kantrowitz, publisher of two authoritative financial aid websites, stated that some parents are getting in completely over their heads when borrowing up to 100 percent of college costs through a federal Parent PLUS Loan (Wang, Supiano, and Fuller 2012). Parents without adverse credit can borrow up to 100 percent of college costs without regard to their income, employment, or any other debt obligations. There is no limit on the amount a parent can borrow on a federal Parent PLUS Loan for all their children, as long as they do not have adverse credit and the total amount is no more than 100 percent of the college's COA. Creditworthy parents can also borrow 100 percent of a college's COA from private lenders; however, private lenders consider an applicant's employment and will analyze existing debt obligations and an individual's income repayment capacity during normal underwriting.

Paying back student loans has become more of a family affair as a greater percentage of private student loans are now cosigned by the students and their parents or the students and their grandparents (Post 2010). Grandparents are not eligible to borrow from the federal Parent PLUS Loan program unless they have formally adopted the grandchild. A legal guardianship is not sufficient. However, there are more grandparents turning to private student loans and cosigning those loans with their grandchildren. Some creditworthy grandparents are also cosigning federal Parent PLUS Loans when the parents have adverse credit and do not qualify on their own.

There has been an increase in grandparents applying for private student loans over the past two years for a variety of reasons: the parents were already at their maximum private loan amounts when borrowing for college for other children or due to high education costs for one particular child (for example, over a $150,000 limit), the grandparents may qualify for a better interest rate than the parents, the parents may simply not be willing to apply, or the parents may not qualify for credit-based loans. For those grandparents challenged by a private lender's online-only application process, representatives are available by telephone to help guide them through that process (SunTrust, telephone inquiry, August 23, 2013). Income from retirement accounts, Social Security income, and disability benefits are included in the income repayment ratios for grandparents agreeing to sign private student loans. For those parents opposed to helping their children pay for college or for those parents who cannot afford to help their children, the possibility that the grandparents would elect to spend their own money to help pay college costs for their grandchildren and bypass their children's inheritance is a noteworthy trend.

With the heightened compliance rules since the HEOA, college students are being left alone, some by their own families, to seek out the multitude of financial aid sources and then decipher and compare the differences in federal and private student loans and in federal and private lenders. Statistics are beginning to show that the financial decisions made by students regarding college loans could negatively affect them and their parents sooner or later. There are parents who just did not realize that their children could incur so much debt while going to college until their children lost their financial independence and moved back home, even those who were fully employed. A study completed by Pew Research in December 2011 found that 39 percent of all adults ages 18 to 34 say they either live with their parents now or moved back in temporarily in recent years, including 53 percent of those 18 to 24. The study found that 1 in 10 college-educated adults between the ages of 30 and 34 are living at home with their parents (*Huffington Post* 2012).

Based on 2012 student loan debt statistics from the American Student Assistance, approximately one-third of recent college graduates, if they could do it all again, would have pursued more scholarships or financial aid options, selected a major that would have led to a higher-paying job, worked while in college, and started saving earlier. It would have simplified their lives (American Student Assistance n.d.).

Simplifying Financial Aid and Student Loans

Anything that we have is on our website. With everything that happened with the student loan industry, and Cuomo, and all of that, we really can't have that information. What we do have is on our website, and even that is under review with our office and our general counsel to make sure that what we're doing is in compliance with what the new information act is causing us to do. Basically, we can't counsel families, really, on the financial aid process, especially loans, primarily because it then gives the impression that we're pushing students in one direction of one bank versus another. And, that's really not what we do, but that's what the perception came out to be. And so what information we can provide students is very limited. The only thing we can do is students can come to us and say, "This is what I'm looking at doing," and we can talk to them about that, but we, as an institution, can't provide anything to students.

—*Financial aid counselor, 2008*

OLLEGE STUDENTS may find colleges that have simplified their application for enrollment process by working under the umbrella of one admissions and financial aid office, with a seamless separation of duties. College employees work tirelessly to satisfy their customers and enroll college students into their colleges of choice. Students may even select a college that they cannot afford to attend and then look to college counselors to find a way for them to be able to pay for it. Students may then receive a financial aid award letter from each college that they apply to that lists any grants, scholarships, and loans all under the same simple heading of "Award." It is up to students and their families to decipher the differences between college award letters.

> *It's going to be bad for us, as institutions. Why? Because the student's going to think about it and he's going to say, "Huh? If I do $10,000 and I do this over four years, there's going to be $40,000, and based on this interest rate my payments are going to be this, and if I do the federal loans, it's going to be that, and together it's going to be...HOLY CRAP...I'm going to pay $900 a month on student loan payments? Hmmm..." I think they might look and say, "Maybe I should go to a community college for a couple of years."* —Financial aid counselor, 2008

In reality, the majority of colleges' financial awards are neatly packaged loans, with names like Perkins, Stafford, and PLUS. Federal financial aid includes the following loan options for borrowers:

1. Federal Perkins
2. Direct Stafford—Subsidized and Unsubsidized
3. Direct PLUS—Direct Parent PLUS for parents of undergraduates; Direct PLUS for professional and graduate students

Other student loans are available through state or private sources and are referred to as nonfederal, private, direct-to-consumer, direct-to-student (DTS), school-channeled, and alternative loans. Federal student loans that are available to students alone are not contingent upon their college major, their current income, their future income, or whether they complete college. Private student loans are available to students and creditworthy cosigners based on their reported credit history and repayment capacity from income. Some college financial aid packages include private student loans, some do not. When combining federal aid and private loan options, college financial aid offices work diligently to certify that college students, parents, and their creditworthy cosigners can simply borrow up to 100 percent of a college's COA. The trend in federal and private student loan defaults supports the fact that the ease of the current financial aid process has left borrowers with debts they cannot or will not pay, even those who are fully employed.

> *It's probably been too easy to borrow, because sometimes they'll go, "Oh, I can get up to $16,000," or whatever it might be. Sometimes they just did that without thinking.*
> —Financial aid counselor, 2008

There has been little effort to reduce the amount that students and parents can borrow to something less than 100 percent of college costs. Counselors indicated back in 2008 that the current financial aid structure was mainly squeezing middle-income consumers. When *The Two Income Trap: Why Middle-Class Parents Are Going Broke* was written, college debt was in its infancy and was not included in the financial challenges for the middle class (Warren and Tyagi 2003). The increase in student debt amounts in the past decade has become another predominant financial factor for the middle class. The government plan "Bargain for the Middle Class: Making College More Affordable" proposes to give colleges a bonus based upon the number of Pell students that they graduate, which will exclude the middle-income applicants who do not qualify for a need-based Pell Grant (Jaschik 2013).

> *Low-income kids are doing OK...they seem to be able to make it with grants and the loans that they can get. Now they just barely eke by, but they can make it. The higher income kids, mom and dad can usually help them out, take out a PLUS loan or have saved and can pay it. But the middle-income kids, the parents are just making ends meet on their own and don't have the extra money to help them ...they're the ones getting into the [private] alternative program.* —Financial aid counselor, 2008

> *We get information back from the federal government, and it's rare to see any substantial numbers in the savings investment section even for middle- to middle-to-higher-income families, which amazes me.* —Financial aid counselor, 2008

> *The Pell program hasn't kept up with the increase in costs. We do have a state grant program, but it is need-based like the Pell. So for those students whose parents are middle income, they're not receiving that.* —Financial aid counselor, 2008

Simplifying the Financial Aid Process

The American Dream 2.0 recommends that the financial aid process be simplified and made transparent (HCM Strategists 2012). A similar financial literacy effort for housing occurred in 2011 when the CFPB announced "Know Before You Owe," an attempt to combine two federally required mortgage disclosures into a single, simpler form that makes the costs and risks of the loan clear and allows consumers to comparison-shop for the best offer (Meyerowitz 2011). Also, in 2011 the Department of Education and the CFPB teamed up for the "Know Before You Owe: Student Loans Project" (Consumer Financial Protection Bureau 2011). They created a financial aid shopping sheet (see Appendix A) that colleges can use to help students better understand the type and amount of grants and loans that they qualify for. It also can be used to help students easily compare financial aid packages offered by different colleges and universities.

> *I think they need to do, you know, a lot more comparisons because their lender is probably not always the best choice for their alternative-type loans.* —Financial aid counselor, 2008

There are legislative efforts to simplify and improve the current financial aid structure to better inform consumers and to reduce federal student loan defaults and collection costs for taxpayers. Here are some of the most recent efforts:

Understanding the True Cost of College:
An Effort to Simplify a College's Award Letter

In May 2012, Senator Al Franken introduced a legislative bill, Understanding the True Cost of College Act of 2012 (GovTrack.us 2012), an effort to simplify the financial aid process and create a uniform financial aid award letter. An amendment, Understanding the True Cost of College Act of 2013, was introduced by Senator Franken in June 2013. One goal of the 2013 amendment is for colleges to have to clearly label *loans* on college financial aid award letters. If it is passed, colleges will continue to be able to label loans as awards on college financial aid award letters; students and parents should be prepared to continue to read the small print when comparing their offers.

Earnings Contingent Education Loans (ExCEL) Act of 2013: *Simplifying Federal Student Loan Payments and Reducing Student Loan Defaults*

Recently, some politicians have attempted to reduce federal student loan defaults and be more assured of future federal student loan payments by tying federal student loan payments to a borrower's income and federal tax return. A bill known as the Earnings Contingent Education Loans (ExCEL) Act was first proposed in 2012 by Representative Tom Petri (Gray 2012), with a revision proposed in 2013 (H.R. 1716). The legislation is intended to *simplify* and improve student loans for borrowers, encourage responsible borrowing, and save significant taxpayer dollars. The ExCEL Act is expected to reduce federal student loan defaults and the associated collection costs for those borrowers unable or unwilling to repay on their unsecured federal student loans. Anyone who has ever tried to collect on unsecured debt from a customer, friend, business partner, or family member will understand the intent of this bill and how it could simplify current federal student loan collection efforts. If approved, the plan involves a solution for new federal student loans, already implemented successfully in Great Britain, New Zealand, and Australia, that allows automatic monthly payments to be drawn from a borrower's paycheck to pay back federal student loans. This proposal will affect federal student loan borrowers, along with their future employers, income tax preparers, and U.S. taxpayers. The pending 2013 revision can be tracked at https://www.govtrack.us/congress/bills/113/hr1716/text. If it is passed in the United States, federal student loan payments will be managed directly by the U.S. Department of Education and the IRS. Here are some of the highlights of the ExCEL Act:

1. The proposed ExCEL Act eliminates the Stafford subsidized loan whereby the government pays the interest for undergraduate

students while they are in college, with the exception of those students active in the military. (The subsidized Stafford Loan for graduate and professional students was already eliminated on July 1, 2012.) Beginning July 1, 2014, these loans would be replaced by variable-rate loans named as Income Dependent Education Assistance Loans (IDEA Loans). IDEA Loan rates would be determined by the U.S. 10-year Treasury notes on June 1 plus 3 percent; loan fees would range from 1 to 4 percent.

2. Employees will be required to notify all employers of their monthly federal student loan repayment amounts that need to be automatically deducted from their wages; the exact amount will be determined by the Department of Education. Employees will not need to disclose their total federal student loan debt to their employers; they will just need to disclose the required monthly payment amounts. The employer will simply need to withhold the federal student loan repayment amount, combine the withholdings for the loan with the amounts withheld for federal and state taxes, and send that entire sum to the IRS. An employee's W-2 will include a section on how much was withheld for federal student loan payments.

3. There is no time limit for borrowers to repay federal student loans under the proposed ExCEL Act. Borrowers will have as many years as they need and will be expected to coordinate payments with as many employers as they have until the debt is paid in full through the ExCEL income-contingent requirements. A borrower who fails to indicate to their employer that they have a federal student loan could be subject to significant penalties for failing to meet at least 90 percent of their repayment obligation by the final day of the tax year.

4. The ExCEL Act proposes to replace an array of loans, subsidies, deferments, forbearances, and repayment options. It would simplify

federal loan options for undergraduate and graduate students by limiting them to one take-it-or-leave-it choice, an income-contingent loan. As proposed, the ExCEL Act would not replace the federal Parent PLUS Loan or the Perkins Loan. The federal Perkins Loan is a loan available to undergraduate, graduate, and professional students with exceptional financial need. The federal Parent PLUS Loan is available to one parent who has no adverse credit history. An example of adverse credit is when the parent has one unpaid medical collection.

5. The proposed ExCEL Act would combine the federal subsidized Stafford, federal unsubsidized Stafford, and Graduate PLUS (Grad PLUS) loans into a single income-contingent loan, with repayment requirements of up to 15 percent of an employee's gross income (after subtracting an allowed exemption amount).

The effective percentage rate of gross income that student borrowers would pay on their federal student loans would be progressive. For example, for a single individual with no dependents, the exemption amount in 2012 would have been $16,755 (150 percent of the poverty line for a household size of one). Exemptions for married individuals, filing jointly, with both spouses having federal student loans, would allow each one to get the same exemption. If ExCEL is passed, new federal student loan borrowers earning $35,000–$50,000 out of college need to know that they will be expected to repay nearly 8–10 percent of their gross income just on their federal student loans. This does not include any repayment obligations they incur for private student loans. The table *(shown on the facing page)* shows the effective rate of gross income that an individual could be expected to pay at various salary levels under the proposed ExCEL Act.

The Department of Education will determine the borrower's repayment obligations and have a repayment plan tailored to their income level, by adding together any salary or wage income and

Annual Wages/Salary	Annual Obligation	Effective Rate of Income to Be Paid
$10,000 per year	$0 per year	0.00% of gross income
$20,000 per year	$486 per year	2.40% of gross income
$35,000 per year	$2,736 per year	7.80% of gross income
$50,000 per year	$4,986 per year	9.90% of gross income
$80,000 per year	$9,486 per year	11.80% of gross income

any nonsalary or nonwage income, such as self-employment income, interest income, dividend income, and capital gains above $3,000. If more than $3,000 of self-employment income is anticipated, taxpayers can calculate that additional taxable amount and send it as part of their estimated taxes to the IRS.

6. New federal student loan borrowers would be eligible only for this newly proposed income-contingent loan. Borrowers with active Stafford Loans or Graduate PLUS Loans could continue to borrow those types of loans for a limited time.

The ExCEL Act implies that federal student loan limits for college students may already be near what the government believes many college graduates can likely afford to repay without any other (private) student loans. The increasing number of federal student loan defaults would suggest that federal limits for subsidized and unsubsidized loans are already higher than what many college students commit to repaying. A dependent undergraduate student may borrow up to $31,000 in aggregate. An independent undergraduate student may borrow up to $57,500 in aggregate. Graduate students can borrow up to 100 percent of the COA for their institution (Federal Student Aid n.d.-j).

This bill was assigned to a congressional committee on April 24, 2013, which will consider it before possibly sending it on to the House or Senate as a whole. There is only a minimal chance that it will be enacted; however, it highlights the need for college students and their families to try to understand the ramifications for all of the debt they incur for college and to be financially prepared to repay on their federal student loans. The undercurrent is that future federal student loan repayments will be contingent upon income. The bill for the ExCEL Act can be found online at http://petri.house.gov/sites/petri.house.gov/files/documents/ExCELAct-BillLang-113th-4-24-2013.pdf.

Under the ExCEL Act, the repayment decisions made by college students could be greatly simplified to the monthly repayment amount that the Department of Education requires them to pay based on income. The mandate for federal student loan exit counseling could simply shift from notifying students on a variety of repayment options to notifying students of their income-contingent monthly payment amount that needs to be reported to their employers and deducted from their wages until it is paid in full.

"A Better Bargain for the Middle Class: Making College More Affordable"

Another plan, "A Better Bargain for the Middle Class: Making College More Affordable," was announced in August 2013. Starting in 2014, the Department of Education and the Department of Treasury will work to help borrowers learn about and enroll in Pay As You Earn and Income-Based Repayment plans when they file their taxes. The Pay As You Earn plan caps loan payments at 10 percent of income for federal student loans. The Pay As You Earn payment plan is being proposed to be available to all student borrowers (Jaschik 2013). The plan does not include nonfederal private student loans. The existing Income-Based and Pay As You Earn repayment plans do not involve federal Parent PLUS Loans.

Students who borrow federal loans will find a new undercurrent for federal legislation to incorporate their federal student loan payments with their wages and federal income tax returns. The current trend is for more emphasis on income-driven repayment options. More details of the existing federal repayment plans based on income, including the Pay As You Earn and Income-Based Repayment plans, are included in chapter 6.

Ability-to-Repay and Qualified Mortgage (QM) Rule: *Simplifying Repayment Rules*

Many Americans see a college degree as a necessary investment toward attaining quality employment. In sheer dollars, investing in a college degree ranks as the single largest lifetime investment to be made by college students, next to their house. The decision to invest in college is made by the majority of students and families long before students are in the market to buy a house. Some recent financial indicators suggest that an investment in college could become the single largest lifetime investment for young adults, *instead of* a house. A recent statistic suggests that someone with student loan debt is 36 percent less likely to own a home (Condon 2013). Large student loan debt amounts crowd out other consumption (Gray 2012). In 2011, first-time home buyers, with a median age of 31, fell to the smallest percentage of total home purchasers since 2006 (Fairchild and Keene 2012).

On January 10, 2013, the CFPB announced a new set of ability-to-repay mortgage rules. Collectively, these rules are known as the *qualified mortgage*, or QM. In short, a qualified mortgage is a home loan that meets certain criteria designed to minimize risk. The debt-to-income ratio is one of eight required criteria (CFPB Web Team 2013). According to CFPB and with few exceptions, QM loans "generally will be provided to people who have debt-to-income ratios less than or equal to 43 percent. This cap on debt ensures consumers are only getting what they can likely afford."

Lenders will now have less flexibility in what repayment risks they can approve for new and existing customers, based on QM rules. This new mortgage rule is simple in that QM home loan applicants that fall within the 43 percent repayment ratio may qualify for QM loans based on their ability to repay; applicants exceeding the 43 percent ratio will not. There will be little room for exceptions to the rule, and this is scheduled to take effect for qualifying applications on or after January 10, 2014 (Cornett 2013).

College students, parents, and cosigners who borrow too much money for college or have a college loan repayment plan that does not allow them to meet the 43 percent ratio may find that they will no longer qualify for QM home loans for future house purchases or refinances. Also, parents who intend to sell assets or liquidate cash accounts as part of their loan repayment plan may find that they will first have to obtain that cash before they can qualify under the 43 percent QM rules. Any monthly repayment amounts required for student loans and parent loans will be included in the 43 percent house repayment ratio, even those loans that are cosigned. QM may cause signers of college loans to reconsider whether or not they will accept the legal ramifications for signing on those loans. Parents may limit their financial responsibilities and begin to lower the total student loan amounts that they agree to sign or cosign for in order to meet their own housing ratio requirements.

The 43 percent QM rule can be broken down to a maximum of 28 percent for monthly principal, interest, taxes, and insurance payments for a house loan and 15 percent for all other monthly payments combined, such as student loans, vehicle loans, and credit card debt. Here is a 43 percent QM example for the college undergraduate student working full time and earning $14.90 per hour (over twice the amount of federal minimum wages in July 2013) or $31,000 their first year out of college. It is calculated for those students wanting to live independently by buying (or renting) a house, needing to buy a used car to get to and from work, having minimal credit card debt, having college debt at only half of the expected $31,000 salary, and having student loan payments limited to 7 percent of their gross income. The $31,000 average income for a college graduate's first year of gross wages is supported by Marc Scheer in his book *No Sucker Left Behind* and by Zac Bissonnette in *Debt Free U*. In 2002, Nellie Mae studied the impact of student loan debt and found that borrowers who require less than 7 percent of their monthly gross income to pay their education debt generally did not feel financial difficulty (Bissonnette 2010). Also, a 7 percent monthly repayment supports the federal government's 10-year standard repayment plan when total loan amounts are limited to half of gross income.

	Purchase Price	Down Payment	Loan Amount	Interest Rate	Loan Years	Monthly Payments	Percentage of $2,583.33 Monthly Gross Income
House	$117,500	$23,500	$94,000	4.50%	30	$721.25	27.92%
Car	$7,000	$700	$6,300	8.12%	3	$197.75	7.65%
Student Loans			$15,500	7.00%	10	$180.01	6.97%
Credit Cards			$100	10.00%		$11.82	0.46%
Total						$1,110.83	43.00%

In this example, house payments include principal, interest, real estate taxes, and insurance. Real estate taxes are calculated at 2 percent of the house purchase price; insurance was calculated at ½ percent of the purchase price of the house. The house loan assumes a 20 percent cash down payment. (The car loan assumes a 10 percent down payment with a trade-in or cash.) The American Community Survey states that the average rent in the United States is $804 per month. Students who do not intend to buy a house may still need an amount near a house payment to be financially independent and to be able to pay monthly rent costs (FindtheData n.d.).

According to a 2012 telephone survey of 507 college graduates of four-year degree programs, 43 percent expected to receive a higher starting salary for their first job out of college than they actually received. The number of people with college degrees in professions that do not require them has increased. By 2008, more than one in five clerical sales workers had a college degree; one in 20 laborers as well as 10 percent of service workers had one. Some 17,000,000 Americans with a college degree are doing jobs that the Bureau of Labor Statistics (BLS) says require less than the skill level associated with a bachelor's degree. Over 317,000 waiters and waitresses have college degrees (over 8,000 of them have doctoral or professional degrees), along with over 80,000 bartenders and over 18,000 parking lot attendants (Vedder 2010).

> *They may think as a teacher that they are going to make $40,000, but really they're going to be making $29,000.*
> —Financial aid counselor, 2008

According to the 2011 Project on Student Debt, 37.8 percent of working young graduates had jobs that did not require a college degree, depressing their wages (The Project on Student Debt 2012). Using data from the U.S. Bureau of Labor Statistics regarding 2011 college graduates, an economics professor, Andrew Sum, reported that as many as 50 percent of college graduates under the age of 25 are underutilized, meaning they are either working no job at all, working a part-time job, or working a job outside of the college labor market (Fairbanks 2011). According to William J. Bennett and David Wilezol in their book, *Is College Worth It?*, half of all college graduates in 2010–

2011 were unemployed or dramatically underemployed (Bennett and Wilezol 2013).

In addition, parents who ask their children to focus specifically on high-paying majors, such as computer science, nursing, engineering, biology, and accounting, said they expect them to earn an average of $70,300 upon graduation. Overall, parents said they expect their child to graduate with an average $14,600 in student loan debt—much lower than the $25,250 debt that the average college student owed in 2010. And they anticipate that it will take their child about eight years to pay off the debt (Ellis 2012). Members of the class of 2013 are graduating with an average $35,200 in college-related debt (Ellis 2013). College debt is steadily increasing, and the volume of student loan delinquencies is one reliable indicator that the average debt has become too high for many students to be able to repay.

American Student Assistance, a nonprofit organization based in Boston, has offered a financial guideline for student borrowers that states that the total amount of student debt that is incurred while attending college should not exceed the anticipated annual salary for the first year out of school (Couch 2011). Based on current economic conditions, this equal-to-wages guideline is too high for students; however, it could work for those parents who have little or no debt, continue to work, have maintained employable skills, do not have enough in savings to be able to pay for college without borrowing, and agree to the standard 10-year repayment plan.

Total student loan debt should not exceed *half* of the anticipated first year of wages.

College students, on the other hand, should refrain from borrowing up to the amount of their first year of wages, considering unemployment rates, underemployment factors, and optimistic starting-salary expectations. Due to the declining economy, escalating college costs, and the unemployment and underemployment trends in the United States, the financial one-size-fits-all guideline for this book has been downsized to a new 50 percent rule. College financial aid counselors revealed that college students resort to loans no matter how much they discourage it; however, college students should borrow no more than *half* of their anticipated first year of wages.

> *We sit down with the student and figure out they really only need $7,700. The student says, "I want $10,000 anyway." "Well, why?" "Well, because I want this, this, and this." "You know, you're a college student...hate to break it to you but you're supposed to be poor. You know, borrow as little as you possibly can. Quite honestly, I didn't even like the fact that you're borrowing any money, but this is an investment and it is going to pay off." Now they still might do it, but I can sleep at night knowing that I, at least, I tried. And those that trim it back, hey, if they trim it back $1,000, if they go from $10,000 to $9,000, they just trimmed back $1,000. At $100 a month, that's 10 months of payments.* —Financial aid counselor, 2008

> *We tell them they're going to have to pay it back and it is based on their credit and that could impact it in the future. They usually take it out anyway, but just as long as we make them aware of how it will impact them.* —Financial aid counselor, 2008

The standard repayment plan for federal student loans is 10 years. If students who have exited college are struggling financially, they could then consider extending the student loan repayment term to a longer federal loan payment plan; however, 10 years should be the student loan repayment plan when first determining a budget and selecting a college. Here are the same variables of $31,000 in annual wages, a house loan, a car loan, credit card debt, and a student loan with a 20-year extended repayment plan in place of the previous federal 10-year standard repayment plan:

	Purchase Price	Down Payment	Loan Amount	Interest Rate	Loan Years	Monthly Payments	Percentage of $2,583.33 Monthly Gross Income
House	$117,500	$23,500	$94,000	4.50%	30	$721.25	27.92%
Car	$7,000	$700	$6,300	8.12%	3	$197.75	7.65%
Student Loans			$15,500	7.00%	20	$120.22	4.65%
Credit Cards			$100	10.00%		$11.82	0.46%
Total						$1,051.04	40.68%

In this example, the extended 20-year repayment plan results in the borrower paying more in interest than in the previous 10-year student's loan repayment plan. The total interest paid on a $15,500 student loan at 7 percent for 10 years = $6,101.20. The total interest paid on a $15,500 student loan at 7 percent for 20 years = $13,352.80. The difference is $7,251.60.

**Student loan payments should not exceed
7 percent of monthly gross income**

Assuming the 43 percent QM rule and an annual income of $31,000, $13,330 per year, or $1,110.83 per month, would be needed to be available to repay all monthly debt obligations. This would leave only $17,670 a year (or $1,472.50 a month) to pay state, federal, and Social Security taxes, utilities, fuel, day-care costs, house and car maintenance, food, clothing, insurances, health-care costs, general living costs, and retirement savings. The 43 percent rule is an optimistic housing repayment plan for most households to be able to comfortably maintain while paying typical day-to-day living costs. It could further squeeze the middle class.

The 43 percent rule tends to simplify the gamut of financial obligations for borrowers into a one-size-fits-all answer. For someone having any college debt and making $31,000 out of college, they will find it next to impossible to buy a house on their own and be able to maintain their financial independence. Repaying 43 percent, or 43 cents of every dollar, is too much money for most consumers to be able to budget and commit to for monthly payment amounts. A 43 percent ratio could prove too high a repayment ratio even for someone earning $60,000 a year, let alone a college graduate entering the workforce with a starting income of $31,000 per year. As is, the 43 percent QM could shut out consumers from the housing market if applicants agree to borrow too much money to go to college. Students and families who accept the 10 percent repayment terms under the federal Pay As You Earn repayment ratio on just their federal student loans under the pending "Better Bargain for the Middle Class: Making College More Affordable" plan (Jaschik 2013) could further delay their ability to qualify for a home loan under the 43 percent QM rules.

Bipartisan Student Loan Certainty Act:
Simplifying Federal Student Loan Rates

On July 24, 2013, the U.S. Senate approved and amended the Bipartisan Student Loan Certainty Act legislation, also known as the Smarter

Solutions for Students (SSS) Act, to propose changes to federal student loans from fixed interest rates to variable interest rates for new student loans made on or after July 1, 2013. The stated purpose of the bill, enacted August 9, 2013, was to "make students' loans cheaper, *simpler*, and more certain" (Nawaguna 2013). Initially this change resulted in cheaper stated interest rates than the previous federal student loan fixed rates, with the exception of subsidized Stafford Loans, and only for as long as those variable interest rates do not increase to an amount exceeding the fixed interest rates that they replaced.

Direct federal Stafford Loans and PLUS loans for undergraduate, graduate, and professional students, and Direct PLUS Loans for graduate students, professional students, and parents of dependent undergraduate students, changed from having fixed interest rates to having variable interest rates that are designed to change annually. The index used for the variable-rate option is the 10-year Treasury rate. The cap rates on those variable-rate federal loans are 8.25 percent on Direct unsubsidized and subsidized Stafford Loans for undergraduate students, 9.50 percent on Direct unsubsidized Stafford Loans for graduate and professional students, and 10.50 percent for Direct Graduate PLUS Loans for graduate and professional students and Direct Parent PLUS Loans for parents of dependent undergraduate students. Each of these cap rates exceeds the fixed rates for the categories that they replaced.

The Bipartisan Student Loan Certainty Act amends the Higher Education Act to change the interest rate on all new Direct Stafford subsidized, Stafford unsubsidized, Graduate PLUS, and Parent PLUS Loans disbursed on or after July 1, 2013, to variable rates that rescore annually. College students, parents, grandparents, cosigners, and any other borrowers should not view variable interest rates on any loans, including their college loans, as "simpler and more certain" than fixed-rate loans. This would be equivalent to believing that house loan payments that can change every year to some unknown amount will be simpler to prepare for financially than having a fixed-rate house loan where the monthly payment amount never changes for up to 30 years. No one can be certain of what a 10-year Treasury rate will be on June 1 of a future year; it is only certain that the interest rate is scheduled to change annually on July 1 (based on the previous June 1 10-year Treasury rate index). This plan allows for variable interest rates on federal student loans to change annually; payment amounts can increase or decrease whenever rates change with the market. College students and parents now need to be financially prepared for an unknown payment amount, especially when the time comes that variable interest rates and their monthly loan payments increase.

Here is an accounting of variable interest rate increases for the prime rate index during one month only, December 1980. It is intended to show borrowers of student loans that any variable interest rate index can increase. While this is an unusual time in the history of the prime rate, it is also unusual that, at the time of this writing, the current prime rate of 3.25 percent has not changed since December 16, 2008. Prior to that date, the prime rate had not been below 3.25 percent since March 17, 1954 (FedPrimeRate.com n.d.).

Variable Prime Interest Rate History—December 1980

Variable Prime Interest Rate	Effective Date of Rate
17.75 percent	December 1, 1980
18.50 percent	December 2, 1980
19.00 percent	December 5, 1980
20.00 percent	December 10, 1980
21.00 percent	December 16, 1980
21.50 percent	December 19, 1980

The following example incorporates the Bipartisan Student Loan Certainty Act, with new variable-rate federal Direct student loans disbursed on or after July 1, 2013, and before July 1, 2014. The 10-year Treasury note index is determined each prior June 1. These rates are an example of the variable interest rates that replace the current fixed interest rates for Stafford and PLUS loans. The greatest financial risk to students and parents is that the interest rates can increase on each individual loan to the cap rates of 8.25 percent for undergraduate subsidized and unsubsidized loans, 9.50 percent for graduate unsubsidized loans, and 10.50 percent for Graduate PLUS and Parent PLUS Loans for parents who borrow for their undergraduate children. The 10-year Treasury rate is subject to change. For students and parents who eventually apply for consolidation of their Direct federal student and parent loans, there is no interest rate cap. The consolidated rate will be determined by the weighted average of the loans being consolidated and then rounded up to the nearest 1/8 percent.

Direct Loans	10-Year Treasury		Added Spread		Interest Rate 7/1/2013– 6/30/2014	Variable Interest Rate Cap
Undergraduate— Stafford (subsidized and unsubsidized)	1.81%	+	2.05%	=	3.86%	8.25%
Graduate—Stafford (unsubsidized)	1.81%	+	3.60%	=	5.41%	9.50%
Graduate— PLUS	1.81%	+	4.60%	=	6.41%	10.50%
Parent— PLUS	1.81%	+	4.60%	=	6.41%	10.50%
Consolidation	Weighted average rounded up to nearest 1/8%					No cap

Source: http://ifap.ed.gov/eannouncements/080913DirectLoanInterestRate
  2013t2014Eff070113.html

Smarter Borrowing Act:
to Provide Effective Financial Aid Counseling

U.S. Senators Richard Blumenthal, Tom Harkin, and Barbara Mikulski introduced the Smarter Borrowing Act in an effort to protect and empower student loan borrowers with effective loan counseling (DefendYourDollars.org 2013). The senators highlight the concern that students and families often report to them about having difficulty figuring out the differences between grant aid, which does not need to be repaid, and student loans, which do need to be repaid. The legislation is intended to strengthen and reform the current mandatory entrance and exit loan counseling requirements for federal student loans and to *notify* students annually of their cumulative debt, including their remaining eligibility for loans and grants (HometownSource 2013). There is no indication that students will be required to complete any part of the mandatory federal exit counseling session proposed under the Smarter Borrowing Act.

The Smarter Borrowing Act requires the exit counseling that institutions of higher education (IHEs) provide to student loan borrowers of Federal Family Education Loans (FFELs), Direct Loans (DLs), and Perkins Loans to do the following (Congress.gov 2013):

1. Include personalized information reflecting each borrower's actual borrowing circumstances.
2. Include a statement that such loans must be repaid even if students are dissatisfied with their education.
3. Be provided in a simple and understandable manner that includes comprehension checks.
4. Be conducted in person or online.

Simplifying Counseling

College students are now on their own to research and select their own private lender(s) and private loan options. The major reason that colleges are no longer recommending specific private lenders, according to the college counselors interviewed in 2008, is due to the nationwide investigation concluded by New York Attorney General Andrew Cuomo in 2007. The private lending practices that Cuomo investigated involved "preferred lenders" bribing college employees, lenders posing as college employees, and lenders giving donations to schools in exchange for colleges marketing student loan borrowers who needed alternatives to finance higher-education costs. Some college employees were found guilty as charged; others were not involved or charged. The findings resulted in New York's Student Lending Accountability Transparency and Enforcement (SLATE) Act (Benjamin 2007). The legislation was simply intended to halt all controversial conflict-of-interest practices rampant in the student loan industry at the time. It established civil penalties of up to $50,000 for lending institutions and colleges and $7,500 for employees engaging in these practices (New York State Assembly 2008).

In May 2007, Chapter 41 of the Laws of 2007 was enacted in New York. The SLATE Act led to a strict code of conduct set forth in the national Higher Education Opportunity Act (HEOA). The HEOA, signed into federal law in 2008, directly affected colleges and the job responsibilities of their college financial aid counselors with its increased regulations and heightened compliance requirements. The law requires that a school's code of conduct must prohibit a conflict of interest with the responsibilities of an officer, employee, or agent of a school regarding loans. The law further specifies that the code must be displayed prominently on the institution's website (New York State Office of Higher Education 2008). Some colleges simplified their own compliance risks and stopped their financial aid counselors from recommending specific private lenders who offered private student loans. Colleges no longer risked having their financial aid counselors offer specific information and counseling to students and families when financial aid involved private student loans.

> *Everything that's happened has not happened to the benefit of the student; it has really worked against the student.*
> —Financial aid counselor, 2008

> *I think it's going to remain that schools cannot advocate one private loan over another.* —Financial aid counselor, 2008

"Preferred lenders" became a negative term, and many colleges elected to no longer recommend private lenders to college students. While financial aid counselors stated that they were challenged with the difficulty in staying up to date when comparing all of the different private (alternative) loan variables themselves, HEOA left college students with a full range of education-funding options to research on their own, without much guidance or assistance.

> *We published a brochure on alternative loans, and, of course, we had the naughty word "preferred lenders" on there. And one of the preferred lenders even published it for us. You know, printed it for us. So a change we've had to do, of course, is to no longer offer that alternative loan brochure. Because it did have the lender's name on there, that they had published it. We now have a lot of information on our website. They should read everything on our website. It really is a counseling tool for the student. Whenever we talk to a student who is thinking about an alternative loan, we always tell them to, again, go to our website. We tell them*

they should go in, do their homework, and compare the various lenders that are out there. —Financial aid counselor, 2008

There are a lot of different marketing techniques used in alternative loans where the costs are difficult to discern because, in some instances, they're upfront in terms of origination fees, and in other loan products they're imbedded in the back end in terms of late payment penalties and surcharges. They vary significantly more than the federal loans and are harder to discern and compare. —Financial aid counselor, 2008

I do admit, with the variety of loan options out there and all the different options available, it is hard to keep up to date on all the information out there. —Financial aid counselor, 2008

We are in the process of revamping that stuff right now because we used to have an alternative loan sheet. And, it just became impossible to keep current with the interest rate changes and so on. —Financial aid counselor, 2008

College financial aid offices have a unique opportunity to help students and families with financial aid options regarding private student loans; however, colleges no longer risk the possibility of compliance violations and fines since Cuomo's investigation. The likelihood that colleges would support their own financial aid counselors and allow them to steer college students toward any particular private lenders is now very minimal. When asked, financial aid counselors will more likely direct students toward a limited amount of general information that they can find online.

We provide very limited counseling for the alternative loan program because the student seeks out that lending on their own. We don't do any processing of the alternative loans.

> *The only thing we actually do is certify it. We do try to counsel them to seek other forms before resorting to the alternative loans. We are much more general in the information we provide to students.* —Financial aid counselor, 2008

Colleges simplified their financial aid counseling and directed students to look online for most anything having to do with private lenders and private student loans. Some colleges no longer package private student loans when offering financial aid awards. Students should be prepared to do their own research and be able to recognize the differences between private and federal student loans.

> *We have no more loan brochures because we no longer pay all that money for something that is going to be obsolete tomorrow. We do have, at this point, an 8½-by-11 sheet of paper with some various lenders on there as well as website information. It is not very pretty at this point; it's just functional because that's really the world we live in. We had a written document drawn up on Thursday morning that became obsolete that day and had to be redone for a visit day on Friday. That is how fast things are changing.... Students should look online.* —Financial aid counselor, 2008

Counselors are not privy to the details of all private student loans that are obtained by borrowers. Private lenders, students, parents, grandparents, and other cosigners do not consistently share all of their private loan information with counselors; this may be intentional or unintentional.

> *There are a wide range of students who won't disclose private loan information, for competitive reasons. So there is a limit to what we can offer in the way of counseling. We*

> won't know what the terms of the loan are until after the
> student's been approved. —Financial aid counselor, 2008

Colleges provide minimal training for their own financial aid counselors to be able to offer in-depth counseling to college students who elect private student loans. Colleges typically do not train their counselors to be able to counsel specifically on private student loans. Students can turn to their private lenders with their questions, or they can turn to financial aid counselors that may or may not be able to help them. College students should be prepared to provide full disclosure and information regarding all of the terms and conditions of their private student loans as they search for financial help.

> There needs to be more training for our profession in that
> area—more banking background, know interest rates a little
> bit better as far as the different types of private loans more
> than we do, as far as interest rates on the private side. This
> is opposite of when we had to get more tax knowledge and
> do more conflicting information verification. —Financial aid
> counselor, 2008

Private lenders generally do not require borrowers to attend loan counseling. They may offer it, and more private lenders are beginning to offer brochures and online counseling options; however, they do not typically require borrowers to attend counseling in order to receive loan funds. Borrower acknowledgments and signatures on private college loans are acceptable proof that all borrowers have read, understood, and agreed to all of the terms and conditions of their private student loans, including the details shown in small print. The use of electronic signatures allows the entire private loan process to simply be completed online. Students and private loan cosigners (typically the parents, and also some grandparents) should plan to read the small print of their college loans or find outside help, such as a local accountant or community banker, to help them understand the details of their college loans.

> *Private loan borrowers are not required, actually, to go through an entrance or an exit counseling process.*
> —Financial aid counselor, 2008

> *Currently, private loan counseling is not mandatory.*
> —Financial aid counselor, 2008

> *It would be beneficial that the family be mandated by the federal government to come in [for private loan counseling]. Although I hate to say this because it would really burden our office, they should have more information or at least try to grasp more information. If mandated by the federal government, then staffing would be in place at institutions.*
> —Financial aid counselor, 2008

Parent PLUS Loans Have a Simple Approval Process

The federal Parent PLUS Loans for parents are remarkably simple to get. Using Education Department data, the *Chronicle of Higher Education* and ProPublica analyzed colleges and the average PLUS loan amounts that parents took out. With an average annual loan of $27,305, New York University (NYU) ranked 11th in the nation in 2011, and parents borrowed more than $116 million through the Parent PLUS program (Penn State University's amount was $160 million in one year). "Getting a PLUS loan shouldn't be so easy," says Randall Deike, vice president for enrollment management at NYU (Wang, Supiano, and Fuller 2012).

While parents report their income on the FAFSA, their income is not considered when Parent PLUS Loan amounts are offered up to 100 percent of a college's COA. A Parent PLUS Loan is approved when one parent does not have adverse credit; it is that simple. If the parent has adverse credit, a Parent PLUS Loan can be cosigned with them by someone who does not have adverse credit. The approval is not contingent on income. The government does not check employment status. It does not check how much other debt—such as other student loan debt, a car loan, a home mortgage, or credit cards—the borrower is already obligated to pay. One parent qualifying without adverse credit can borrow up to 100 percent of a college's COA through a federal Parent PLUS Loan. If a student has received any other financial aid, then the Parent PLUS Loan limit is simply the total COA minus any other financial aid, without regard to repayment ability. There are no federal loan counseling requirements for parents who obtain a federal Parent PLUS Loan. According to David Palmer, the New York Conservatory for Dramatic Arts' chief executive, when acknowledging families who borrow too much in PLUS loans, "I don't know that it's the institution's responsibility to say we'll take a glimpse of what your individual situation is and say maybe this isn't a good idea" (Wang, Supiano, and Fuller 2012).

The Parent PLUS Loan is an unsecured loan, and there is no collateral required for this loan. From July 1, 2013, through June 30, 2014, the variable rate on a Parent PLUS Loan is 6.41 percent; the loan can increase annually up to a maximum interest rate of 10.50 percent. The maximum rate for consolidating PLUS loans into a Direct Consolidation Loan would be 10.625 percent. There is a standard repayment term of 10 years, and repayment begins 60 days after the loan is disbursed. The Parent PLUS Loan has forbearance and deferment options that are typically not available on private loans from private lenders (ParentPLUSLoan.com n.d.-a).

The Parent PLUS Loan offers additional protection for college students and parents in that it is a federal loan that may be discharged due to total or permanent disability or death. It is one of the main selling points used by financial aid counselors, and it is an option that is available with federal loans that is not typically available with private student loans. However, loan forgiveness due to death and disability is considered taxable income, with few exceptions. Families should expect that when a federal student loan is erased due to a student's death (the student whom the PLUS loan was intended for), a parent's death (the parent signed on the PLUS loan), or a parent's total and permanent disability (the parent signed on the PLUS loan), the amount would then be taxed as income in the year the debt was forgiven (Federal Student Aid n.d.-i). They will be receiving notice of the forgiven amount on IRS tax form 1099c. Failure to pay taxes on taxable income is subject to federal IRS collection procedures. While this same tax law pertains to debt erased by private lenders, it would be unlikely that a private lender would forgive the debt under the same terms. The tax repayment risk on federal student debt forgiveness due to death could be minimized with life insurance protection, for those who are insurable. For debt forgiveness due to total or permanent disability, families will need to rely on savings or liquidation of assets to pay any taxable income obligations. Even if they have disability insurance and receive monthly payments, the payments would unlikely be enough to repay a lump sum income tax obligation.

The Parent PLUS Loan is the loan that many financial aid counselors will turn to when filling a financial gap, as they find unsecured Parent PLUS Loans to have clear advantages over unsecured private loans; in some cases the Parent PLUS Loan is the only parent loan that is offered by colleges in the financial aid process. It offers the simplest approval because the Parent PLUS Loan is not contingent on a parent's income, on employment, or on the amount of any other debt.

Credit scores are not considered for Parent PLUS Loans; the primary applicant just cannot have adverse credit. In contrast, private lenders depend on credit history, credit scores, and repayment capacity from income for private loan approvals.

Families start the federal financial aid application process when they complete the FAFSA, and colleges are eager to help families find financing. Colleges may package and label Parent PLUS Loans as awards on a student's financial aid award letter. The Parent PLUS award can be an amount equal to 100 percent of COA, repayment begins 60 days after the final disbursement, and the standard repayment plan is 10 years. Only one creditworthy parent is needed to sign a Parent PLUS Loan, and that parent cannot have adverse credit to qualify. A college undergraduate student does not sign a Parent PLUS Loan and is not legally responsible to repay it. For those parents who have side agreements with a child that the child will be the one to make the payments on the Parent PLUS Loans once they exit school, the original Parent PLUS Loans would be a legal agreement between the federal lender and the parent. And a student cannot consolidate a federal Parent PLUS Loan with their own federal student loans. Any failure to pay on a PLUS loan will negatively affect the credit score of the parent (and any creditworthy cosigner) who signed the loan.

During the 2008 interviews, counselors stated that they overwhelmingly recommended the federal Parent PLUS Loans over nonfederal private student loans. Since July 1, 2013, Parent PLUS Loans are offered only as variable-rate loans at 6.41 percent, with a 10.50 percent cap rate.

> In 2004, we changed from offering private loan options to only offering PLUS loans to parents if there was a gap in the financial aid package...we saw a $7 million increase in PLUS loans and $7 million decrease in private loans.
> —Financial aid counselor, 2008

> *We will encourage their parents to take out a federal PLUS loan before we allow them to proceed with securing a private alternative loan.* —Financial aid counselor, 2008
>
> *We do a lot more talking about the death and disability benefits of the PLUS loan and that private loans do not have these benefits.* —Financial aid counselor, 2008
>
> *The PLUS loan has built-in protections for the family that the private loans do not.* —Financial aid counselor, 2008

Here is a well-publicized example of a counselor favoring the federal Parent PLUS Loan over private student loans. According to Alison Rabil, while she was the director of financial aid for Barnard College, a one-on-one conversation was effective in their goals of having more parents accept Parent PLUS Loans over private student loans. In 2006, she made a policy change that required students or their parents to have an actual conversation with a financial aid counselor when planning to borrow money through private lenders. This change resulted in a 73 percent reduction (more than $1 million) in their private loan volume and shifted the majority of that financial need to federal Parent PLUS Loans. Private loans are theoretically used when parents and students do not think they can pay the expected family contribution (EFC) of a financial aid package, but Rabil said that many families do not understand the potential of PLUS loans. "We were horribly blunt," Rabil said about how students' debt can outlive students' parents. "We had the talk about death and disability. Many parents had not given the issue of their mortality any thought." According to Rabil, "The main thing parents have heard about the Parent PLUS program seems to be that repayment starts 60 days after the last disbursement of funds for a year." According to Rabil, if the family wanted to proceed with borrowing private loans after that one-on-one conversation with a counselor, Barnard did not stand in their way. But for many families, the efforts of the one-on-one talk revealed risks and options they did not know about, and it shifted borrowing from private loans to Parent PLUS Loans (Jaschik 2007).

While the underwriting process for getting a Parent PLUS Loan is relatively simple, once applicants complete the FAFSA, there is no immediate concern on the part of federal student lenders for how much is too much money to borrow. Basically, the Parent PLUS Loan is a viable option used to fill the financial gap for those families who have not saved specifically for their children's college, and they now have somewhere to go to borrow it all in one place and on an unsecured basis. The Parent PLUS option can work quite well for those parents who maintain enough income to steadily repay the debt and gives them an opportunity to help pay college costs. Parent PLUS Loans, like all federal and nonfederal (private) student loans, are next to impossible to discharge in bankruptcy.

> *Families have not saved as they have in the past. They might have more debt out there and, again, less savings. Savings has not kept up with the increase in expenses.* —Financial aid counselor, 2008

Estimates from survey results in 2010 and 2011 by American Community Survey (ACS), an ongoing Census Bureau survey, show that household income has continued to decline. According to the U.S. Census Bureau, the real median household income in the United States for 2011 was $50,502 (Noss 2012). For those parents who are earning at least $50,000 in annual gross income, are committed (on a united front) to helping their children pay for college, and are looking for a simple financial guideline as far as how much money might be a safe amount for them to borrow, the financial recommendation for parents is the same as the recommendation for college students: (1) the combined total loan amounts that are borrowed for college should not exceed *half* of their annual income, and (2) the monthly payment amount should not exceed 7 percent of their monthly gross income. Parents who consider an unsecured Parent PLUS Loan may also consider a secured home equity loan to fill the financial gap (FinAid n.d.-f).

The added assumption when limiting the amount parents borrow for their children is that many parents will be making monthly house payments on their home loan while their children are going to college (parents without house debt could likely manage more college debt). If those home mortgage payments for principal, interest, real estate taxes, and insurance are at the maximum 28 percent of income, then total monthly payments would be 35 percent of gross monthly income (28 percent for the house and 7 percent going toward student loan payments). There should be no other monthly payment obligations, as this already represents 35 percent of total income. For a household earning $50,000 a year, that would be approximately $14,000 per year (or $1,167 a month) for mortgage payments and $3,500 per year (or $291 a month) for college loan payments. It would leave $32,500 or about $2,700 a month for their basic living costs (assuming no major medical expenses), house and vehicle maintenance, Social Security and retirement savings, and income tax obligations. It leaves very little room for trading vehicles, which is why a commitment to borrow money for college should be on a united front by both parents, even if only one of them is required to sign the federal Parent PLUS Loan. It could require a decline in lifestyle for parents for a decade, longer for those who extend their repayment obligations beyond 10 years or commit to Parent PLUS loans for multiple children.

Here is an example assuming a Direct Parent PLUS Loan with a 10-year Standard Repayment Plan, an average 7 percent interest rate, and a $25,000 loan (half of $50,000 gross annual income). The 7 percent interest rate used in this example is somewhat optimistic considering that the current variable interest rate on a federal Parent PLUS Loan is already at 6.41 percent and it can increase up to 10.50 percent. (The Direct Parent PLUS Loan program also offers a 25-year extended repayment plan when borrowers have more than $30,000 in outstanding loan programs.)

Monthly Gross Wages	Maximum Loan Amount	Average Interest Rate	Number of Payments	Monthly Payment Amount	Percent of Gross Income
$4,166.67	$25,000	7.00%	120	$290.33	6.97%

The U.S. Department of Education does not know how many parents have defaulted on the Parent PLUS Loans. It does not analyze default rates for the PLUS program with the same details that it does for other federal education loans. It estimates that of all Parent PLUS Loans originated in the 2011 fiscal year, about 9.4 percent, or about 1 in 10, will default over the next 20 years (Wang, Supiano, and Fuller 2012). For those parents who are trying to help their children, want their children to go to college, and need to borrow money, they will be relatively safe under the combined rules of borrowing no more than *half* of their annual income in total college loans and committing to monthly payments no greater than 7 percent of their gross monthly income. Money needed in addition to the half-of-annual-income rule will need to come from savings, liquidation of assets, or other cash sources. Parents who sign on Parent PLUS Loans or any private student loans should plan to repay them and include them in their budget. Any creditworthy cosigner who signs with a parent on a PLUS loan should plan to repay them in their own budget. The amount of Parent PLUS Loans added to a college student's debt may prove too much for the college student to have to repay while they work full time and if they intend to maintain financial independence once they exit college, even with the best of intentions.

Private Lenders Simplified Their Repayment Risks by Requiring Creditworthy Cosigners

The population of college students greatly increased during the 1960s and '70s, with the baby boomer generation heading to college. By the 1980s, there was a shift from the reliance on state and federal government funding for education to more family contributions and student loans. The federal government began funding fewer need-based grant programs. Credit scoring was widely used for credit-based consumer lending, including both loans to college students and loans to parents. In addition, family savings did not keep pace with the steady increases in education expenses. These changes resulted in the need for more college students to continue to borrow more money, with a creditworthy cosigner.

> *Parents, years ago, could get a job out of high school. Or they could go into manufacturing or a trade school. And those just aren't available anymore. One of the common responses is, "Why, I just never thought they'd go to college. I just never thought they would want to go to college, so I didn't save and I just don't have anything."* —Financial aid counselor, 2008

By 2011, the investor demand for private student loan asset-backed securities had fallen sharply after the 2008 credit crisis, constraining funding options for student lenders. Due to the decline in the U.S. economy, the loss of jobs, and the increase in private loan defaults, some lenders abruptly left the private student loan industry. This made it much more difficult for students to borrow money on their own from private lenders because there were fewer lenders taking that risk and the remaining lenders starting requiring cosigners to help mitigate the risk. This was a significant change in private student loans that directly affected college students.

> *A fairly prominent provider decided to exit the business. They basically told us that day, and that was the last day they were doing business—no warning, no anything. We received a letter that they were no longer doing business because they wanted to focus money and effort on the federal loan volume.* —Financial aid counselor, 2008

> *A lot of private lenders, a lot of Stafford Loan lenders, have gotten out of the private loan business.* —Financial aid counselor, 2008

> *Lenders who once lent money for alternative loans are no longer able to do that.* —Financial aid counselor, 2008

There were varied reactions from parents when the financial obligations of paying for college shifted from students being able to sign for both federal and private loans on their own to students needing to have parents become legally responsible and sign their names with their children on private student loans or sign alone on federal Parent PLUS Loans. For those students who felt they had no other choice but to ask their parents to sign loans in order for them to be able to stay in school, the reactions from parents began to form a negative undercurrent, according to the financial aid counselors.

3 The Undercurrent

There's unable and then there's unwilling. I'll work with a hundred of those [unable] to the one that's unwilling. The parent says, "Look, I know I'm supposed to come up with $10,000. I know I have an expected family contribution of $45,000. I should be able to write out a check for this because I make $130,000 a year. But, I'm not gonna do it." So the student has a $3,500 Stafford Loan, a $1,500 Perkins Loan, he has $5,000 in loans, and mom and dad are asking him to come do another loan for $8,000–$10,000 in a private loan. So he's going to have $13,000–$15,000 in loans the first year. Can we multiply by four? I think we can. And the parents, you know, are good with that. —Financial aid counselor, 2008

THE FEDERAL GOVERNMENT and colleges consider it primarily the family's responsibility to pay for school. They may be able to provide some financial assistance when the family is unable to pay; however, parents are expected to have a greater responsibility toward their children than the government or the schools. The conflict occurs when the child is directed toward college, and the parents feel that their financial responsibility ends when the student turns 18, graduates from high school, or enters college.

> *Parents had a greater proportion of grants, less amount in loans. They had smaller tuition, fees, room, and board. So we ask parents, "What responsibilities do you want to take out for them to go [to college]?" Parents say, "When I was in school, I went to school by myself. And I pulled myself up by the bootstrap. I did it myself. We want this in his name, and then we'll help him later." I'll believe it when I see it.*
> —Financial aid counselor, 2008

Some parents feel that they cannot afford to pay for college and have enough of their own debt to repay. Some parents refuse to fill out the FAFSA because they think they will not qualify anyway, they are concerned about the privacy of their financial information, or they do not want their children to know their financial business. Some parents do not want their children to go to college or to go to a particular college (e.g., attending college far from home or following a particular boyfriend or girlfriend), so they do not cooperate in the federal financial aid application process. Some parents just do not want to help. The counselors shared a variety of their experiences when working with parents.

1. Some parents willingly sign loans for their children to be able to go to college.

   > *I have parents making $25,000 a year willing to sign an $8,000 PLUS loan because they want their kid in college and having a shot.* —Financial aid counselor, 2008

> *Some kids come in with their parents, and the parents are very good about it. This is what he's going to do, this is how he's going to do it, you know, they walk through it; they're used to managing money.* —Financial aid counselor, 2008

2. Some parents reluctantly cosign loans for their children to go to college.

    > *The undercurrent is there...they just don't want to...they can't or they just don't want to.* —Financial aid counselor, 2008

    > *Parents are either unable or unwilling to incur further debt for the student's education. And so the student is therefore forced to go and get private loans, cosigned often by those parents who are refusing to do PLUS loans.* —Financial aid counselor, 2008

3. Some parents are not creditworthy cosigners.

    > *The fact that they need a cosigner sometimes is an issue for them because we have many parents, unfortunately, that either their debt ratio or their credit history isn't the best. We see where sometimes the students have an issue, getting a cosigner.* —Financial aid counselor, 2008

4. A growing number of parents refuse to sign loans to help their children pay for college.

    > *Time after time after time, I find that the richer the parent, the less likely their willingness to do a loan. The poorer the parent, the more willing but also the more unable. So their willingness is there, their ability is not. It's kind of like what*

> they say about Vegas. Vegas wasn't built on winners. The rich get rich because they don't spend money. The rich didn't get rich by wasting their money. —*Financial aid counselor, 2008*
>
> There are parents who say, "I'm not going do it."
> —*Financial aid counselor, 2008*

Zac Bissonnette, the author of *Debt Free U*, suggests that parents who still have any furniture left in their houses and have eaten anything better than ramen in the past two months are not sacrificing enough to help their children pay for college without the children having to take out student loans. According to counselors, the opposite is more likely to happen.

There are those parents who cannot afford to help their children, and there are some parents who elect not to help. The biggest discovery that counselors highlighted during the interviews was that there were more parents who did not intend to help their children pay for college. Period. Their reasons varied:

> Parents have been adamant about not helping. They did it themselves; the child can do it alone.
> —*Financial aid counselor, 2008*
>
> Parents want children to learn the same lesson, to take it seriously, to do it themselves. —*Financial aid counselor, 2008*
>
> They want their student to stay close to home to go to community college, so they just say, "No, we're not helping because you could get something cheaper." —*Financial aid counselor, 2008*
>
> So we talk about an option for a PLUS loan, and they say, "No, we're not going to do that." —*Financial aid counselor, 2008*

According to the IRS, the typical college student is considered dependent for federal financial aid purposes, no matter how independently a student lives or how they are claimed on federal tax returns. As a dependent, the student must, with their parents, complete and submit the FAFSA to be considered for federal student aid (FAFSA n.d.-a). If a dependent student's FAFSA is not completed by the student and parents, then no federal financial aid is awarded. In addition, most states and colleges now use information from the FAFSA to award nonfederal aid.

Current federal regulation is clear that self-support is not sufficient for filing as independent in terms of financial aid for college. If parents refuse to provide their financial information and a student wishes to be declared independent and would qualify for a dependency override, the student needs to contact the school's financial aid office to start the appeal process. Only in the rarest of situations, when there is documentation of a complete break in the family situation, can the general dependency criteria be overridden.

Some parents mistakenly believe that if they refuse to contribute, the school will declare the student independent and help pick up the parent's share of the college costs. The U.S. Department of Education has guidelines for financial aid administrators indicating that neither parental refusal to contribute financially to a student's education nor parental unwillingness to provide information for federal student aid is sufficient for a dependency status override. This is true even if the parents do not claim the student as a dependent on their federal tax returns.

If a student's parents are divorced, the student will be considered a dependent of the parent they live with. If parental time is split evenly, then the financial information of the parent who provides more support must be on the FAFSA. A 1998 study, *The Unexpected Legacy of Divorce: A 25 Year Landmark Study*, supports the fact that children of divorced parents are less likely to receive parental financial support for college than children of intact marriages (FinAid n.d.-n).

If the supporting parent remarried, the stepparent's financial information is required on the FAFSA as well, even if the stepparent does not or will not support the student. Sometimes stepparents do not feel responsible to help pay for their stepchildren to go to college and feel it is unfair that the government requires them to pay.

Prenuptial agreements are ignored in the financial need analysis. A prenuptial agreement is an agreement between the husband and wife and is not binding on any third party, such as the college, a lender, or the government. A prenuptial agreement cannot negate the obligation to help children pay for a college education. If the prenuptial agreement includes this type of clause, courts could consider it null and void (FinAid n.d.-n).

Colleges follow the law when awarding federal and state student aid, as well as their own college aid. Many colleges will consider the custodial parent and stepparent's income and assets, as well as the income and assets of the noncustodial parent.

The Higher Education Opportunity Act of 2008 amended the Higher Education Act of 1965 to allow colleges to offer unsubsidized Stafford Loans to dependent students without requiring the parents to file a FAFSA, provided that the financial aid administrator is able to verify that the parents have ended financial support and refuse to file the FAFSA (FinAid n.d.-n). When parents refuse to pay, it does not constitute an unusual circumstance for the student; there has to be sufficient justification. The financial aid administrator will need evidence that the student is self-supporting, such as copies of tax returns and pay statements. For example, if the student's earnings are not even close to the poverty line, they are going to need additional documentation on how the student was able to live. They will also verify whether or not the student is living at home or if the student stopped living at home recently. They will want to see canceled rent checks (having the student pay rent to the parents will not help). Additionally, the aid administrator will want all statements confirmed by third-party documentation. The financial aid administrator will then have the final decision and determine whether or not the student is independent. Their final decision is not subject to appeal (FinAid n.d.-n).

Veterans and active duty military personnel are automatically considered independent for federal need analysis purposes. Military personnel should verify the interpretation of their military status, as those can vary. The federal government, as well as nonprofit organizations, offers money for college to veterans, future military personnel, active duty personnel, and those related to veterans or active duty personnel (Federal Student Aid n.d.-c).

The federal requirements for independent student status changed in 1992. According to FinAid, students must satisfy at least one of the following criteria to be considered independent:

- The student is 24 years of age or older by December 31 of the award year.
- The student is an orphan or ward of the court or was a ward of the court until the student reached the age of 18.
- The student is a veteran of the Armed Forces of the United States.
- The student is a graduate or professional student.
- The student has legal dependents other than a spouse (example: children). (For an individual to be considered a dependent, more than half of their support must come from the student.)
- The student is married.

What counts is the student's marital status as of the date the student submitted the FAFSA. If the student gets married after that date, they will not be considered independent until the subsequent year. Federal law prohibits schools from changing a student's marital status midyear. Students who are married are considered financially independent from their parents, but students who are under 24, divorced, and not remarried are typically considered dependent. Marriage is one of the few variables that college students have control of within the rules of federal student aid (FinAid n.d.-n).

Students who do not meet the criteria for independent status are considered dependent, and their parents' income and resources will determine the eligibility for federal financial assistance. If parents refuse to pay, students will have to make up that difference by working, finding other payment sources, or attending college in nontraditional ways. The college and the government cannot help based on the current financial aid rules. Financial aid counselors stated that more parents are refusing to help.

This information is not intended to insult hardworking parents; it is intended to address a very real financial problem faced by many students. Current federal law does not provide many federal financial aid options for dependent students who go to college at least halftime and have no support from parents.

Selecting Colleges

A Fidelity survey of 2,000 families with children 18 and younger found that only 31 percent of parents have spoken with their children about the total costs of college and future job opportunities, earnings potential, and possible debt load—meaning that 69 percent have not tackled the topic (Ellis 2012).

> *I end up seeing a student or I end up talking to a parent. I'm not seeing them together a lot. It's either the student handling it or it's the mom or dad. It's rarely, unless we're talking to someone at the orientation program, it's rarely*

> them together. If they're coming in October because they can't pay the bill, mom and dad are usually somewhere else. Or, mom or dad always handles the financial stuff, so the student just says take care of it and they're willing to do it. I don't think that's necessarily a benefit for either of them because they're not really knowing, not all of them are knowing, what the other hand is doing. —Financial aid counselor, 2008

Students can begin researching their college options by first talking to their parents and highlighting what they personally plan to do to help pay for their own college costs. Students can show how much money they have saved, how much they will earn, how many hours they will work while in college, how they plan to budget their living costs, and what colleges they can possibly afford to attend based on those numbers. If gaining parental support and the numbers suggest enrolling in a lower-cost school, after grants, scholarships, and gifts are determined, then students may need to limit their college search to lower-cost schools after gifts, grants, and scholarships are awarded. A report on college dropout rates revealed that nearly 46 percent of all those who enter a U.S. college fail to graduate within six years due, in part, to the debt burden (HCM Strategists 2012). College students without any family support have a greater risk of dropping out of school.

One area where parents can help their children, where it would cost them more in time than in money, would be to complete the FAFSA and apply with their child for federal financial aid. Students and parents can turn to financial aid counselors for assistance in completing the FAFSA. This is a free application that parents are required to complete with students to be able to obtain financial aid and for students to be able to sign for some federal student loans on their own. Completing the FAFSA may also help in obtaining other federal, state, and college aid.

A student's financial aid and the family's expected family contribution (EFC) are determined annually. Students and families have no guarantees on financial aid awards and EFC in future years; aid packages could improve or get worse.

$$COA - EFC = \text{Financial aid award}$$

In this example, a college's COA is $22,000, a family's EFC is $16,500, and the student is awarded $5,500 in a federal unsubsidized Stafford Loan (the unsubsidized Stafford Loan is not based on need or credit).

$$\$22,000 \text{ (COA) minus } \$16,500 \text{ (EFC)} =$$
$$\$5,500 \text{ (federal loan through financial aid)}$$

For example, the federal unsubsidized Stafford Loan, which is not credit-based or based on need, is currently at an aggregate limit of $31,000 (there are also various annual limits) for dependent undergraduate students. This $31,000 aggregate limit is more than what most college undergraduate students should be borrowing based on this book's guideline that they should not be borrowing more than *half* of their expected gross income in their first year out of college.

How does the balance get paid? Students and parents need to first identify ways to pay more of their college costs from sources outside of borrowing money. They can agree to the following: earning more money through working additional hours or jobs, tapping into savings, applying for more scholarships and grants, finding cash through other family sources, selling unused assets, and planning to save additional room and board costs by living at home (Yee 2011). For those students planning to work more hours or work full-time jobs, federal financial aid requires that students attend college at least half-time. According to a Fidelity survey, more parents are asking their college-bound children to live at home and commute to classes or major in areas of study that will lead to more lucrative careers (which can be difficult to forecast for the next four or five years) and are asking their children to start saving for college when they are as young as 13. The survey discloses that more parents are considering shared sacrifices (Ellis 2012).

At a minimum, undergraduate students should discuss the following with their parents:

1. Where to live while going to college.
2. The colleges that students can possibly afford to attend and that parents can support emotionally and/or financially.
3. Their willingness to complete the FAFSA to be able to apply for federal financial aid.
4. The amount of savings and wages that will be earmarked for college costs.
5. Who is paying what.
6. The parents' willingness to help them with the financial aid process.
7. The parents' willingness to sign or cosign loans.

> *If they do have a cosigner, then that opens up a lot of doors. Now which lender has the best loan?* —Financial aid counselor, 2008

College students can benefit from knowing answers to these basic financial questions, and it could simplify the college-selection process. One father shared, "We all have cell phones, but no one communicates around here anymore." College students have been known to be home for an entire holiday break and not say one word about needing money to be able to stay in school. The day they return to campus, they text a parent, "Need $—can't enroll in classes." That gives parents only three days instead of three weeks to come up with some money. Students who cannot pay (for college) cannot stay. Students who want to earn a college degree cannot afford to stop communicating with their parents.

> **Students who cannot pay cannot stay.**

Grandparents

What about college students looking to grandparents when their parents cannot or will not help them pay for college? Actuaries support the fact that people are living longer; today's young people are likely to live to be 90 (Hacker and Dreifus 2011). Grandparents will need to have enough money to support their own living costs and medical costs for their retirement. But how much money is enough money? It is a difficult question to answer because lifestyle is a personal choice at all ages. Some professional financial advisors specialize in retirement planning and offer basic financial advice; they often recommend that grandparents put their own financial needs first and ahead of helping their grandchildren pay for college. They emphasize that lenders will loan grandchildren money to go to college but will not loan grandparents money for retirement, for example. This advice should be updated to today's student lending environment. Dependent college students cannot qualify for federal loans on their own without the cooperation of their parents completing the FAFSA. The maximum federal loan amounts available to students alone typically will not cover a college's COA. Private lenders offering private student loans have become much more selective in how they loan money to college students, and it typically is no longer to the student alone, meaning that lenders will not automatically loan money solely to the grandchildren to help them pay for college. These changes in loan options can leave grandparents with their own financial decisions on whom to bet on and where they will invest their money—on their grandchildren or on the financial returns of their savings and retirement accounts.

Helping grandchildren pay for college has been a goal for some grandparents for years. Back in 2003, the American International Group's SunAmerica Mutual Funds conducted a survey that found that 54 percent of grandparents said they were either helping with college costs or planning to do so. Unfortunately the value of many stocks dropped, some 40 to 50 percent in a year, and the investment accounts set aside to help grandchildren with tuition payments were destroyed (Ritt n.d.). However, there have been indications recently that with the rising cost of tuition and the lagging economy, grandparents are pitching in more. The theory is that parents are suffering in this economy and grandparents, even though their savings may have declined with the market, are more financially stable. Even Warren Buffett committed to "homespun" values in his grandchildren and agreed to pay for their college, school expenses only—and nothing more (Goodman 2008).

Financial issues are often difficult to discuss with families. Many students avoid it and would sooner resort to borrowing too much money, if they could, than having to work through the finances and find other sources. It is a common reaction to a seemingly complicated college financial aid structure. If college students determine that their parents cannot or will not help financially, they then need to decide if anyone else can help, what they can afford on their own, where and when they can go to college, and for how long.

Analyzing Options

According to the Best Colleges website, in a poll of college graduates, the one thing that stood out as playing a vital role in how a student perceives college was the campus setting: "College campuses rule the day" (The Best Colleges 2013). Colleges are competing for students by beautifying their campuses. There are five-star college campuses with state-of-the-art residence halls, dining centers, recreational facilities, and numerous other amenities; however, students should be financially savvy when first selecting a college.

> *Basically, it is a life choice.*
> —Financial aid counselor, 2008

Students can begin the college application process by searching college options and limiting their search to those with a cost they can afford to pay, a class structure and delivery that they can manage while working, and a college budget they can live within. They should plan to complete the FAFSA along with their parents so that they can compare their financial aid options. Loans should not be considered awards when comparing college options; the comparisons should be limited to the college's total COA minus awarded grants and scholarships.

Parents who are unwilling to complete the FAFSA, in order for their students to be able to qualify for financial aid and for federal loans that they can sign alone, force their children into an à la carte, pay-as-you-go option under the current financial aid rules. Students can work and save money, then pay for a college course and course materials whenever they have enough (time and money) to enroll. Some employers still offer college reimbursement programs for part-time and full-time employees. Students can apply for scholarships along the way on their own, if the scholarship application processes do not require the FAFSA. Donors of scholarships could help more college students by specifically stating that their scholarship is not contingent upon completion of the FAFSA.

The Reality of College Readiness 2013 by ACT Research provides the following characteristics of undergraduate students:

- Eleven percent of students simultaneously enrolled in more than one institution.
- Forty-one percent of graduates attended more than one institution.
- Thirty-eight percent enrolled part-time.
- More than 2 million students brought college credit with them at the time of first full-time enrollment (dual credit, advanced placement [AP], online, or College-Level Examination Program [CLEP]).
- Thirty percent delayed enrollment for a year or more.
- Twenty-five percent of undergraduates were over age 25.
- Thirty percent of undergraduates enrolled in an online course.
- Twenty-nine percent of community college students transferred to four-year colleges.
- Fourteen percent transferred from four-year to two-year colleges.

A typical college-age student who has no parental financial support could also wait until age 24 to enroll in college. Based on the current federal financial aid rules, a 24-year-old could qualify as independent in order to borrow more money through federal student loan options; however, total borrowing needs to be limited to *half* of the expected first year of wages out of college no matter how many people are pushing for 100 percent financing. Students need to be saving their own money between the ages of 18 and 24 to be ready to attend college at age 24. There is always that risk that these federal financial aid rules may change for college students during the six years it takes before a typical 18-year-old college student reaches

24 years of age; however, six years of savings will help independent young adults to be able to attend college.

> Students will either have to enroll at a very low-cost local alternative, a community college or something of that nature, or simply wait to go to college until they are independent students at age 24. At that age they can borrow more from the federal government, as an independent student. —*Financial aid counselor, 2008*

Students may or may not initially want to attend a college located close to home. The option of enrolling in college and attending full time and outside of commuting distance from home may not be realistic for a student without some family support. It may not be realistic even for the student who has financial support from their family. Room and board typically accounts for one-quarter to one-half the total annual cost of U.S. colleges. The average cost for room and board for full-time undergraduates at public, four-year schools in the 2012–2013 academic year was $9,205 a year, according to the College Board, a nonprofit that promotes higher education. Private universities average $10,462 a year for room and board only (College Board Advocacy & Policy Center n.d.-b). Students who are able to live at home and can save on those costs are getting substantial support from their family, valued at about $10,000 a year. Students will have to reassess whether or not they will apply to any colleges that require them to live on campus and pay room and board costs, even if it is for only one year.

The traditional college landscape of graduating from high school and attending four years of college on a campus away from home may change for many college students due to the lack of finances alone; however, students can also earn a college degree by working while going to college. It could mean working full time and attending college either part-time or full time. Students and families are already resorting to these financial alternatives in order to pay for college. Elizabeth A. Armstrong and Laura T. Hamilton, authors of *Paying for the Party*, completed a case study of 50 students who attended a large Midwestern residential university and discovered that students who left that university to attend community colleges actually fared better; they accomplished more academically and were happier (Armstrong and Hamilton 2013).

A variety of college course delivery options are also available to students, more choices than were available when their parents were in college. Some colleges offer multiple locations in addition to their main campuses. Accredited colleges also offer online courses that are flexible and allow students to attend classes while working one or more jobs and supporting a family. Online classes are available to undergraduate and graduate students at many different accredited public, nonprofit, and for-profit colleges and universities.

In the fall 2010 semester, about 6.1 million students across the nation took at least one online college course, and the Sloan Consortium reports that the number of students taking online courses continues to rise each year. According to a 2010 CNN article, in the past, many employers were not familiar with online programs, which accounted for their sense of skepticism and distrust. Today, this apprehension is slowly disappearing, as Web-based degree programs become more common (Groux 2012). Twenty-three percent of leaders in academia say that online learning is inferior to face-to-face learning—down from 43 percent in 2003 (Reif 2013).

For those students who need to borrow money to attend college, they should borrow a total of no more than 50 percent of their gross income, an amount they can reasonably expect to earn their first year out of college. Students who borrow any money to attend college will join some national student loan debt statistics; here are some recent ones (American Student Assistance n.d.).

How many Americans borrow or have borrowed for college?

- As of the first quarter of 2012, the under-30 age group had the most borrowers at 14 million, followed by 10.6 million for the 30–39 group, 5.7 million in the 40–49 category, and 4.6 million in the 50–59 age group. The over-60 category had the smallest number of borrowers at 2.2 million.
- Nearly 20 million Americans attend college each year.
- Of that 20 million, close to 12 million, or 60 percent, borrow annually to help cover costs.

How much do Americans borrow or have they borrowed for college?

- As of the first quarter of 2012, the average student loan balance for all age groups was $24,301. About one-quarter of borrowers owed more than $28,000; 10 percent of borrowers owed more than $54,000; 3 percent owed more than $100,000; and less than 1 percent owed more than $200,000.
- Among all bachelor's degree recipients, median debt was about $7,960 at public four-year institutions, $17,040 at private not-for-profit four-year institutions, and $31,190 at for-profit institutions.
- As of October 2012, the average amount of student loan debt for the Class of 2011 was $26,600, a 5 percent increase from 2010. High-debt states are mainly in the Northeast and Midwest, with low-debt states mainly in the West and South. The 10 high-debt states are New Hampshire, Pennsylvania, Minnesota, Rhode Island, Connecticut, Iowa, Ohio, Vermont, the District of Columbia, and New Jersey. The 10 low-debt states are Utah, Hawaii, California, Arizona, Nevada, Tennessee, North Carolina, Oklahoma, Texas, and Washington. Multiple factors influence average college debt levels, such as endowment resources available for financial aid,

student demographics, state policies, institutional financial aid packaging policies, and the cost of living in the local area.

How many student loan borrowers struggle with repayment?

- Only about 37 percent of federal student loan borrowers between 2004 and 2009 managed to make timely payments without postponing payments or becoming delinquent.
- For every student loan borrower who defaults, at least two more borrowers become delinquent without default.
- Two out of five student loan borrowers, or 41 percent, are delinquent at some point in the first five years after entering repayment.
- As of 2012, there was more than $8 billion in defaulted private loans, or 850,000 loans in default.

Who struggles most?

- As of early 2012, borrowers in their 30s had a delinquency rate (more than 90 days past due) of about 6 percent, while borrowers in their 40s had a delinquency rate of about 12 percent. Borrowers in their 50s had a delinquency rate of 9.4 percent, and those over 60 had a delinquency rate of 9.5 percent.
- Students who drop out of college before earning a degree often struggle most with student loans: From 2004 to 2009, 33 percent of undergraduate federal student loan borrowers who left without a credential became delinquent without defaulting, and 26 percent defaulted, versus 21 percent with a credential who became delinquent without defaulting and 16 percent who defaulted. A loan becomes delinquent the first day a payment is missed. For most federal student loans, default means a payment has not been made for 270 days (nine months).

- The number of dropouts is on the rise: Nearly 30 percent of college students who took out loans dropped out of school, up from less than 25 percent a decade earlier.
- More than half of students who take out loans to enroll in two-year for-profit colleges never finish. At traditional nonprofit and public schools, the percentage of students with loans who started college in 2003 and dropped out within six years was about 20 percent.

Why do they struggle?

- Forty-eight percent of 25-to-34-year-olds say they are unemployed or underemployed.
- Fifty-two percent describe their financial situation as just fair.
- Seventy percent say it has become harder to make ends meet over the past four years.
- Forty-two percent of those under 35 have more than $5,000 in personal debt that does not include a mortgage.
- Student loans account for the most common form of increasing debt among ages 18–24 (54 percent have seen increased school loan debt), while those in the older group attribute increased debt equally to school loans (37 percent) and credit cards (37 percent).

How is student debt affecting borrowers and the U.S. economy?

- A college degree does increase an individual's potential for earnings. In 2010, people ages 25–34 with a bachelor's degree earned 114 percent more than did those without a high-school diploma.
- College graduates earned 50 percent more than did young adults who completed only high school and 22 percent more than did those with an associate degree.

How well do students and alumni understand their options to minimize borrowing and manage the debt once they have it?

- As of 2012, only 700,000 borrowers had enrolled in Income-Based Repayment to reduce monthly payments.
- About 65 percent of high-debt student loan borrowers misunderstood or were surprised by aspects of their student loans or the student loan process.

Cost of Attendance and Free Application for Federal Student Aid

The difficult part is a lot of them come in with a lot of bills they are paying themselves. You know, they just graduated from high school and they want a nice car. It's like, why do you want a nice car now? And it's $250 a month for their payment, it's like…[sigh]…you're just insane for doing that. I've counseled a couple kids in trying to get rid of their car because it was just too much. Do you want the car or do you want your education? It just came down to that. They're driving a better car than I'm driving. And, all you need is something that when you turn the key it starts and moves you from point A to point B. —Financial aid counselor, 2008

COLLEGE STUDENTS are faced with a tremendous amount of temptations and can find themselves falling into a debt trap when they do not plan financially. In a must-see video, *Cautionary Tales of the Student Debt Crisis*, produced by Virginia Blackburn of Iowa State University, college students share their personal finances and offer financial advice to college peers based on their own experiences. According to Blackburn, "I walk through the [college] union and I see students signing up for 10 credit cards just so they can get 10 free T-shirts. They don't think about what they're doing or how it will affect them later" (Jerousek 2003). The video contains 27 minutes of real-life testimonies—some of the most convincing evidence on the need for students to pay very close attention to their spending while attending college. Indebted college students, some starting college with full scholarships, share the aftermath of some of the financial decisions that they made while attending college. One college accounting major shared, "It took me, I'd say, probably $60,000 before I figured out the difference between a need and a want. And then I started figuring it out and it still took me another $5,000 or $10,000 before I figured out, OK—really, seriously—these are needs, these are wants, and I have to separate the two." Some colleges offer the content of this video as part of their entrance counseling requirements. It is available for viewing at the Buena Vista University website (http://www.bvu.edu/admissions/financial-assistance/credit-management.dot).

> *Borrow as little as you possibly can...we try and counsel them that way.* —Financial aid counselor, 2008

The College Board found that for the 2008–2009 school year, the average published tuition and fees for in-state students at public four-year colleges and universities was $6,585. By the 2011–2012 school year, the average tuition and fee costs had increased to $8,244. That is an increase of slightly over 25 percent in three years. When adding in room and board, tuition and fees plus room and board rose from $14,333 to $17,131 over the same period, nearly a 20 percent increase (Ma and Baum 2012). These figures are not adjusted for inflation. The National Center for Education Statistics reported for the 2010–2011 academic year that the average total costs for tuition and room and board charged to full-time undergraduate students across all four-year degree-granting institutions was $21,657 (National Center for Education Statistics n.d.-b).

> *In the time I was a student, tuition went up 50 percent from the day I started to the day I graduated [in 2005]. Federal aid can't keep up with that.* —Financial aid counselor, 2008

The College Board also offered data for other types of schools. Here are the percentages of tuition and fee increases for several other types of institutions:

- *Public, four-year institutions*—up 19 percent
- *Public, two-year colleges*—up 23 percent
- *Private, four-year institutions*—up 13 percent
- *For-profit institutions*—up 11 percent

The College Affordability and Transparency Center has resources for students in search of colleges (http://collegecost.ed.gov). Here are some of the options this website offers:

1. College Scorecard: Students can use the College Scorecard to find out more about a college's affordability and value to make more informed decisions about which college to attend.

    Within the "Better Bargain for the Middle Class: Making College More Affordable" plan and before the 2015 school year, the Department of Education plans to develop a new ratings system to help students compare the value offered by colleges. The ratings will be based upon such measures as access, affordability (e.g., average tuition, scholarships, and loan debt), and outcomes (e.g., graduation rates, transfer rates, and graduate earnings). The results will be published on the College Scorecard (Jaschik 2013).

Students will be able to continue to choose whichever college they want, but taxpayer dollars will be steered toward high-performing colleges that provide the best value. The Department of Education is to develop and publish a new college ratings system that would be available for students and families before the 2015 college year.

2. Net Price Calculator Center: Net price calculators helps students estimate how much a college costs after scholarships and grants. Loans should not be included when determining a college's net price.

3. College Navigator: Students are able to search for and compare colleges on all sorts of criteria, including costs, majors offered, size of school, campus safety, and graduation rates.

4. College Affordability and Transparency List: This list helps students find information about tuition and prices at postsecondary institutions. The website highlights institutions with high and low tuition and fees as well as high and low net prices. It also shows institutions where tuition and fees and net prices are increasing at the highest rates.

5. State Spending Charts: Students can find information on the changes in state appropriations for postsecondary education, state aid for students, and tuition and fees.

Students can also access College Navigator through the National Center for Education Statistics (http://nces.ed.gov/collegenavigator/). It offers an array of options for students when deciding a career and locating possible college options.

An alternative to College Navigator for students and their families to be able to compare the true cost estimates of a college's financial aid offer (College Navigator is operated by the U.S. Department of Education and may be unavailable during a government shutdown) is a fairly new and free, one-stop online application called College Abacus. Once personal financial and educational information is entered into College Abacus, this website can compare net costs based on a college's full COA minus scholarships. College Abacus does not limit the number of colleges a student can select to compare; however, the comparison feature is limited to three colleges or universities at one time (Schoof 2013). College Abacus is available at https://college abacus.com.

College students can beat the odds of losing their financial independence in several ways:

- Borrow as little as possible.
- Be accountable to live within a well-defined budget while in college and work with parents to figure out the finances.
- Select a college with a COA that they can afford to pay.
- Borrow no more, on a combined basis for both federal and private student loans while in college, than half of what is expected in gross wages during the first year after college.
- Select a payment plan in which monthly student loan payments are no more than 7 percent of their monthly gross income.

> *We bring in their potential income, and I think that really opens their eyes, too.... Instead of saying, "I'm here to take out a $10,000 loan because I need it," after talking to them, they may say, "Hmmm...after seeing all that, I guess I only need $6,000, and I can put some money in from working."*
> —Financial aid counselor, 2008

> *We just try to counsel our students on wise borrowing. You know, if you don't need the money, don't borrow it because the interest starts now, and it's going to cost you a lot more in the end than you ever think.* —Financial aid counselor, 2008

High school students should not have debt, or should have very little debt, when entering college. Income from wages will be needed to pay college expenses along the way and to keep interest paid monthly on their student loans. Some parents are willing to work additional jobs and lower their own standards of living during the time that their children are in college. The decade of kids, cars, and college can require additional jobs for everyone, especially the parents, to make it all work financially. According to counselors, some students work three or more jobs while in college. The sacrifices are enough to keep their college borrowing to a minimum, which increases the potential for financial independence for the students after college.

> *We want to counsel them out of as many loans as possible. You know, the old "Live like a college student now and spend it like a college student forever" kind of thing and go with that. I don't want them to have a lot of money now. I don't want them to have, you know, tons left over. We have a difficult enough time, the two of us, the financial aid office and the student and family, you know, just paying for school. We don't need fancy stuff to go along with it. So, we try and counsel them out of that stuff as much as possible.*
> —Financial aid counselor, 2008

Students should plan to earn enough income to pay interest monthly while attending college. No interest should be capitalized on any college loans. Federal and private lenders capitalize interest when interest is not paid on loans while going to school, unless it is a subsidized federal Stafford Loan where the government pays the interest. If interest is capitalized, it is typically capitalized monthly, quarterly, semiannually, or annually. With all other things being equal on a loan, a fixed interest on a loan that is capitalized annually will result in a lower amount than interest that is capitalized monthly, quarterly, and semiannually.

> *We let them know that the $20,000 they borrow now is going to be $100,000 in the future, when they go back to repay it or however it ends up being.* —Financial aid counselor, 2008

> *I think generally what is most helpful to students is when we start showing the repayment charts and when we start showing the amount of interest that can accumulate on that loan over the life of the loan. So, if we're visiting with a group of freshmen students and we indicate to them that you've borrowed, let's say, $3,000 this year and you're at a variable rate but it's changing quarterly, we're trying to indicate to them what that's going to cost them in interest, and then if they're not paying that interest while they're in school and it capitalizes on an annual basis or worse, on a quarterly basis, what that is going to cost them when they get out of school.* —Financial aid counselor, 2008

> *We do have some charts that we give them, that give them estimates of what they will end up paying back at the end, and that's a real eye-opener for them.* —Financial aid counselor, 2008

Here *(on the following page)* is an example of interest on an $8,000 student loan that is capitalized annually. This example shows interest that has capitalized as a result of not being paid while attending college. The interest rate of 6.80 percent is shown and calculated as .0680.

In this example, the principal loan amount began at $8,000 and interest of $2,762.06 was annually capitalized interest during the four years of college attendance and the six-month grace period, during which time no interest was being paid. The loan amount increased by

Freshman Year		
Beginning loan amount	$8,000.00	
Interest rate (fixed)	6.80%	
Interest for *Year 1*	$544.00	($8,000 x .0680)
Sophomore Year		
Year 2. Capitalized loan amount	$8,544.00	($8,000 + $544)
Interest on capitalized amount	$580.99	($8,544.00 x .0680)
Junior Year		
Year 3. Capitalized loan amount	$9,124.99	($8,544 + 580.99)
Interest on capitalized amount	$620.50	($9,124.99 x .0680)
Senior Year		
Year 4. Capitalized loan amount	$9,745.49	($9,124.99 + $620.50)
Interest on capitalized amount	$662.69	($9,745.49 x .0680)
Six-Month Grace Period		
Year 4.5. Capitalized loan amount	$10,408.18	($9,745.49 + $662.69)
Interest on capitalized amount for six months	$353.88	($10,408.18 x .0680/2)
The capitalized loan amount after 4.5 years	$10,762.06	

$2,762.06, a 34.5 percent increase in the balance owed due to capitalized interest in 4.5 years. The capitalized loan amount that must now be repaid is $10,762.06. Interest begins accruing on the capitalized amount of $10,762.06. For college students who stay in school longer than four years and do not pay the interest on a loan, the capitalized amount will be greater than the amount shown in this example. The capitalized amount will be even more for those students who return to college and elect to defer payments on a loan longer than the 4.5 years shown in this example.

> *I don't think it would be bad to have some sort of entrance counseling required for alternative loans, to make them aware of what it's costing them or what kind of repayment they'll end up with. Because I don't think they realize the reality of that.* —Financial aid counselor, 2008

Students should know the COA for a typical academic year on all colleges they are interested in attending. Some students select colleges they cannot afford, have little or no savings to pay for it, do not apply or qualify for scholarships, assume they will have little time to work while attending college, and first look to financial aid counselors to help them solve their financial deficit. The financial solution that financial aid counselors are left to offer will likely be a majority of neatly packaged loans that students may qualify for and will eventually need to pay back with interest.

A college's financial aid office administers a variety of federal and state financial aid programs to assist students with paying for the college of their choice. As college employees, financial aid counselors are instrumental in the following: helping students and their parents apply, receive, and maintain eligibility for various types of financial aid; determining financial aid awards; ensuring financial aid compliance with all federal, state, and college regulations; helping both students and colleges meet enrollment goals; and offering federal work-study resources to help eligible students. According to counselors, college students and parents can benefit from having a united front when it comes to figuring out the finances and meeting with financial aid counselors early in the college-selection process.

> *We're really encouraging students to spend a little bit more time researching what they're doing, initially coming in and having a conversation with us to determine whether or not they are getting financial aid, scholarship aid possibly.*
> —Financial aid counselor, 2008

COA

Public colleges are those that are largely supported by state or federal funds. In-state tuition (for students who are residents of the state that the institution is in) at public institutions is less than out-of-state tuition (although some state institutions do have reciprocal agreements with other nearby states). About three-quarters of college students attend a community college or public university, and declining state funding has been the biggest reason for rising tuition at public institutions.

Private colleges, on the other hand, are supported by tuition, endowments, and donations from alumni and friends, rather than by public funds. Private colleges are usually more expensive than public colleges, but this does depend on the particular schools. The availability of scholarships also varies from college to college. The College Board determined that a moderate budget for the 2012–2013 school year would be approximately $22,000 at a public university and near $43,000 for a private institution (Holland 2013).

When selecting a college, students can begin by finding the college's COA (cost of attendance). The COA is the cost for an academic year. Each college determines its own COA for in-state and out-of-state students. The COA includes modest living costs. College financial aid limits are calculated based on each college's COA. The COA can be found by calling the college or searching on the college's website. The COA typically includes the following:

1. Tuition and fees
2. Housing and meals (room and board)
3. Books and supplies
4. Transportation
5. Personal Costs

Tuition and fees in a college's COA are estimates for students enrolled full time (12 or more credit hours per semester). The total amount of tuition and fees in the COA covers a full nine-month academic year. Students are billed half of this cost at the beginning of the fall semester and half at the beginning of the spring semester, assuming two semesters per academic year.

On-campus housing and meals are typically based on a shared dorm room (double or triple occupancy) with a full meal plan. On-campus housing is often billed on a semiannual basis. Off-campus housing and meals will vary based on personal housing choices. Living off-campus requires monthly rent payments (unless the student is living at home) and paying daily food costs.

The purchase price of new and used textbooks and supplies varies depending on the classes a student takes. Students often have a choice of where to buy required course materials. Online textbook rental (versus purchase) options are also available, such as Chegg (http://www.chegg.com) and BookRenter (http://www.bookrenter.com). Technology fees are often included in the costs for books and supplies. Additional fees may also be required to download instructor lecture notes. The COA does not include costs for tutors, although students may want to consider those costs in their budget.

Transportation costs are the estimated amounts needed for traveling to and from classes and going home over college breaks. They do not include the costs of consistent weekend travel or travel to and from any off-campus jobs. The COA does not include the additional costs for a spring-break trip, an ineligible study-abroad trip, a different car, or three months off during the summer. The COA does not include budgeted money to repay existing debt obligations, such as a car payment.

> *We don't provide aid for their off-campus or study-abroad programs, and that's an additional cost to the student. It*

> is an out-of-pocket expense for them, and so that is the primary reason our students will borrow. Either that, or to help cover the expected family contribution if they don't have an adequate amount of savings or if the parents are simply unwilling to assist them in any other way, is usually the reason our students will borrow. —Financial aid counselor, 2008

Personal costs in the COA cover items that include, but are not limited to, personal hygiene, entertainment, laundry, rental or purchase of a personal computer, costs related to a disability, dependent care, and reasonable costs for eligible study-abroad programs. These are the most variable expenses in the COA, since they depend on personal spending habits. If the amount spent on these items exceeds the budgeted COA, some students may elect to pay by credit card. Students should avoid carrying any unpaid balances on credit cards; it is financially important to pay off all credit card balances each month. While establishing good credit should begin very early in adulthood and is essential throughout a person's lifetime, unpaid credit card balances could negatively affect a person's credit score.

The financial responsibility for paying for college ultimately rests with the college student who is seeking the experiences and services of higher education and will reap the benefits from obtaining a college degree. It begins with selecting colleges that have a COA that they can reasonably afford to pay, after determining what amounts will be awarded annually in grants and scholarships.

> We encourage students to be very selective and be very thoughtful of what they're doing. —Financial aid counselor, 2008

For students and parents who are not quite ready to complete the FAFSA, Federal Financial Aid offers FAFSA4caster (http://studentaid.ed.gov/fafsa/estimate) as a free financial aid calculator that provides an early estimate for federal student aid. The intention of FAFSA4caster is to help families plan ahead for college. It is a source that college students and families can use prior to completing the FAFSA for federal student aid. The FAFSA4caster's estimate will be displayed on a College Cost Worksheet where applicants can also provide estimated amounts of other student aid and savings intended for a college education. To get those results, applicants will need to answer the following basic questions in FAFSA4caster in order for the program to estimate federal student aid eligibility for grants, scholarships, federal work-study, and federal student loans.

- Are you a U.S. citizen?
- What is your date of birth?
- What is your marital status?
- When you begin college, what will be your grade level?
- How many people are in your household?
- How many people in your household will be college students?
- Have you filed taxes recently?
- What was your (and your spouse's) adjusted gross income from the most recent tax return?
- What is your total current balance of cash, savings, and checking accounts? (This amount is limited to $999,999.)
- What is the net worth of your investments, including real estate (not your home)? (This amount is limited to $999,999.)
- What is the net worth of your current businesses and/or investment farms? (This amount is limited to $999,999.)
- What is your state of legal residence?
- How much does the college cost? (Naming the college is optional.)

Source: FAFSA4caster (http://studentaid.ed.gov/fafsa/estimate)

Eligibility for Federal Student Aid

To be eligible for federal student aid, applicants must meet these general eligibility requirements:

- Demonstrate financial need (for almost all programs—the unsubsidized Stafford Loan, for example, is an exception, as it is not based on financial need);
- Be a U.S. citizen or an eligible noncitizen;
- Have a valid Social Security number (with the exception of students from the Republic of the Marshall Islands, Federated States of Micronesia, or Republic of Palau);
- Be registered with Selective Service, if male (must register between the ages of 18 and 25);
- Be enrolled or accepted for enrollment as a regular student in an eligible degree or certificate program;
- Be enrolled at least half-time to be eligible for Direct Loan Program funds;
- Maintain satisfactory academic progress in college or career school;
- Sign a statement on the FAFSA stating (1) you have not defaulted on a federal student loan, (2) no money is owed on a federal student grant, (3) federal student aid will be used only for educational purposes; and
- Show qualifications to obtain college or career school education by (1) having a high school diploma or a recognized equivalent such as a General Educational Development (GED) certificate or (2) completing a high school education in a homeschool setting approved under state law.

For a student to be considered an eligible noncitizen, one of the following categories must apply:

- Applicant is a U.S. national; or

- Applicant is a U.S. permanent resident with a Form I-551, I-151, or I551C (Permanent Resident Card, Resident Alien Card, or Alien Registration Receipt Card), also known as a green card.

- Applicant has an Arrival-Departure Record (I-94) from U.S. Citizen and Immigration Services (USCIS) showing: refugee, asylum granted, Cuban-Haitian entrant (status pending), condition entrant (if issued before April 1, 1980), parolee (must be paroled for at least one year and provide evidence from the USCIS of intention to become a U.S. citizen or permanent resident).

- Applicant holds a T-visa or parent holds a T-1 visa.

- Applicant is a battered immigrant–qualified alien.

- Applicant is a citizen of the Federated States of Micronesia, the Republic of the Marshall Islands, or the Republic of Palau.

Source: http://studentaid.ed.gov/eligibility/basic-criteria

FAFSA

The completion of the FAFSA by parents of dependent undergraduate students and current and prospective college students (undergraduate and graduate) in the United States is required annually to determine their eligibility for federal financial aid. Although the FAFSA is not the only way to apply for money to pay for school, it is required in order to be considered for federal aid. The federal government uses the FAFSA to determine eligibility for federal assistance. Despite its name, the application is not for a single federal program, but rather is a gateway of consideration for several federal student aid programs, for various state student-aid programs, and for most of the available institutional aid.

> *It's going to be much quicker to apply for private loans than applying for federal aid. But I think so many of them are caught up in the old days of applying for aid when it did take several months for things to go through. But now with the Web application, if it's a clean application and they're not chosen for verification, we can offer them money within probably two weeks of their application.* —Financial aid counselor, 2008

Some families view the FAFSA process as financially invasive and avoid applying for federal student aid. When that happens, they miss out on federal student aid options and also lose opportunities for state and school aid, including scholarships and grants.

> *We do have students, surprisingly, that come from families that don't want to divulge or disclose income information required in the federal financial aid process and go directly to private [alternative] loans. There are some students who use the alternative loans as a means of supplementing or replacing the lack of support from family, parents in particular.* —Financial aid counselor, 2008

Federal financial aid includes the following:

1. Pell Grant
2. Federal Work-Study
3. Federal Perkins Loan
4. Direct Stafford Loans—Subsidized and Unsubsidized
5. Direct PLUS Loans—Direct Parent PLUS for parents of undergraduates; Direct PLUS for professional and graduate students

Schools Have Different Rules

Each school has its own financial aid filing date, and each has its own Federal School Code. Students should contact all of the schools they plan to apply to and find out their financial aid filing dates. The U.S. Department of Education accepts the FAFSA beginning January 1 of each year for the upcoming academic year. Although the application period is technically 18 months long (until June 30 of the next year), students are advised to submit their FAFSA as early as possible to be eligible for the maximum amount of financial assistance available. Most federal, state, and institutional aid is provided on a first-come, first-served basis.

There may be additional eligibility deadlines for some state aid (in California, for example, some aid is available only to students who apply by March 2 before the academic year starts). The FAFSA website provides details that are particular to the resident state of the student. The FAFSA can be submitted even if all of the required information and copies of income tax returns are not available by the deadline; adjustments and corrections can be made after the application is submitted.

Students and parents should locate the following documents and information before completing the online or paper version of the FAFSA:

1. Social Security numbers (U.S. citizens) or alien registration numbers (non-U.S. citizens) of students and parents.
2. Driver's license numbers, dates of birth, and date of parents' marriage/divorce.
3. Most recent federal tax forms, including W-2 forms.
4. Current bank account and investment statements.
5. Last year's business and farm records.

The FAFSA form asks applicants over 100 questions. While some FAFSA questions are personal, most are financial. The FAFSA does not include questions related to the race, ethnicity, sexual orientation, disability, or religion of the student or parents.

Students and parents can order free U.S. Department of Education publications of the FAFSA form (up to three copies) in English, Spanish, and Braille at https://www.edpubs.gov/default.aspx. Delivery for in-stock items can be expected within 10 days. The English and Spanish versions of the FAFSA are shown in Appendices B and C. All publications are provided at no cost to the general public by the U.S. Department of Education. This website offers more than 6,000 titles. Items include brochures, compact discs (CDs), grant applications, newsletters, posters, research reports, videotapes, and financial aid products. Along with the FAFSA form, the booklet titled *Funding Education Beyond High School: The Guide to Federal Student Aid*, which is used by many high school counselors, is available for free.

Here are three options available for students and parents to obtain the FAFSA form (FAFSA n.d.-b):

1. Online (FAFSA on the Web) at http://www.fafsa.ed.gov. Applicants (college student and at least one parent) should obtain a personal identification number (PIN) at http://www.pin.ed.gov before applying online. Federal School Codes are available online.
An online application is the quickest way to complete the FAFSA.

2. PDF FAFSA (download file) at http://www.studentaid.ed.gov/PDFfafsa.

3. Paper FAFSA—call 1-800-4-FED-AID or 1-800-433-3243. A completed paper copy of the form can be mailed to: Federal Student Aid Programs, P.O. Box 4696, Mt. Vernon, IL 62864-0066.

The U.S. Department of Education recommends that students use the IRS Data Retrieval Tool (DRT), which is available through the

FAFSA process. This tool retrieves most of the student's tax information, excluding wages, directly from the IRS and automatically fills in the information on their application. The DRT may be used by both students and parents alike.

Applicants who have completed a FAFSA in previous years may submit a renewal FAFSA. Any information that has changed can then be updated annually.

Expected Family Contribution (EFC)

The Expected Family Contribution (EFC) is a measure of a family's financial strength and is calculated according to a formula established by law. The federal analysis methodology for the 2014–2015 academic award year can be found online at http://ifap.ed.gov/fregisters/FR052013.html. The formula is somewhat complicated. Section 478 of Part F of Title IV of the HEA requires an annual update of four tables for general price inflation: the Income Protection Allowance (IPA), the Adjusted Net Worth of a Business or Farm, the Education Savings and Asset Protection Allowance, and the Assessment Schedules and Rates. The IPA is the amount of living expenses for an individual or family that can be offset against the income. The annual changes are based, in general, upon increases in the Consumer Price Index (CPI).

A family's taxed and untaxed income, assets, and benefits (such as unemployment or Social Security) are all considered in the formula. The U.S. Department of Education plugs in the answers that applicants submit through the FAFSA into a formula that determines the EFC. The EFC is not the amount of money a family will have to pay for college, nor is it the amount of federal student aid a college student will receive. EFC is the number used by a college to calculate the amount of federal student aid for which a college student is eligible (FAFSA n.d.-a). A number of factors are used when determining the EFC, including household size, income, number of students in the household in college, and assets (not including retirement and 401[k] funds). This information is required because of the expectation that parents will contribute to their child's education, whether that is true or not.

The following circumstances could lower a student's EFC:

1. Additional family members supported by the head of the household (siblings or grandparents who are part of the household).
2. Additional siblings in college.
3. Low income.
4. Few assets.
5. Parents are enrolled in college.

The IPA for the dependent student is $6,260 for the 2014–2015 award year. The IPA for independent students and parents of dependent students for 2014–2015 can be found at https://www.federalregister.gov/articles/2013/05/20/2013-11982/federal-need-analysis-methodology-for-the-2014-15-award-year-federal-pell-grant-federal-perkins-loan. For the 2014–2015 award year for parents of dependent students, each additional family member is valued at $4,180 and each additional college student is valued at $2,970. Additionally, some colleges will lower the EFC if an appeal is filed at the financial aid office and approved due to special circumstances. The recent loss of a job could qualify as a special circumstance.

Student Aid Report (SAR)

Following the submission of the FAFSA, the student will receive a Student Aid Report (SAR), which is a document that summarizes the information from the FAFSA. The SAR is generated by the U.S. Department of Education after the FAFSA has been processed and sent to the schools of choice that were listed on the application. This form officially notifies the student that the FAFSA was received. The student should review the SAR carefully and make necessary corrections. If there are errors, the student can go to the FAFSA website, enter their PIN, and make the necessary corrections. Once the SAR is accurate, the student should keep a copy of the form. The SAR also contains a four-digit Data Release Number (DRN). Students will need the DRN if they choose to allow a college or career school to change information on their FAFSA.

An electronic version of the summarized FAFSA content can be sent directly to the institution; this is called the Institutional Student Information Record (ISIR). The term ISIR refers to all processed student information records that are sent directly to the institutions. The schools that the student lists on the FAFSA will receive the ISIR automatically. The ISIR is also sent to state agencies that award need-based aid. SARs and ISIRs contain the same processed student information in different formats.

Verification

The student and parents may be asked to verify the information they provide on the FAFSA, which could require additional documentation regarding their debts, accounts, or sources of income. There is no need for applicants to be alarmed by this request; it is quite common. The response may be as simple as providing a copy of a tax return to the college financial aid office. Students need to send the requested documentation promptly to avoid delays in processing the financial aid award. A college cannot officially award financial aid until verification is complete. College policies vary, and some financial aid offices may require 100 percent verification (meaning they would request copies of tax returns) from all applicants, while other colleges may make fewer verification requests.

Any financial aid awarded to an eligible student through the FAFSA process may be paid directly to the college first and applied toward any balance owed by the student. Excess funds can then go from the college to the student when the award is disbursed in that order. Students can ask their financial aid office how they handle their financial aid awards, such as loans, scholarships, and grants.

Pell Grant

Federal student loan limits are not keeping pace with colleges' increasing costs of attendance. The vast majority of students who complete the FAFSA on time are eligible for some sort of financial aid. Federal, state, or institutional grant funds are very limited and do not need to be repaid when terms of the award are followed. Pell Grants are the largest source of aid for the neediest students and are awarded to eligible undergraduate students and some postbaccalaureate students with the most financial need.

Where the maximum Pell Grant once covered the entire cost of obtaining a two-year degree and 77 percent of the cost at a public university in 1980, it now covers only 62 percent of the cost of a two-year degree and 36 percent toward a public four-year degree, according to a 2012 report by the *Huffington Post*. States have scaled back higher education support, and tuition is growing faster than the Pell Grant can keep up with. The cost of obtaining a college degree has increased about five times the rate of inflation since 1980, a rate that the Pell Grant simply has not be able to follow (Kingkade 2012).

The federal Pell Grant program was designed to help low-income families afford college without being buried in debt. The Pell Grant now covers less than one-third of the cost of attendance at a public four-year university, the lowest in its history (Kingkade 2012). A recent study, commissioned by the nonprofit College Board, revealed that even the Pell Grant, a federally funded program, must now serve two equally needy but very different populations—young and old. There are now many students who are not the traditional Pell Grant students—they are not young people from low-income families but rather are adults who have already spent time in the workforce and are seeking to improve their own skills and labor force opportunities.

Politicians agree that Pell Grants no longer provide enough aid for students, but they disagree on how to address the problem (Debt.org n.d.). Some politicians believe that increasing the Pell Grant would fuel tuition inflation; some believe it should be reserved for the "truly needy." The eligibility requirements for Pell Grants were tightened in December 2011. No long-term decisions have been made yet on the fate of the Pell Grant, although the "Better Bargain for the Middle Class: Making College More Affordable" plan proposes to give colleges a bonus if they enroll large numbers of students who are eligible for need-based Pell Grants (Jaschik 2013).

Students and families who do not qualify for grants may qualify for federal loans or federal work-study. For example, the Direct Stafford Unsubsidized Loan is federal aid that is not based on financial need or credit qualifications and is available to the student alone if the student and parents (of the dependent student) complete the FAFSA. A college student may also qualify for federal work-study, which essentially gives them an on-campus job, such as working in the college's cafeteria. The only way to know for sure whether or not a student qualifies for the benefits of federal financial aid is for the student and family to complete and submit the FAFSA.

Award Letters

Students will receive an award letter from the colleges whose Federal School Codes they included on the FAFSA. The award letter is part of the school's financial aid package, which may also include loan documents prepared for signatures. Every award package is unique to the student and the school packaging the various sources of financial aid. Financial aid terminology used by colleges in the financial aid structure can confuse some recipients. Award letters are subject to change, especially when a FAFSA is initially filed with estimated numbers and is revised once the actual numbers are known.

Financial aid award letters can also include some scholarships and grants. Often, scholarships will have contingencies, such as participating in a certain major, meeting specific criteria, and/or maintaining a certain grade point average (GPA). Scholarships do not need to be repaid if the rules for each particular scholarship are fully followed. Some scholarships are renewable, which means that they can be awarded for multiple years, while others are nonrenewable.

The majority of total financial aid dollars are offered in the form of student loans and parent loans, neatly packaged by the college's financial aid office and labeled as awards. Students and parents should plan to read the small print of a college's financial aid award letter or get help in reading a college's award letter, if needed. Students do not need to accept any loan that is offered. They can also choose to accept a lower loan amount than what is initially offered. College award packages include federal student loans and can also include private student loans, although not all colleges package private student loans.

> *At a recent conference, there was concern that if they wouldn't package private loans anymore, that it would hurt recruiting efforts, as some schools just package the Parent PLUS Loans.* —Financial aid counselor, 2008

Award letters will typically begin with the COA. Some colleges will split the COA into direct costs and indirect costs, billed expenses and estimated expenses, or fall and spring semesters. There is no consistency in how colleges categorize their COA, and there is currently no mandate to require colleges to provide consistent terminology in their award letters.

Direct costs, such as tuition, fees, and room and board (for the student living in a college's dormitory), are billed by the school. Indirect costs are estimated expenses that students may have throughout the year, such as books, transportation, and personal expenses. While indirect costs may appear on the award letter, they are not typically billed by the school.

Below is an example of a school that shows the COA for resident and nonresident students and divides total costs in two categories: billed (direct) expenses and estimated (indirect) expenses:

	Living on Campus	
	Resident	Nonresident
Billed Expenses:		
Tuition and Fees	$8,061	$26,931
Housing and Meals	$9,424	$9,424
Subtotal of Billed Expenses	**$17,485**	**$36,355**
Estimated Expenses:		
Books and Supplies	$1,040	$1,040
Personal ($164.66 per month for 9 months)	$1,482	$1,482
Transportation	$684	$684
Subtotal of Estimated Expenses	**$3,206**	**$3,206**
TOTAL (Billed and Estimated Expenses)	**$20,691**	**$39,561**

Source: http://www.uiowa.edu (June 2, 2013)

Loan packaging offers colleges a way to show students that the entire COA can be met through state and college aid along with federal financial aid: work-study, grants, scholarships, and loans; usually, the packages are mostly loans. Students and families can make an informed college decision after knowing how to dissect the pieces of a financial award letter, although each college's award letter could have a different appearance and format for consideration. Here is an example of the information that could be included in an award letter with a $20,691 COA. The aid amounts are shown in parentheses, while the expenses are not. This is intended to show students and families how to decipher a college award letter.

	College Award Letter	
	Fall	Spring
Billed expenses	$8,742.50	$8,742.50
Estimated expenses	$1,603.00	$1,603.00
Pell Grant	($500.00)	($500.00)
Perkins Loan	($500.00)	($500.00)
Direct Stafford Subsidized Loan	($1,000.00)	($1,000.00)
Direct Stafford Unsubsidized Loan	($1,750.00)	($1,750.00)
Expected Family Contribution— Direct Parent PLUS	($6,595.50)	($6,595.50)
Unmet Need	$0	$0

It is typical for colleges to divide the COA equally for the fall and spring semesters. If the awards are loans, the award letter does not include who is expected to sign for the loan and who is responsible to repay it. The award letter does not include loan interest rates, fees, and repayment terms. Scholarships and federal work-study awards were not included in this example.

To analyze this example further, the federal student aid awards are categorized by which awards are grants that do not need to be repaid and which awards are loans that need to be repaid in full with interest.

Grant	Loans
Pell Grant	Perkins (to the student based on financial need, not based on credit)
	Direct Stafford Subsidized (to the student based on need, not based on credit)
	Direct Stafford Unsubsidized (to the student, not based on need or credit)
	Direct Parent PLUS (to one parent, based on having no adverse credit)

Acceptance of any financial aid awards is voluntary. In the case where a parent does not agree to a Direct PLUS Loan, students who accept their own federal loans (Perkins, Stafford) would then need to find alternative sources for the remaining $13,191 balance ($20,691 minus $7,500 in this example). Those college students who resort to private student loans to cover this balance typically need a creditworthy cosigner (Wegmann, Cunningham, and Merisotis 2003). The $19,691 balance (total COA less the $1,000 Pell Grant) could be paid through a combination of financial sources as long as the total amount does not exceed the $20,691 COA. These sources could include work-study, additional grants, loans, and scholarships. Some colleges may allow students to make monthly payments throughout the academic year for those billed expenses not covered by financial aid. College students should borrow as little as possible and should consider any available savings and future wages as payment sources prior to accepting loans.

On the following page is a real-life example of an award letter. This *award* includes no grants, no scholarships, and no work-study; it is all loans—$2,625 for the qualified student to sign and $8,076 for a creditworthy parent. The recipients would be expected to know that

1998–99 UNIVERSITY AWARD NOTIFICATION

A. DETERMINING FACTORS

The following information was obtained from your University Verification Form.

Change any incorrect item(s) and return this notification to the Office of Student Financial Aid immediately.

Type of Tuition:	**Resident**
Housing:	**On Campus**
Classification:	**Undergraduate**
Enrollment Hours:	Fall: **12 or more**
	Spring: **12 or more**

B. ESTIMATED COST OF ATTENDANCE, FAMILY CONTRIBUTION, AND FINANCIAL NEED

Tuition	$ 2,666.00
Health/Computer Fees	202.00
Books/Supplies	818.00
Room/Board	4,152.00
Personal	2,415.00
Transportation	448.00
TOTAL COST OF ATTENDANCE	$10,701.00
Federal Student Contribution	− 1,749.00
Federal Parent Contribution	− 7,978.00
FINANCIAL NEED	$ 974.00

C. FINANCIAL AID AWARD

(1) Read both sides of this notification and the enclosed important information About Your 1998-99 Financial Aid brochure. (A brochure will not be enclosed if this is a revised award notification.)

(2) Return this notification if you are: changing items in Section A, informing us of other aid in Section E, or declining/reducing aid in Section F.

(3) Complete and return one copy of any enclosed loan promissory note(s).

	FALL	SPRING	TOTAL
AWARDED FINANCIAL AID			
Federal Direct Student Loans (Optional):			
Federal Direct Stafford/Ford Loan**	$ 487.00	$ 487.00	$ 974.00
Federal Direct Unsubsidized Stafford/Ford/Loan**	825.50	825.50	1,651.00
Federal Direct PLUS (Parent) Loan**	4,038.00	4,038.00	8,076.00
TOTAL DIRECT STUDENT LOANS			$10,701.00
UNMET COST OF ATTENDANCE*			$ 0.00

**The amount of this loan is the maximum amount of your eligibility. You must complete and return your loan promissory note. Loan fees will be taken out before your loan is disbursed. Review your loan promissory note for exact amounts.

***The Unmet Cost of Attendance cannot be met by financial aid funds from the University Office of Student Financial Aid due to lack of funds or program maximums. This need may be met through part-time employment and/or outside assistance.

the Stafford is a loan directly to the student and that the Parent PLUS is a loan for a parent who does not have an adverse credit history.

Colleges offer students their best financial packages based on available funding, college policies and enrollment goals, and federal and state regulations. When comparing award letters from different schools, students can quickly determine what balances they would have to pay by totaling the amounts awarded through grants and scholarships and subtracting that number from the college's COA. This will help students determine how much of the COA remains and whether or not they will need to earn more money, live a lifestyle lower than the costs budgeted on the COA, resort to borrowing money from federal or private loan sources, find other cash sources, eliminate room and board costs and commute back and forth from home, or look for other college options. This is when students and families should identify their cash down payment sources and refrain from borrowing total loan amounts that are more than *half* of their anticipated first year of wages after exiting college.

Here are the maximum annual loan amounts that undergraduates should be obtaining to pay for college when borrowing $15,500, or half of the $31,000 in expected earnings the first year out of college. This also means that students should be budgeting to pay the monthly interest on their student loans while they are in college to keep the principal loan amounts from capitalizing to amounts greater than the original loan amount—$15,500 in this example.

Earning a college degree in four years:	$3,875.00 per year— maximum combined loans
Earning a college degree in five years:	$3,100.00 per year— maximum combined loans
Earning a college degree in six years:	$2,583.33 per year— maximum combined loans

Rules of Thumb When Borrowing Money

The rule for college students to borrow no more than *half* of what they expect to earn in wages the first year after exiting college also includes any amounts borrowed from other people (parents, grandparents, stepparents, friends of family) who then expect the student to begin making payments after graduation. Some parents borrow money on a Parent PLUS Loan, for example, and then fully expect the student to repay that loan. There may be parents and grandparents borrowing on private loans and anticipating that the student will be able to pay those loans after graduating from college. If that is the agreement, students need to include those balances in their total amount borrowed. Parents and grandparents should know that they will be obligated to repay on any loans for which they have signed, even with the best of intentions from the college student.

> *Borrow as little as you possibly can...we try and counsel them that way.* —Financial aid counselor, 2008

The U.S. Census Bureau reports annually on expected lifetime earnings for students obtaining various degrees, including undergraduate and professional degrees. This data highlights the importance of the undergraduate major. For workers whose highest degree is a bachelor's, median incomes ranged from $29,000 for counseling-psychology majors to $120,000 for petroleum-engineering majors (Chronicle of Higher Education 2011). The contingency, of course, is for college graduates to land a full-time job in their degree area to be able to earn these forecasted wages. And, a degree forecasting high wages when starting college can shift to a degree that cannot demand high wages by the time the student graduates from college.

A 2012 report by the National Center for Education Statistics supports the fact that young females ages 25–34 and working full time in 2010 earned $25,000 with a high school diploma or its equivalent and earned $40,000 with a bachelor's degree. Males in that same age group earned $32,800 in 2010 with a high school diploma or equivalent and $49,800 with a bachelor's degree (National Center for Education Statistics n.d.-c).

According to data compiled by the nonprofit National Association of Colleges and Employers (NACE) from the U.S. Bureau of Labor Statistics, the Census Bureau, and a master set of data developed by the research firm Job Search Intelligence, 2012 data for accepted starting salaries shows that the Class of 2013 predicts an overall starting salary of $44,928. It was $42,666 for the Class of 2012. Average salaries by discipline predicted by NACE for 2013 for those who graduate from college and are able to find full employment within their major are as follows (NACE 2013).

Business	$54,234
Communications	$43,145
Computer Science	$59,977
Education	$40,480
Engineering	$62,535
Health Sciences	$49,713
Humanities and Social Sciences	$37,058
Math and Sciences	$42,724

Financial plans by college students should include the intent to stay in college and to graduate with a degree. Whenever there is an unpaid balance with a college or poor academic progress, it can keep students from being able to attend class, register for upcoming classes, or receive a signed college diploma.

For those students who leave college without a degree due to academic or financial reasons, the rule stating that total debt should not exceed half of the anticipated first year of wages may prove too optimistic, because lifetime earnings will typically be less for someone who has not earned a college degree and still has college debt to repay. There are some very rare exceptions to this earnings rule, such as Steve Jobs, Bill Gates, and Mark Zuckerberg.

> *Students who are not making satisfactory academic progress consequently don't qualify any longer for federal benefits and want private loans. Those would be the highest risk category of students taking out alternative loans.*
> —Financial aid counselor, 2008

Experts in education lending have previously recommended that student loan payments not exceed 8 percent of monthly gross income; some lenders have stretched that rule by supporting a guideline of up to 10 percent of monthly gross income. The proposed ExCEL Act suggests up to 11.80 percent of monthly gross income be available to repay federal student loans; it does not include private student loan amounts. The government announced a renewed emphasis for the Pay As You Earn federal loan repayment plan whereby students would be able to cap their federal loan payments at 10 percent of their monthly income. It does not include private student loan repayments in the calculation (Jaschik 2013). With the depressed job market, the high percentage of students who do not complete their college degree, and the increasing number of student loan defaults, the 8 to 10 percent income guidelines appear too high for those students trying to live independently after exiting college, even those with a college degree. Students should select loan repayment amortizations that limit monthly payments to an amount no greater than 7 percent of their gross monthly income for all federal and private student loans combined. Here is an example of the maximum loan payment amounts based on various annual gross incomes.

Gross Annual Income	Monthly Loan Payments—7 Percent
$15,000	$87.50
$20,000	$116.67
$25,000	$145.83
$30,000	$175.00
$35,000	$204.17
$40,000	$233.33
$45,000	$262.50
$50,000	$291.67
$75,000	$437.50
$100,000	$583.33

Student loans remain a part of a student's financial history long after the student exits college. The loan balances and history of loan repayments are tracked on individual credit reports until the maturity of the loan—longer if the loan is in default. Even if a federal student loan was not a credit-based loan at the time of receiving the funds, the loan history is reported to the three national credit bureau agencies for an individual's credit report. Credit reports typically include unpaid loan balances, expected monthly payments, and the repayment history for each individual signed on the loan. All loans are accruing interest each day. Some loans require payments while the student is in college; some loans delay payment requirements until after the student exits college. The status of student loans that are in deferment or in default will also show on an individual's credit report.

An analysis of 10 million credit files released from the Fair Isaac Corporation (FICO) found that the average student debt load ballooned 58 percent from 2005 to 2012—from $17,233 to $27,253. In the same period, the number of consumers with two or more open student loans on their credit report grew from 12 million in 2005 to 26 million in 2012, according to the *Wall Street Journal* (Kingkade 2013).

If there is a cosigner on a student loan, the repayment (or lack of repayment) on that loan affects the credit ratings of both the student and the cosigner. Consequently, a cosigner should know the financial status of the person they are cosigning for. A cosigner should also be financially prepared to pay monthly on all of the student loans that they signed and for the entire time the loan is in repayment, which could be as long as 25 years in some cases. All signers on cosigned loans are individually responsible to repay 100 percent of the entire debt, including interest.

If a loan is paid as agreed, both signers will receive a good rating on their credit reports. If there is poor repayment performance on a loan, both signers will receive a failing grade, and it will lower each of their credit scores. Credit reports are objective; borrowers either paid as agreed or they did not pay as agreed. Credit reports do not include reasons why a payment was not made. A credit report is a report card for life; it follows an individual everywhere, linked to their name and Social Security number. There is more information on credit reports in chapter 7.

A credit report is a report card for life.

Parents of a college student may be unaware that the student is having any financial problems and may not even know the total amount of the student's loans. The confidentiality of student records, including financial aid applications, is protected by the Family Educational Rights and Privacy Act (FERPA). In particular, schools will not disclose information submitted by the parent to the student or information submitted by the student to the parent. Due to privacy rights and college students being of legal age, most financial correspondence from the college and from a private lender is sent directly to the primary applicant, the student. The student's privacy is protected by law in consumer transactions. According to counselors, some private lenders will not disclose the details of a student's private loan for the college's certification process.

> *I have the student sitting in my office, and I ask their lender about this direct-to-student loan, and the person says right on the phone, "I can't discuss that loan with you. That's a private, personal loan. I can't discuss that with you. We're not going to tell you...we're not going to say."* —Financial aid counselor, 2008

If a parent is cosigned on a loan, they will eventually be notified by the lender for collection of any past-due loan payments. Any delay in notification may have already negatively affected the credit ratings of both the student and the cosigner(s). It is up to students, parents, and cosigners to notify all lenders each time their address and phone number changes, which could be often for college students. It is up to the college student to communicate with parents and cosigners on their financial status and the possibility of any late loan payments (before they are late) for three main reasons: to protect their individual credit ratings, to protect their family relationships, and to protect their future job opportunities.

Employment screenings increased from 19 percent in 1996 to 42 percent by 2006, and the number of employers obtaining applicants' credit reports during employment background checks has increased. According to a September 2013 report in the *Economist*, 60 percent of employers already check the credit ratings of job candidates (Lexington 2013). Competition for jobs is now based on much more than comparing college degrees and work histories. Employers now use credit reports to assess an applicant's personal character, honesty, and integrity by how they follow through on their financial promises and repay on their financial obligations. In today's competitive job market, students, parents, grandparents, and cosigners need to be aware that there are more employers who are reviewing their individual credit reports these days before making any job offers.

Comparing Federal and Private Student Loan Options

With Iowa Student Loan, you either paid a 9 percent fee or you paid 0 percent. The 0 percent fee had a 1½ percent higher interest rate. Always. That was just the spread between the two. Then other lenders started having no fees but higher rates. —Financial aid counselor, 2008

A N ARTICLE in *Bloomberg Businessweek,* titled "Why Your Student Loan Rate Is So High," highlighted a father of four boys paying 3.50 percent on his home mortgage loan, 1.79 percent on a car loan, and interest rates above 7.00 percent on federal student loans for his college sons. He was nearing 60 years old, and he questioned why the interest rates on unsecured college loans were higher than the interest rates on secured consumer loans. Lenders determine interest rates based on many variables, such as credit history, repayment capacity, collateral value, and repayment risks. Lenders have a much greater risk of not collecting on unsecured loans than on secured loans, and student loans are unsecured while house and car loans are secured. An unsecured federal student loan backed by a repayment guarantee from the federal government has less risk of default for a lender than an unsecured private student loan with no guarantee of repayment. Private lenders look for ways to offset repayment risks, such as a co-signer (parent, grandparent, or other creditworthy cosigner).

> You have a student that has a [federal] Stafford Loan and has a private loan. Assuming he defaults on both of those, a lender can get 95 to 97 percent back from the federal government on the Stafford Loan, and the other [private loan] they're "going to eat." So, private loans need a little higher fee and a little higher interest rate to make up for the risk. If it's cosigned, there's a lot better chance of collecting from them than the student. —Financial aid counselor, 2008

The article supported the fact that Congress sets rates for federal student loans. The author, Karen Weise, added that refinancing loans at lower rates is rarely an option (Weise 2013). What the author was implying is that when students consolidate their federal student loans, the interest rate is based on the weighted average of the interest rates on the federal loans being consolidated, rounded up to the nearest one-eighth percent. Since July 1, 2013, and after the article was written, the cap rate on consolidated federal student loans has been eliminated.

Here are some generalizations for students and parents to use when comparing interest rates:

1. Fixed interest rates are higher than variable interest rates.
2. Fixed and variable interest rates are higher on unsecured debt than they are on loans secured with physical assets that can be repossessed during collection.
3. The interest rates on variable-rate private student loans are open to the market and typically have no maximum cap rate; there is no interest rate limit. Existing federal student loans may have either

fixed rates or a cap on how high the variable interest rates can increase.

4. The longer the loan maturity, the higher the fixed interest rate (for example, a 30-year fixed interest rate on a home loan is higher than a 15-year fixed mortgage rate).
5. Loan fees affect interest rates. Paying more in fees, whether paid upfront or added into the total loan amount, can result in a lower stated interest rate.

Federal student loans typically have fees (with the exception of the Perkins Loan and the Consolidated Loan). These fees allow for lower stated interest rates and higher effective interest rates on federal student loans. Borrowers are actually paying a higher effective interest rate than what is stated on their loan because the effective interest rate is determined on the remaining amount of the loan they have available to pay for college costs after they pay fees. Private lenders may or may not charge origination fees on their private student loans. Private lenders may offer higher interest rates on loans when they do not charge fees.

Congress set the federal student loan interest rates in 2001, when overall interest rates were higher, and they had not changed much until the July 1, 2013, change from fixed to variable interest rates based on a predetermined spread added to the 10-year Treasury rate. The fixed interest rate had been 7.90 percent from July 1, 2006, to June 30, 2013, on Direct Parent PLUS Loans, which is a decrease from the previous 9.00 percent cap on these variable-interest-rate loans. There are Federal Family Education Loan (FFEL) PLUS Loans that have a 7.90 percent fixed rate, which was lowered from the 8.50 percent fixed rate. These loans would have been obtained prior to the FFEL Program ending July 1, 2010 (FinAid n.d.-b). Fixed interest rates on loans help students and parents accurately budget monthly repayment requirements. Students and parents can now obtain only variable-rate federal student loans, with the exception of the Perkins Loan, and that fixed-rate loan is based on financial need.

Unsecured federal student loans did not always have fixed interest rates. Beginning July 1, 2006, and ending June 30, 2013, all newly issued Stafford Loans and PLUS loans had fixed interest rates; fixed interest rates on federal Stafford Loans were available for only seven years. The Stafford Loans already in repayment and borrowed prior to that time kept their variable interest rates. Direct Stafford Subsidized Loans caught national attention recently when the fixed rate of 3.40 percent was replaced by an increased variable rate of 3.86 percent, effective July 1, 2013. From July 1, 2006, to June 30, 2013, the maximum fixed interest rate on unsubsidized Stafford Loans signed solely by college students was 6.80 percent. On new loans with a disbursement between July 1, 2013, and June 30, 2014, the variable interest rate on Direct Stafford Loans is 3.86 percent for undergraduate students with a cap rate of 8.25 percent. The variable interest rate is 5.41 percent for graduate students on new unsubsidized Direct Stafford Loans disbursed between July 1, 2013, and June 30, 2014, with a cap rate of 9.50 percent.

On federal Direct PLUS Loans, signed by parents of undergraduate students or by graduate or professional students, the maximum fixed interest rate was 7.90 percent from July 1, 2006, to June 30, 2013. On July 1, 2013, fixed rates were eliminated, and the variable interest rate on PLUS loans is 6.41 percent with a cap rate of 10.50 percent for new loans disbursed from July 1, 2013, to June 30, 2014.

For existing variable-rate federal student loans, some beginning back in 1987, the cap rates on Supplemental Loans for Students (SLS) and PLUS loans range from 9 percent to 12 percent. In 1997, for example, the small print under the first paragraph of the Variable Interest Rate category of a federal Direct Loans Promissory Note and Disclosure read as follows:

> For Direct Subsidized Loans and Direct Unsubsidized Loans in repayment, the interest rate during any twelve-month period beginning on July 1 and ending on June 30 is determined on the June 1 immediately preceding that period. The interest rate is equal to the bond equivalent rate of 91-day Treasury bills auctioned at the final auction held prior to that June 1 plus 3.1 percentage points, but does not exceed 8.25 percent.

On July 1, 2000, for example, the variable repayment rate on Direct Loans increased to 7.593 percent while a student was in school and during the grace period deferment. By the time the loan came into repayment, the variable repayment rate had increased to 8.193 percent. The Direct Loan office notified borrowers through an Interest Rate Change Notice similar to the example on the following page.

Beginning July 1, 2013, borrowers with new variable-rate federal loans based on a 10-year Treasury rate index should expect to receive annual notifications for interest rate changes and will find wording similar to this on their promissory notes; this is an example of a Direct Unsubsidized loan for graduate and professional students with a 9.50 percent cap rate:

> For Direct Subsidized Loans and Direct Unsubsidized Loans in repayment, the interest rate during any twelve-month period beginning on July 1 and ending on June 30 is determined on the June 1 immediately preceding that period. The interest rate is equal to the equivalent rate of the 10-year Treasury notes auctioned at the final auction held prior to that June 1 plus 3.60 percentage points, but does not exceed 9.50 percent.

Loan fees are typical for federal Direct Stafford, federal Direct PLUS, and private (nonfederal) loans. Origination fees will increase the stated interest rate on a loan to a larger effective interest rate, known as the annual percentage rate (APR). Fees on federal Stafford

Direct Loans

William D. Ford Federal Direct Loan Program

INTEREST RATE CHANGE NOTICE

06/06/2000

ACCOUNT#:

Reason for Notice The interest rate(s) on your Direct Loan(s) may change once a year on July 1. This is your notice of the interest rate(s) in effect on your Direct Loan(s) from:

July 1, 2000 – June 30, 2001

Loan ID	Loan Status	Interest Type	July 1, 1999 – June 30, 2000		On or After July 1, 2000	
			In-School, Grace, Deferment Rate	Repayment Rate	In-School, Grace, Deferment Rate	Repayment Rate
#1	IN-SCHOOL	Variable	6.320%	6.920%	7.593%	8.193%
#2	IN-SCHOOL	Variable	6.320%	6.920%	7.593%	8.193%
#3	IN-SCHOOL	Variable	6.320%	6.920%	7.593%	8.193%
#4	IN-SCHOOL	Variable	6.320%	6.920%	7.593%	8.193%

If your monthly payment amount is changing as a result of interest rate changes, we will be informing you of the new amount. Borrowers repaying loan(s) under the Income Contingent Repayment (ICR) plan should be aware that annual recalculations done at this time may affect monthly payment amounts. (You cannot repay PLUS Loans and PLUS Consolidation Loans under the ICR plan.) Questions? If so, please call the toll-free telephone number shown on the back of this Notice.

VAR2AV05

Our Mission is to Ensure Equal Access to Education and to Promote Education Excellence Throughout the Nation
U.S. Department of Education

and PLUS loans previously ranged from 1.00 percent to 4.00 percent. Since July 1, 2013, fees on federal Stafford and PLUS loans range from 1.051 percent to 4.204 percent, and, according to one counselor, including those fees in an APR disclosure to federal loan borrowers is not required (Baker 2013). Private student loans with fees require private lenders to disclose the APR to borrowers based on truth-in-lending laws. For a fair comparison of interest rates paid on college loans, borrowers should compare the APRs.

> *I was shocked to learn recently that federal student loans are not subjected to truth-in-lending laws. For the federal loans, there was some belief that because the rates and things were set by Congress that they didn't need to have truth in lending because they were so highly regulated in other ways. I think we could go a lot further in terms of more disclosing so it's easier for students to see where the cost is in the loan product, whether it's in the front end in origination fees or interest rates or in timely repayment incentives or rebates on the back end, or penalties for late payment. I think all of that needs to be fully disclosed. It's just very difficult to compare apples to apples.* —Financial aid counselor, 2008

The Truth in Lending (TIL) Act is a federal law that regulates and sets guidelines for consumer credit, such as credit cards, house loans, and certain student loans. The counselor is revealing that the 4.204 percent fee charged on federal Parent PLUS Loans, for example, would not need to be disclosed to borrowers in the same way that private lenders are required to disclose fees on private student loans. This makes it difficult for students to compare effective interest rates on federal student loans with effective interest rates (APRs) on private student loans. The act was intended to reduce confusion by requiring private lenders to disclose certain information to consumers so that they can make informed financial decisions. The act was established in 1968 and is implemented by Regulation Z, which contains the rules to carry out the TIL Act (Federal Reserve 2012). The law does not determine or limit interest rate charges or fees; rather, it was intended to provide a uniform means of presenting information to consumers before entering into a credit arrangement.

TIL establishes a consistent way of providing disclosures to consumers who are seeking credit. It gives a consumer certain rights to cancel, or rescind, a loan. Special regulations have been established for private student loans, and private student loans are subject to TIL. Under the TIL Act, consumers have a three-day period after signing a loan and entering into a credit transaction to cancel the transaction and have all fees and early payments reimbursed. A provision in the law also allows borrowers to rescind the entire transaction after up to three years have passed, if the lender did not comply with the TIL disclosure requirements.

Private student loans barely existed 20 years ago. This was a time when financing higher education was simpler, as the vast majority of all student loans were issued through federal loan programs. Interest rates on federal student loans were regulated, and borrowers were given specific protections, such as income-based repayment and loan deferment, if they returned to school. Students and families will now find that private student loans are much different than federal student loans, once they do their research. Today there are many more choices, which may add to the confusion, but it also encourages competition among the lenders. Due to competition, lenders may also waive some fees.

Based on federal student loan requirements back in 1997, the loan fee charged for each Direct Subsidized Stafford Loan and Direct Unsubsidized Stafford Loan was 4 percent of the amount borrowed. The loan fee was disclosed in small print on the back of a promissory note under the loan fee paragraph. Stafford Loan fees have since been reduced from 4 percent to the current 1.051 percent. A reduced loan fee benefited all college students obtaining subsidized and unsubsidized federal Stafford Loans. The example on the following page highlights Direct Subsidized and Direct Unsubsidized Loans when they included a 4 percent loan fee. It does not disclose the annual percentage rate (APR) including the fee.

Student loans are typically unsecured, and the loan rates reflect that additional risk for lenders. This is why interest rates for an unsecured student loan are typically higher than for a secured car or secured house loan, for example. While borrowers who have multiple federal loans can consolidate them, the rate on the consolidated loan will be limited to a weighted average of the rates on the existing loans and rounded up to the nearest one-eighth percent. There is no interest rate cap on federal consolidated student loans under the 2013 change in law. Direct Consolidation Loans have no origination fees (Federal Student Aid n.d.-g).

Private loans can consolidate in theory, but few private lenders offer that option. Private lenders offer less flexibility in changing loan terms, in part because of accounting regulations that force private lenders to reduce the value of their student loan receivables when the loan terms are modified. This causes private lenders to be cautious when modifying private student loans. Students and parents should ask private lenders whether their private loans can be consolidated. If the lender cannot consolidate loans, then borrowers will have multiple loans with multiple monthly payments for all the years prior to loan payoff. Private student loans cannot, in general, be consolidated with federal student loans (FinAid n.d.-g).

Some private lenders will consolidate all private student loans; however, many will not. For those private lenders that do consolidate loans, private lender consolidations can include both fixed-rate and variable-rate loans. Lenders of private student loans may or may not charge consolidation fees.

Direct Loans

William D. Ford Federal Direct Loan Program
U.S. Department of Education

OMB No. 1840-0667
Form Approved
Exp. Date 12/31/98

William D. Ford Federal Direct Loan Program

WARNING: Any person who knowingly makes a false statement or misrepresentation on this form shall be subject to penalties which may include fines, imprisonment or both, under the U.S. Criminal Code and 20 U.S.C. 1097.

Federal Direct Stafford/Ford Loan
Federal Direct Unsubsidized Stafford/Ford Loan
Promissory Note and Disclosure

Section A: To Be Completed By The Borrower

1. Name (last, first, middle initial) and Address (street, city, state, zip code)

2. Social Security Number

3. Date of Birth
   MM/DD/YYYY

4. Area Code/ Telephone Number

5. Driver's License Number
   (List state abbreviation first.)

6. References: You must list two persons with different U.S. addresses who have known you for at least three years. The first reference should be a parent or legal guardian.

Name 1. _____ 2. _____
Permanent Address _____ _____
City, State, Zip Code _____ _____
Area Code/Telephone Number ( ) _____ ( ) _____

Section B: To Be Completed By The School

7. School Name

8. Loan Period   From: MM/DD/YYYY   to   MM/DD/YYYY
                 08/24/1998   05/07/1999

9. School Address (street, city, state, zip code)

10. School Code/Branch

The chart below shows anticipated disbursement amounts and dates. Actual amounts and dates may vary. The interest rate for this note is variable.

		Anticipated Disbursement Dates	Loan Amount Approved	Loan Fee Rate	Loan Fee Amount	Net Disbursement Amount
Direct Subsidized Loan	1ST	8/14/1998	$ 626	4.00	$ 25	$ 601
	2ND	01/04/1999	$ 625	4.00	$ 25	$ 600
		Total	$1,251		$ 50	$1,201
Direct Unsubsidized Loan	1ST	08/14/1998	$2,125	4.00	$ 85	$2,040
	2ND	01/04/1999	$2,124	4.00	$ 84	$2,040
		Total	$4,249		$169	$4,080

I promise to pay the U.S. Department of Education all sums (hereafter "loan" or "loans") disbursed under this Promissory Note plus interest and other fees which may become due, as provided in this Promissory Note. If I fail to make payments on this Promissory Note when due, I will also pay collection costs including attorney's fees and court costs. I understand that I may cancel or reduce the size of my loan by refusing any disbursement that is issued to me. I certify that the total amount that I receive under this Promissory Note will not exceed the allowable annual maximum or cumulative maximum under the Higher Education Act of 1965, as amended.

I understand that this is a Promissory Note. I will not sign this Promissory Note before reading it, even if I am advised not to read this Promissory Note. I am entitled to an exact copy of this Promissory Note and a Statement of the Borrower's Rights and Responsibilities. My signature certifies that I have read, understand, and agree to the terms and conditions of this Promissory Note and the statement of Borrower's Rights and Responsibilities. My signature on this

Promissory Note will serve as my authorization for my loan proceeds to be credited to my student account by the school identified in Section B.

Under penalty of perjury, I certify that the information contained in the Borrower Section of this Promissory Note is true and accurate. The proceeds of this loan will be used for authorized educational expenses at the certifying school for the specified loan period. I certify that I do not owe a refund on a Federal Pell Grant, Basic Educational Opportunity Grant, Supplemental Educational Opportunity Grant or a State Student Incentive Grant and that I am not now in default on any loan received under the Federal Perkins Loan Program (Including National Defense Student Loans) or the Federal Family Education Loan Program, or Direct Loan Program, or if I am in default, I have made repayment arrangements that are satisfactory to the holder of my loans.

I UNDERSTAND THAT THIS IS A FEDERAL LOAN THAT I MUST REPAY.

11. Identification Number(s)

12. Signature of Borrower   Date   MM/DD/YYYY

Retain a copy of this signed promissory note for your records.

This includes both Direct Subsidized and Unsubsidized Loans with a 4.00% loan fee in 1998-1999.

04/08/1998 07 :31 :59 SERVICER COPY

The Higher Education Act of 1965 sets the maximum interest rates and fees on federal student loans. However, nothing prevents a lender from charging lower interest rates and fees. Since the repeal of the single holder rule in 2006 by the Emergency Appropriations Act of 2006, an anticompetitive rule that limited a student's choice of lenders for consolidation, borrowers are allowed to consolidate their loans with any lender (FinAid n.d.-j). The originating lender, the lender who financed the first loan, faces the risk of losing its borrowers to other lenders. Lenders of both private student loans and federal student loans offer discounts to encourage borrowers to obtain their education loans from them. Lenders are increasingly competing with each other for potential profits in the student loan market. This encourages competition among lenders and some common loan discounts (FinAid n.d.-k):

- Lenders may waive origination fees; they may also waive default fees.
- There is a .25 percent interest rate reduction when automatic monthly loan payments are deducted from a bank account.
- On-time payment discounts are given (for example, a 1 percent interest rate reduction after 36 months of consecutive on-time payments).
- Graduation credits are given (the principal amount is reduced when repayment begins—reduction amounts typically vary from $250 to $750).
- Principal loan amounts are forgiven (for example, some lenders forgive loan amounts, such as the last five or six payments or when the remaining loan balance is less than $600).

College students can reduce the amount they repay lenders by allowing automatic monthly payments. When borrowers agree to have automatic monthly payments directly withdrawn from their bank account, they will need to have enough money in that account on the lender's first attempt for it to be reported as an on-time, prompt payment to be eligible for future repayment discounts. According to FinAid, less than 15 percent of borrowers sign up for direct monthly payments because they want to maintain control over their accounts. Less than 10 percent of borrowers qualify for prompt-payment discounts throughout the full term of the loan (FinAid n.d.-k).

Some lenders may require borrowers to repay any rebates and discounts if they consolidate their loan(s) with another lender within a given timeframe; borrowers should read the small print of their loan agreements. Many of the discounts require borrowers to have a minimum loan balance, and the best discounts are reserved for those who borrow the most.

The prime rate is a variable interest index used by many banks to set rates on consumer loan products. The prime rate can increase or decrease, and historically it has done both. The variable prime rate last changed to its current 3.25 percent rate on December 16, 2008, as reported by the *Wall Street Journal*. The spread that needs to be added to the variable index (in this example, the prime rate) would be identified on the promissory note and varies between lenders and loan options.

Interest rates are the most talked-about loan characteristic; however, stated interest rates can be reduced when borrowers elect to pay fees in order to reduce the interest rate. Applicants often search for the lowest stated interest rate, which leads them to variable rates that may start low but can increase over time. Paying fees to get the lowest interest rate can make good coffee-shop talk for consumers and, at times, lead to poor financial decisions.

> A good rule of thumb is that 3 to 4 percent in fees
> is about the same as a 1 percent higher interest rate.

If they have a parent or a cosigner with excellent credit, the student can actually see a private loan with better rates and better terms than a federal student loan. But from there the terms and rates can definitely be at a higher cost for the student, with some lenders adjusting their fees based on a credit score on the borrower or cosigner for a private loan. And, those rates and fees can be almost double what the federal loan program is. —Financial aid counselor, 2008

The following example shows the relationship between stated interest rates and loan fees and how they affect effective interest rates.

Loan Amount	Stated Interest Rate	Number of Months	Loan Fee Amount	Effective Interest Rate (APR)
$8,076.00	7.90%	120 months	1%	8.134%
$8,076.00	7.90%	120 months	4%	8.842%
$8,076.00	7.90%	120 months	11%	10.628%

In this example, each borrower has an unsecured loan amount of $8,076.00, and each loan has a stated interest rate of 7.90 percent and a 10-year maturity; however, the effective interest rates range from 8.134 percent APR to 10.628 percent APR, based on the different loan fees.

A loan in the amount of $8,076.00, with a stated fixed rate of 7.90 percent and a 4 percent loan fee, would have an effective interest rate of 8.842 percent APR on a 10-year maturity. With a 4 percent loan fee, the borrower is paying interest on $8,076.00, is paying a fee of $323.04, and would have only $7,752.96 left to pay the college costs that the loan was intended for.

Using the $8,076.00 loan amount, with the same 7.90 percent stated fixed interest rate and 10-year maturity, a fixed-rate loan with a 1 percent loan fee has an effective APR of 8.134 percent.

If a lender, such as a private lender, charges a fee of 11 percent on an $8,076.00 loan with a borrower and a creditworthy cosigner at the 7.90 percent stated interest rate, the effective interest rate climbs to a 10.628 percent APR. In addition, a private student loan would likely have a variable interest rate that could increase anytime over the 10-year repayment period.

The amount of money a borrower would actually be given to pay their college costs after signing a loan for $8,076.00 would range from the lowest amount of $7,187.64 to the highest amount of $7,995.24. Because loan fees effectively reduce the amount available to the borrower, no borrower would receive the total loan amount of $8,076.00. They would be paying interest on the full $8,076.00, but they would not be getting that entire amount to pay their college costs because the fees were subtracted first. Very few student loans are offered by lenders without fees, unless fees are waived due to competitive marketing. Even federal loans have fees, with the exception of the Perkins Loan and the federal consolidation loan. In predicting private loan fee options in the future, one counselor forecasted:

> *Private loan costs will increase, probably not in the interest rate because there is so much attention focused on interest rates by the public, by Congress, and so forth. I'm betting more on the fee side. I can imagine the lenders implementing front fees, disbursement fees, and back-end fees—especially back-end fees so it's not so obvious up front to the student. Once they start to repay the loan, an extra 5 percent is tacked on, for example.* —Financial aid counselor, 2008

There are more loan variables to consider when comparing student loans than just the stated interest rate, although that is the one area most discussed by consumers. The fees alone can result in higher effective interest rates for both fixed-rate and variable-rate unsecured student loans. Some other loan variables to consider are the repayment terms, forbearance and deferment options, credit score requirements, loan forgiveness options, tax consequences when loans are forgiven, and whether repayment is required while the student is in school or deferred until they exit school. While interest rates remain at the forefront of conversations and news media reporting, students and parents can benefit from understanding loan fees as they compare and select between private and federal student loan options.

Many of the differences between current federal and private student loan options, excluding TIL and interest rates, are highlighted in the chart below, with more specific loan details to follow in the chapters detailing federal student loans and private student loans. Parents who agree to help their children pay for college are often deciding between federal Parent PLUS Loans that they solely sign or private student loans that they sign with their college student. College students and parents may find this chart for comparing categories between federal student loans and private student loans a quick and helpful resource.

Federal Student Loans	Private Student Loans
Students do not have to start repaying Perkins or Stafford Loans until they graduate, leave school, or change enrollment status to less than half-time.	Many private student loans require payments while the student is in school. However, some private loans do have deferred payment options.
From July 1, 2006, to June 30, 2013, new federal student loans had fixed interest rates. Direct Stafford and Direct PLUS Loans disbursed on or after July 1, 2013, have variable rates fixed for a maximum of one year and have interest rate caps. Federal Perkins Loans have fixed interest rates.	Private student loans offer both variable-rate and fixed-rate loan options. Fixed-rate private loans typically have a higher interest rate than federal fixed-rate loans. Fixed interest rates on private student loans vary by lender.
The standard repayment term for federal student loans is 10 years. Loan repayment plans with extended maturities are available.	Private lenders typically have repayment terms up to 20 years, some as long as 25 years.

(Table continued on the next page)

Federal Student Loans	Private Student Loans
Undergraduate students with financial need could qualify for a subsidized loan, for which the government pays the interest during qualifying times (e.g., when the student is enrolled full time in school).	Private student loans are not subsidized. No one else pays the interest for the borrower(s).
Federal student loans are not based on full creditworthiness. Direct PLUS Loans are credit-based to the extent that borrowers cannot have an adverse credit history. A parent who has adverse credit can have a cosigner without adverse credit to help qualify for the Parent PLUS Loan.	Private student loans are credit-based and require an established credit record. The interest rate and fees for obtaining a private student loan depend on the credit score of the student, the credit score of the cosigner, and other factors, such as income and repayment capacity.
Federal loans can be consolidated into a Direct Consolidation Loan. The fixed interest rate is determined by the weighted average of the loans being consolidated and then rounded to the nearest ⅛ percent. Direct Consolidation Loan applications received on or after July 1, 2013, do not have an interest rate cap.	There are few options for private student loan consolidation. Private student loans cannot be consolidated with a federal Direct Consolidation Loan. Private lenders who consolidate private student loans typically offer variable and fixed interest rates.
Federal student loans offer forbearance and deferred payment options. For example, a student may qualify for an in-school deferment on their federal student loans when they return to school at least half-time.	Private student loans may not offer forbearance or deferment options. Each lender's policies vary.
The FAFSA is required for all federal loan applications.	Each private lender has individual application requirements for credit-based loans. Overall, the application process for private student loans is quicker and easier than for the FAFSA.
Perkins and Stafford Loans are signed solely by the student. A Direct PLUS Loan is signed by the parent of an undergraduate student or directly by a graduate or professional student (and cosigner if needed due to adverse credit rules).	Most private student loans require both the college student and a creditworthy cosigner to sign the loan documents.
The FAFSA can be completed online and has over 100 questions that are required to be answered by applicants.	Private student loan applications can be completed online.

Federal Student Loans	Private Student Loans
Students may be eligible to have some portion of their student loans forgiven if they choose to work in public service. The amount forgiven may be taxed as income.	It is unlikely that a private lender will offer any loan forgiveness program for working in public service.
There is no prepayment penalty fee on federal student loans.	Private lenders may or may not have prepayment penalty fees on their private loans.
If the student borrower dies, the loan will be discharged. The forgiven loan amount may then be taxed as income in the year the amount was forgiven.	Private loans are usually not discharged upon the death of the borrower. The student's estate and any cosigner are then responsible to pay the balance of the loan.
If the parent who signed on a Parent PLUS Loan becomes permanently disabled or dies, the loan can be forgiven. The forgiven loan amount may then be taxed as income in the year the amount was forgiven.	If a parent who cosigned on a private student loan becomes permanently disabled or dies, the loan is not forgiven.
Loan fees range from 1.051 percent to 4.204 percent for Stafford and PLUS loans disbursed on or after July 1, 2013. The federal Perkins and consolidation loans do not have fees.	Loan fees vary and have been reported to be as high as 11 percent prior to default.
Federal student loans are usually nondischargeable in bankruptcy. The 1998 law requires proof of undue hardship.	In 2005, the 1998 bankruptcy laws were updated so that private educational loans also could not be readily discharged in bankruptcy.
There is a limit in the amount that can be borrowed each year in Direct Subsidized and Unsubsidized Loans. The limit depends on the student's grade level and whether the student is dependent or independent. Borrowers can obtain up to 100% of the COA from a PLUS loan.	A student borrower and creditworthy cosigner can borrow up to 100% of the COA. Students may need to prove they are enrolled in college.
There is no grace period for Direct PLUS Loans. Repayment begins 60 days after the funds are fully disbursed.	Private student loans may have grace periods. Sometimes loan payments are deferred until after the grace period; others require repayment to start immediately.

(Table continued on the following page)

Federal Student Loans	Private Student Loans
Parent PLUS Loans may be deferred when the parent is attending school at least half-time, when the student is attending school at least half-time, while the parent is unemployed for up to three years, or while the parent is experiencing economic hardship for up to three years. Graduate students may defer repayment on PLUS loans while they are in school.	Private lenders may or may not offer payment deferment options.
Interest begins accruing on the first day of a loan. Borrowers are required to pay all accrued interest, principal, and fees. The interest on a subsidized Stafford Loan begins accruing immediately; however, the government pays the interest for the student during the subsidized period.	Interest begins accruing on the first day of the loan. Borrowers are required to pay all accrued interest, principal, and fees. No interest payments are subsidized.
Income and repayment ability is not analyzed for federal student and parent loans.	Income and repayment ability is analyzed for private student loan applicants and cosigners.
Credit scores are not analyzed for federal student loans.	Credit scores are analyzed as part of the underwriting requirements for private loans.

Without including interest rates, one counselor compared federal and private loans in this way:

> *Federal loans are much more attractive: the terms of the loan, repayment options, deferment benefits, forbearance benefits, loan forgiveness option—loan is canceled if the student is totally and permanently disabled or deceased. Private loans don't offer that.* —Financial aid counselor, 2008

Another counselor added:

> *We provide default counseling...meaning that we tell them about their credit history, how it can impact them in the*

future, how to be debt-wise. We do that to all of our students, not particularly those that are private borrowers. We really encourage them to go with the federal loans prior to seeking out private. —Financial aid counselor, 2008

College students and parents should know that financial aid counselors typically favor federal student loans over private student loans. This is expected to continue even with the recent law changing most federal student loans from fixed rates to variable interest rates (the exception is the federal Perkins Loan remaining fixed at 5 percent). The deferment and forbearance options available on all federal loans are preferred over the limited number of private student loans offering those features. The income tax implications for forgiveness of debt pertain to both private and federal student loans.

Options for Counseling

For those students accepting first-time federal Direct Stafford and Graduate PLUS Loans, entrance counseling is required. Entrance counseling can be completed in a college's financial aid office by appointment, or it can be completed online at http://www.studentloans.gov. Entrance counseling takes approximately 30 minutes for students to complete. The Office of Student Financial Aid then receives entrance counseling results and will not disburse federal loans to a student until that student has completed entrance counseling. Entrance counseling is not required for parents (or a creditworthy cosigner) signing a Parent PLUS Loan for up to 100 percent of a college's COA (Federal Student Aid 1997a).

Possible topics covered during entrance counseling include the following:

- Disbursement of loan funds to the student
- Delivery of loan funds to the student
- Borrower rights and responsibilities
- Future borrowing and managing debt
- Obligations of loan repayment
- Consequences of loan delinquency or default

Federal regulations also require financial aid offices to notify students of available exit counseling for all Federal Stafford Loan and Direct Loan borrowers who graduate, drop below half-time enrollment, or leave the college. Some colleges encourage attendance by requiring their students to attend the exit counseling in order to be able to do something else, such as obtain a copy of their official transcript. It is unknown how effective exit counseling could be in deterring federal student loan defaults if students would be required to complete it.

Information for Financial Aid Professionals (IFAP) states that exit counseling is for federal student borrowers who graduate, withdraw, or attend less than half-time and includes information on issues like student loan repayment, discharge, deferment, consequences of default, repayment plans, and loan consolidation. IFAP states that schools are to *notify* students of exit counseling and *strongly encourage* them to attend. The school may take stronger measures and develop institutional policies that keep students from receiving diplomas or obtaining academic transcripts until they have completed exit counseling; however, such measures are taken at the discretion of the institution or the state and are not regulated by the U.S. Secretary of Education. Loan funds cannot be withheld for students who elect not to attend federally mandated exit counseling based on federal rules (Federal Student Aid 1997b).

Collection costs are expenses charged on defaulted federal student loans that are added to the outstanding principal balance of the loan. These expenses can be up to 18.5 percent of the principal and interest for defaulted Direct Loans or FFEL Program loans and may exceed 18.5 percent for defaulted federal Perkins Loans (Federal Student Aid n.d.-l).

Financial aid counselors suggested financial literacy counseling and consumer credit-building for students starting in high school, recommended parental involvement in the financial aid process, and overwhelmingly suggested the addition of verbal one-on-one counseling as improvements to the current loan counseling requirements (Jensen 2010).

> *I think private loan counseling should start earlier, in high school. High school discussions about credit would allow students to start building their credit before they're 18. It would be helpful for many students that don't have a cosigner option or any family support. It would help them to be able to fund their education.* —Financial aid counselor, 2008

> *Understand when they say your interest rate is going to be 13.5 percent what that looks like for you over a 2-, 3-, 4-year period while you're enrolled. What that looks like if you go into a 10- or 15-year repayment plan.* —Financial aid counselor, 2008

> *It really does seem that students are not responding very well to written materials. I mean, we will give them brochures and things, and they just don't seem to absorb that as well.* —Financial aid counselor, 2008

> *If parents are willing to come in and have that conversation with us, that's the most effective way for us to communicate to our students.* —Financial aid counselor, 2008

First of all, it's up to them to come and see us. I mean, in theory we're supposed to know about all private loans. We do know about the school-channeled ones. It's the non-school-channeled ones that we don't necessarily ever know about. Some of the lenders actually provide us with some types of exit counseling packets. —Financial aid counselor, 2008

Most effective is one-on-one with the financial aid officer, because every student has a different situation. There's not a private loan that's what I would say is "cookie cutter" for every student's situation. I think it's probably the most beneficial for the student, and it's probably the most beneficial for us because we know exactly what the student's looking for. —Financial aid counselor, 2008

We recommend one-on-one, to talk about the specific terms of private nonfederal loans through individual lenders, what the terms are as far as interest rates, what options are available, credit issues with the student and/or cosigner, what's involved in that credit review, what their repayment is going to be like while they're in school or after school. —Financial aid counselor, 2008

There should be a verbal counseling in addition to what's online, because so many of these kids go online. —Financial aid counselor, 2008

We do provide loan counseling if they come in.
—Financial aid counselor, 2008

I try to do at least one on-campus, all-campus, open-door, come in and ask any financial aid questions you may have. That, for us, is the most effective. We've learned that students don't necessarily read everything that we send out.

> *But if you do have an open forum, conversation with students can go back and forth. Or, even with parents, if parents are willing to come in and have that conversation with us, that's the most effective way for us to communicate to our students.* —Financial aid counselor, 2008

College students and parents could benefit financially by having a one-on-one conversation with a counselor from the student's college of choice (Reed et al. 2011). The financial aid counselors found that the one-on-one approach is most effective when it includes the parents, and the verbal discussion is more effective than online counseling. For those students who want to learn more about their loan options and borrowing money for college than what online counseling provides, they should initiate and schedule a one-on-one counseling session in the financial aid office and attend with their parents. Students and their parents could also benefit financially by completing online financial aid counseling even when it is not required.

Federal Student Loans

There are generally more options in the federal program: interest rate, deferment options, forbearance options, less in terms of fees on federal loans, so it's better all the way around. —Financial aid counselor, 2008

THE DIRECT LOAN PROGRAM is the federal student loan program that exists for new loans to parents, undergraduates, graduate students, and professional students. Under the current Direct Loan Program, the government lends money directly to qualified applicants using federal funds provided to it by the United States Treasury. All federal student aid, including loans, requires completion of the FAFSA. To be awarded a federal student loan, students and parents of dependent students must complete the FAFSA. Students may not be eligible for federal student loans if they have any federal student loans in default, if they do not maintain satisfactory academic progress in school, or if they have been convicted of a drug offense. Parents must also complete the FAFSA for the federal Parent PLUS Loan and can qualify if they do not have adverse credit. The FAFSA is available online at http://www.fafsa.ed.gov.

The federal Stafford Loan Program allows students to obtain subsidized and unsubsidized federal loans solely in their own name, provided that they and the parents of dependent students complete the FAFSA. Direct Subsidized and Unsubsidized Stafford Loans are available to undergraduate students. Approximately 40 percent of all federal Stafford Loans are awarded based on need, with the taxpayers paying the interest on subsidized loans while students are in school.

The Budget Control Act of 2011 eliminated subsidized Stafford Loans for graduate and professional students effective July 1, 2012 (College Board n.d.-a). Graduate and professional students can still apply for federal Stafford Unsubsidized Loans. Unsubsidized loans do not require proven need, and applicants do not need to be creditworthy. Approval is not based on the student's income, future income, or college major, or on whether or not a degree is obtained.

Colleges typically include student loans as part of the financial aid package that is offered to students applying for financial aid. Generally there are two types of student loans:

- Federal student loans: These loans are funded by the federal government.
- Private student loans: These loans are nonfederal loans, made by a lender such as a bank, credit union, state agency, or school.

The U.S. Department of Education has two federal student loan programs:

1. **The Federal Perkins Loan Program:** The Federal Perkins Loan Program is a school-based loan program for undergraduates and graduate students with exceptional financial need. Under this program, the school is the lender. The federal Perkins Loan has a 5 percent fixed interest rate and no fees. The repayment terms are determined by the school. An undergraduate student may

be eligible to receive up to $5,500 a year. The total amount that an undergraduate can borrow is $27,500. The total amount that a graduate student can borrow is $60,000, which includes amounts borrowed as an undergraduate.

2. **The William D. Ford Federal Direct Loan (Direct Loan) Program:** This is the largest federal student loan program. Under this program, the U.S. Department of Education is the lender (Federal Student Aid n.d.-e). Direct Loans are generally included as part of a college financial aid package. Four types of Direct Loans are available:

   - Direct Subsidized Stafford Loans
   - Direct Unsubsidized Stafford Loans
   - Direct PLUS Loans
   - Direct Consolidation Loans

The U.S. Department of Education (ED) uses several loan servicers to handle the billing and other services for borrowers within the federal student loan program, specifically on loans obtained through the William D. Ford Federal Direct Loan (Direct Loan) Program and for loans originally made under the Federal Family Education Loan (FFEL) Program (now owned by ED) (Federal Student Aid n.d.-a). This means that students may receive billing notices from different loan servicers assisting the federal government in servicing their federal student loans. An unrecognizable name on a mailing should not cause it to be automatically discarded by recipients prior to opening it; it should be reviewed to be sure that it does not pertain to them and their college loans. Since July 1, 2013, Direct federal loan borrowers should expect an increased amount of important mailings and notifications due solely to the fact that their variable interest rates are scheduled to change annually, based on the market. Currently, the variable interest rates are determined for the year beginning July 1, 2013, and ending June 30, 2014, and are based on the following assumptions:

Variable-Rate Federal Direct Interest Rates and Origination Fees—July 1, 2013 through June 30, 2014

	Origination Fee	Variable Interest Rate	Interest Rate Cap
Undergraduate— Direct Subsidized Stafford Loan	1.051%	3.86%	8.25%
Undergraduate— Direct Unsubsidized Stafford Loan	1.051%	3.86%	8.25%
Graduate— Direct Unsubsidized Stafford Loan	1.051%	5.41%	9.50%
Direct PLUS— Graduate PLUS Loan	4.204%	6.41%	10.50%
Direct PLUS— Parent PLUS Loan	4.204%	6.41%	10.50%
(Federal Perkins Loan remains fixed at 5 percent, no fees)			

Variable interest rates are scheduled to change annually on July 1, based on the previous June 1 10-year Treasury rate plus the predetermined spread.

Federal student loans have annual and aggregate limits for subsidized and unsubsidized loans *(shown on the facing page)*. They may be forgiven, canceled, or discharged. For federal loan borrowers (students and parents), a physician must certify total and permanent disability. The physician must certify that the borrower is unable to engage in any substantial activity by reason of physical or mental impairment that can be expected to result in death, has lasted a continuous period of 60 months or more, or can be expected to last for a continuous period of at least 60 months. For federal student loan discharge, if the student borrower dies, then the federal loans will be discharged.

Year	Dependent Students (except students whose parents are unable to obtain PLUS loans)	Independent Students (and dependent undergraduate students whose parents are unable to obtain PLUS loans)
First-Year Undergraduate Annual Loan Limit	$5,500—No more than $3,500 of this amount may be in subsidized loans.	$9,500—No more than $3,500 of this amount may be in subsidized loans.
Second-Year Undergraduate Annual Loan Limit	$6,500—No more than $4,500 of this amount may be in subsidized loans.	$10,500—No more than $4,500 of this amount may be in subsidized loans.
Third-Year and Beyond Undergraduate Annual Loan Limit	$7,500—No more than $5,500 of this amount may be in subsidized loans.	$12,500—No more than $5,500 of this amount may be in subsidized loans.
Graduate or Professional Students Annual Loan Limit	Not applicable (all graduate and professional students are considered independent).	$20,500 (unsubsidized only).
Subsidized and Unsubsidized Aggregate Loan Limit	$31,000—No more than $23,000 of this amount may be in subsidized loans.	$57,500 for undergraduates—No more than $23,000 of this amount may be in subsidized loans. $138,500 for graduate or professional students—No more than $65,500 of this amount may be in subsidized loans. The graduate aggregate limit includes all federal loans received for undergraduate study.

Source: http://studentaid.ed.gov/types/loans/subsidized-unsubsidized#how-much-can-i-borrow

If the borrower of a Parent PLUS Loan dies or the student on whose behalf the loan was obtained dies, then that Parent PLUS Loan will be discharged. The amount discharged will be reported as income and may be taxable under IRS rules (Federal Student Aid n.d.-i). *(See table on following page)*

Type of Forgiveness, Cancellation, or Discharge	Direct Loans	FFEL Program	Perkins Loans
Total and Permanent Disability	X	X	X
Death Discharge	X	X	X
Discharge in Bankruptcy (in rare cases)	X	X	X
Closed School Discharge	X	X	
False Certification of Student Eligibility or Unauthorized Payment Discharge	X	X	
Unpaid Refund Discharge	X	X	
Teacher Loan Forgiveness	X	X	
Public Service Loan Forgiveness	X		
Perkins Loan Cancellation and Discharge			X

Source: http://studentaid.ed.gov/repay-loans/forgiveness-cancellation

Taxable Income on Student Loan Forgiveness

Federal student loan amounts can be forgiven. Some loan forgiveness program amounts are taxable and some are not. Loan discharges for closed schools, false certification, unpaid refunds, and death and disability are considered taxable income. The forgiveness of the remaining balance under income-contingent repayment and income-based repayment after 25 years in repayment is considered taxable income. There are no income limitations on the tax treatment of student loan forgiveness. Failure to pay taxes on taxable income is subject to federal IRS collection procedures (FinAid n.d.-m).

Generally, student loan forgiveness is excluded from taxable income if the forgiveness is contingent upon the student working for a specific number of years in certain professions. Under current rules, public service loan forgiveness and teacher loan forgiveness are two examples that may not be taxable income (FinAid n.d.-i).

If a creditor has canceled or forgiven debt, borrowers should expect to receive notification through IRS Form 1099c—Cancellation of Debt. Borrowers are to report the discharged amount on the "Other Income" line of IRS Form 1040. Here is an example of IRS Form 1099-C.

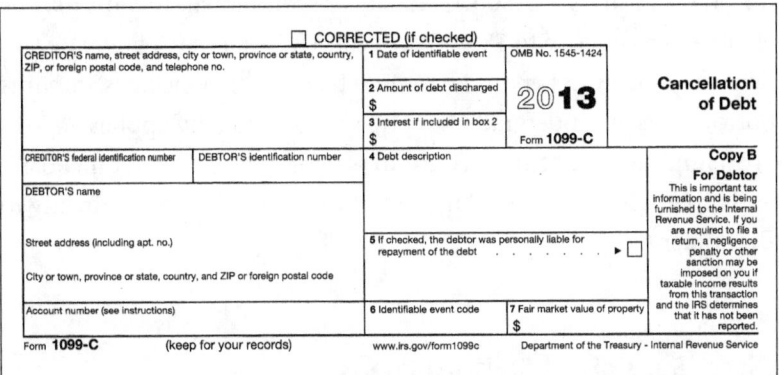

Federal Perkins Loan

The Federal Perkins Loan is available to undergraduate, graduate, and professional students with exceptional financial need who complete the FAFSA. The interest rate for this loan is fixed at 5 percent. There is no loan fee for the federal Perkins Loan. This has not changed with the Bipartisan Student Loan Certainty Act of 2013. Not all schools participate in the Federal Perkins Loan Program. Students should check with their school's financial aid office to see if the school participates and if entrance counseling is required. The school is the lender for the Perkins Loan, so students make payments to the school that made the loan or to the school's loan servicer. Perkins Loan repayment plan options are not the same as those for Direct Loan Program or FFEL Program loans. Students should check with their school for information on Perkins Loan repayment plans, as they vary. Funds available for federal Perkins Loans depend on the student's financial need and the availability of funds at the college.

Undergraduate students may be eligible to receive up to $5,500 a year in Perkins Loans. The total amount an undergraduate can borrow in Perkins Loans is $27,500. Graduate or professional students may be eligible to receive up to $8,000 per year. The total that a graduate student can borrow in Perkins Loans is $60,000, which includes amounts borrowed as an undergraduate. The school generally applies Perkins Loan funds to a student's account to pay for tuition, fees, room, board, and other school charges. Any remaining funds are issued directly to the student.

Direct Subsidized Stafford Loans

Direct Subsidized Stafford Loans are loans made to eligible undergraduate students who demonstrate financial need to help cover the costs of higher education at a college or career school. Undergraduate students and their parents must complete the FAFSA to qualify for a subsidized loan. Graduate students are no longer eligible for subsidized loans (Federal Student Aid n.d.-j).

> *If you have a Stafford Loan, if you have subsidized...*
> *the federal government is paying that [interest] for you.*
> —Financial aid counselor, 2008

Here are the basic rules about subsidized loans:

- Direct Subsidized Loans are available to undergraduate students with financial need.
- Direct Subsidized Loans are not credit-based.

- The school determines the amount that students can borrow, and the amount cannot exceed the financial need determined by the information provided on the FAFSA.

- This is a federal student loan that can be forgiven, canceled, or discharged and is subject to IRS loan forgiveness tax rules.

- Interest begins to accrue on the day the loan is disbursed (the Department of Education pays the interest during the subsidized period). The variable interest rate for loans disbursed between July 1, 2013, and June 30, 2014, for undergraduate students is 3.86 percent.

- The cap interest rate is 8.25 percent.

- Entrance counseling, online or in person, is required for first-time borrowers.

- There is a 1.051 percent loan fee since July 1, 2013.

- Dependent undergraduate students, dependent undergraduate students whose parents were denied a PLUS loan, and independent undergraduate students are limited to $23,000 in Direct Subsidized Loans.

- Graduate students, professional students, and medical school students are limited to $65,500 in subsidized loans, and this aggregate includes all federal loans received for undergraduate study.

- Repayment for subsidized loans can be made through a standard repayment plan, a graduated repayment plan, an extended repayment plan, an Income-Based Repayment Plan (IBR), a Pay As You Earn Repayment Plan, an Income-Contingent Repayment Plan, or an Income-Sensitive Repayment Plan. The repayment period for each of the plans varies from 10 to 25 years. Students can expect to pay less money toward interest when following the standard 10-year repayment plan than under any of the other repayment plans.

For a subsidized loan, the U.S. Department of Education pays the interest:

- While the student is in school at least half-time,
- During a period of deferment (a postponement of loan payments), and
- For the first six months after the student has exited school (referred to as a grace period).

If a Direct Subsidized Loan was first disbursed between July 1, 2012, and July 1, 2014, the borrower will be responsible for paying any interest that accrues during the grace period. If the interest that accrues during any grace period is not paid, it will be added to the principal loan balance (Federal Student Aid n.d.-j).

There are varying annual subsidized loan limits based on the academic levels and eligibility of dependent and independent undergraduate students. These limits do change, and updates can be found on the Federal Student Aid website: http://studentaid.ed.gov. The aggregate lifetime Stafford Loan maximums for subsidized and unsubsidized loans combined for students (including undergraduate borrowing) are currently as follows (FinAid n.d.-l):

Undergraduate Dependent	$31,000	(subsidized limit of $23,000)
Undergraduate Independent Student	$57,500	(subsidized limit of $23,000)
Master's/Doctoral Student	$138,500	(subsidized limit of $65,500)
Medical Student	$224,000	(subsidized limit of $65,500)

Federal student loans are not available for expenses incurred by law, medical, and dental students after they graduate, such as expenses associated with studying for the bar or finding a residency. There are two types of private student loans for these expenses:

- A Bar Study Loan helps finance bar exam costs such as bar review course fees and bar exam fees, as well as living expenses while studying for the bar.

- A Residency and Relocation Loan helps medical and dental students with the expenses associated with finding a residency, including interview travel expenses and relocation costs, as well as board exam expenses.

Direct Unsubsidized Stafford Loans

Direct Unsubsidized Stafford Loans are loans made to eligible un-dergraduate, graduate, and professional students who complete the FAFSA. Students do not have to demonstrate financial need to be eligible for the loan. Also, the Unsubsidized Stafford Loan is not credit-based. Many students and parents who apply through the FAFSA can qualify for the unsubsidized loan because it is not based on need or credit. Parents of dependent students must also complete the FAFSA for Stafford Loans.

Here are some of the rules for unsubsidized loans:

- Direct Unsubsidized Loans are available to undergraduate and graduate students; there is no requirement to demonstrate financial need. It is not based on credit.

- Entrance counseling is required, either online or in person, for first-time borrowers.

- The school determines the amount a student can borrow by considering the COA and any other financial aid the student receives.

- The student borrower is responsible for paying the interest accrued during all periods of repayment of an unsubsidized loan. Interest begins to accrue from the day the loan is disbursed. The variable interest rate for loans disbursed on or after July 1, 2013, for undergraduate students is 3.86 percent from July 1, 2013, to June 30, 2014.
- The cap interest rate is 8.25 percent for undergraduate students.
- The variable interest rate for loans disbursed on or after July 1, 2013, for graduate and professional students is 5.41 percent from July 1, 2013, to June 30, 2014. The cap rate is 9.50 percent for graduate and professional students.
- Dependent students whose parents are ineligible for a Direct Parent PLUS Loan may qualify to receive additional unsubsidized loan funds.
- The repayment plans for unsubsidized loans are similar to the repayment plans for subsidized loans and range from 10 to 25 years.
- If the interest that accrues while the student is in school, during the grace periods, and during deferment and forbearance periods is not paid, then that interest will be capitalized. The interest will be added to the principal amount of the loan during capitalization.
- There is a 1.051 percent loan fee since July 1, 2013.
- The aggregate loan limit for unsubsidized loans is $31,000 for dependent undergraduate students if the parent is able to obtain a PLUS loan.
- The aggregate loan limit for unsubsidized loans is $57,500 for independent undergraduate students and for dependent undergraduate students if the parent is unable to obtain a PLUS loan.
- The aggregate limit for unsubsidized loans for graduate and professional students is $138,500 (which includes undergraduate Stafford loans).

- This is a federal student loan that can be forgiven, canceled, or discharged and is subject to IRS loan forgiveness tax rules.

Direct PLUS Loans

Direct PLUS Loans are federal loans made to graduate or professional students and parents of dependent undergraduate students to help pay for education expenses not covered by other financial aid. To receive a Direct PLUS Loan, applicants must be graduate or professional degree students enrolled at least half-time at an eligible school in a program leading to a degree or certificate, or be the parents (biological, adoptive, or in some cases the stepparent) of a dependent undergraduate student enrolled at least half-time at a participating school and meet the general eligibility requirements for federal student aid. If a parent is borrowing on behalf of a student, the student must also meet these requirements. Applicants must complete the FAFSA to be eligible for Direct PLUS loans.

Here are some basic rules of the PLUS loan for graduate and professional students:

- The borrower must be creditworthy and must not have an adverse credit history.
- A student with adverse credit may qualify for a PLUS loan with a creditworthy cosigner.
- There are no income or collateral requirements.
- There is no employment requirement.
- Existing debt and payment obligations are not analyzed in the PLUS loan approval process if the loan payments are current.
- Repayment typically begins 60 days after the loan is fully disbursed.

- Loan payments can be deferred and unpaid interest can be capitalized.
- The variable interest rate on PLUS loans disbursed between July 1, 2013, and June 30, 2014, for parents of dependent undergraduate students and graduate and professional students is 6.41 percent. The cap interest rate is 10.50 percent.
- One hundred percent of the COA can be borrowed if no other financial aid has been received.
- This loan can be forgiven upon the death of the borrower. The amount forgiven will be reported as taxable income for the year the debt is erased, with few exceptions.
- Entrance counseling, either online or in person, is required for first-time student borrowers.
- There is a 4.204 percent loan fee since July 1, 2013.
- The PLUS loan has a standard 10-year maturity. There is an Extended Repayment Plan that is available for up to 25 years for Direct and FFEL loan program totals individually exceeding $30,000.

Here are some basics on Parent PLUS Loans for parents of undergraduate students:

- One creditworthy parent, who shows no adverse credit history, is required to sign for a Parent PLUS Loan.
- A parent with adverse credit history may qualify for a PLUS loan with a creditworthy cosigner.
- The college student has no legal obligation to repay a Parent PLUS Loan.
- Repayment typically begins 60 days after the loan disbursement.
- There are no income or collateral requirements.

- There is no employment requirement.
- Existing debt and payment obligations are not analyzed in the approval process if the loan payments are current.
- A Parent PLUS Loan cannot be transferred to the student through consolidation.
- Since July 1, 2008, the parent borrower has an additional option of deferring repayment until six months after the dependent student on whose behalf the parent borrowed ceases to be enrolled on at least a half-time basis.
- One hundred percent of the COA can be borrowed if no other financial aid has been received.
- The loan is forgiven at the time of the death of the parent, of the death of the undergraduate student for which the PLUS loan was intended, or upon permanent and total disability of the parent (as determined by a medical professional). The forgiven amount will then be taxable income in the year the debt is erased, with few exceptions.
- The student's biological or adoptive mother or father or a stepparent married to the student's custodial parent is eligible to borrow a PLUS loan.
- Grandparents are not eligible to borrow from the Federal Parent PLUS Loan program unless they have formally adopted the grandchild. A legal guardianship is not sufficient.
- The borrower cannot be in default on any federal student loans.
- Parents are not required to attend entrance counseling.
- The variable interest rate for loans disbursed between July 1, 2013, and June 30, 2014, is 6.41 percent with a cap rate of 10.50 percent.
- There is a 4.204 percent loan fee since July 1, 2013.

- Parent PLUS Loan deferment options can be found on the Federal Student Aid website (http://studentaid.ed.gov/types/loans/plus).
- Dependent students whose parents are ineligible for a Direct Parent PLUS Loan may be able to receive additional unsubsidized loan funds.
- The Parent PLUS Loan has a standard 10-year maturity and repayment term. There is an Extended Repayment Plan that is available for up to 25 years for Direct and FFEL loan program totals individually exceeding $30,000.

Adverse Credit

A credit history may be considered adverse if an applicant has any of the following credit conditions:

- Bankruptcy discharge within the past five years.
- Voluntary surrender of personal property to avoid repossession within the last five years.
- Repossession of collateral within the last five years.
- Foreclosure proceedings started or foreclosure within the last five years.
- Conveying real property that is subject to a mortgage (by deed) to the lender to avoid foreclosure (deed in lieu of foreclosure).
- Accounts that are currently 90 days or more delinquent.
- Unpaid collection accounts (example: medical collections).
- Charge-offs or write-offs of federal student loans.
- Wage garnishment within the last five years.
- Defaulting on a loan, even if the claim has been paid.

- Lease or contract terminated by default.
- County/state/federal tax lien within the past five years.

The federal Parent PLUS Loan allows one parent, without adverse credit, to borrow up to 100 percent of a college's cost of attendance (COA). According to Mark Kantrowitz, publisher of two authoritative financial aid websites, some parents are allowed to borrow far more than is rational (Wang, Supiano, and Fuller 2012). If a parent cannot qualify for a Parent PLUS Loan due to adverse credit, they can find their own cosigner to be able to receive additional federal funding for their child; this person can be the child's grandparent or any other creditworthy cosigner (Higuera n.d.).

> *What 45-year-old wants to ask their mommy or daddy if they'll cosign for a [PLUS] loan? No one, or I mean very, very few.* —Financial aid counselor, 2008

College counselors will recommend Parent PLUS Loans over private student loans. One creditworthy parent can sign a Parent PLUS Loan, and the PLUS loan is not contingent upon the applicant's financial ability to repay it. Aside from completing the FAFSA, it is a simple approval process. A private loan underwriting process includes a simpler application process; however, the analysis for loan repayment ability is based on income, employment, and existing debt obligations. During the 2008 interviews, counselors stated that they overwhelmingly supported Parent PLUS Loans over private student loans.

> *I would much rather that the parent takes out the PLUS loan than for the student to take out the alternative loan.* —Financial aid counselor, 2008

> *We package Parent PLUS Loans; we do not package private loans.* —Financial aid counselor, 2008

> *I've not wanted to publicize private loans very much because honestly, I want as many parents to do the Parent PLUS Loan as possible.* —Financial aid counselor, 2008

> *Part of the counseling of the private loans starts before you even talk about the private loans, and that's talking to the parents about the Parent PLUS Loan.* —Financial aid counselor, 2008

Direct Consolidation Loan

A Direct Consolidation Loan allows students to consolidate (combine) multiple federal student loans into one loan. This results in a single monthly payment instead of multiple loan payments. There is no application fee to consolidate federal student loans into a Direct Consolidation Loan. If students are contacted by someone who offers to consolidate their loans for a fee, they are not dealing with the U.S. Department of Education's loan consolidation servicer. The official website for federal student loan consolidation is http://www.loanconsolidation.ed.gov. This site also offers the list of requirements to consolidate a loan. Loan consolidation can simplify loan repayment by centralizing multiple loans into one loan and can lower monthly payments for up to 30 years. A Parent PLUS Loan made to the parent of a dependent student cannot be transferred to the student through consolidation. Therefore, a student who is applying for loan consolidation cannot include the PLUS loan(s) that the parent took out for the dependent student's education. Direct Consolidation Loans typically cannot include private student loans.

We try and sit down with every one of them...try to explain who the lender is, that it is different than a federal loan, that they can't consolidate the federal with the private but maybe can consolidate a private loan with a private lender.
—Financial aid counselor, 2008

A comparison of stated interest rates for federal student loans can be found online at http://loanconsolidation.ed.gov/help/rate.html (Federal Student Aid n.d.-d). Once loans are combined into a Direct Consolidation Loan, they cannot be separated. The following federal student loans are included in the list of those eligible for consolidation:

- Direct Subsidized Loans
- Direct Unsubsidized Loans
- Direct Subsidized Stafford Loans
- Direct Unsubsidized Stafford Loans
- Direct PLUS Loans
- Federal Perkins Loans
- PLUS loans from the FFEL Program (these loans were available prior to Direct PLUS Loans)

A Direct Consolidation Loan has a fixed interest rate for the life of the loan. The fixed rate is calculated as the weighted average of the interest rates on the loans being consolidated, rounded up to the nearest one-eighth percent. The new Public Law 113-28, effective July 1, 2013, removes the interest rate cap on consolidated loans. Removing the interest rate cap allows the weighted average of the consolidated loan rates, rounded up to the nearest one-eighth percent, to be a rate greater than the previous 8.25 percent cap rate if the variable market rates increase. The federal loans that are being consolidated have interest rate limits, so that offers protection to borrowers. Under the current variable-rate law and assuming that Direct loans are being consolidated, the highest an interest rate could be with a consolidated Parent PLUS Loan, for example, would be 10.625 percent (the 10.50 percent cap rate rounded up to the nearest one-eighth percent). For an undergraduate, the highest consolidated interest rate would be 8.375 (8.25 percent cap rate rounded up to the nearest one-eighth percent). For a graduate or professional student, the highest consolidated interest rate could be 9.625 percent for Direct Unsubsidized Loans and 10.625 percent for Graduate PLUS Loans.

Using the previous 8.25 percent cap rate on a $30,000 consolidation loan as an example, here are the monthly payments and the total interest that would be paid over five different loan periods of 10, 15, 20, 25, and 30 years.

Loan Amount	Number of Years	Monthly Payment Amount	Total Interest	Total Principal Plus Interest
$30,000	10	$367.96	$14,155.20	$44,155.20
$30,000	15	$291.07	$22,392.60	$52,392.60
$30,000	20	$255.66	$31,358.40	$61,358.40
$30,000	25	$236.59	$40,977.00	$70,977.00
$30,000	30	$225.44	$51,158.40	$81,158.40

The total amount of interest varies from $14,155.20 in 10 years to $51,158.40 in 30 years; the difference in interest alone is $37,003.20 (more than the original $30,000 principal amount). The FinAid website has a loan calculator that will estimate monthly loan payments when given the loan amount, interest rate, and loan repayment terms. It can be found at http://www.finaid.org/calculators/loanpayments.phtml.

Repayment Plans

Graduated Repayment Plan: Payments are lower at first and then increase, usually every two years. The maturity is up to 10 years.

Extended Repayment Plan: Payments may be fixed or graduated for up to 25 years.

Income-Based Repayment Plan (IBR): Students must have a partial financial hardship to qualify for this repayment plan. The payment amount changes as the borrower's income changes. The maturity is up to 25 years. Any amount that is forgiven in this repayment plan may be taxed as income. The IBR plan was included in the "Better Bargain for the Middle Class: Making College More Affordable" announcement in August 2013.

The following loans from the William D. Ford Federal Direct Loan Program and the FFEL Program are eligible for IBR: Direct Subsidized, Direct Unsubsidized, Direct PLUS (to graduate or professional students), Direct Consolidation (without underlying PLUS loans made to parents), Subsidized Federal Stafford Loans, Unsubsidized Federal Stafford Loans, FFEL PLUS (to graduate or professional students), and FFEL Consolidation (without underlying PLUS loans made to parents). Those loans ineligible include: PLUS Loans to parents, consolidation loans (with underlying PLUS loans made to parents), and private education loans.

Pay-As-You-Earn Repayment Plan: The maximum monthly payments will be 10 percent of discretionary income. Payments change as income changes. The loan maturity is up to 20 years. The "Better Bargain for the Middle Class: Making College More Affordable" plan commits to ensuring that all borrowers who need it can have access to the Pay As You Earn Plan, which caps loan payments at 10 percent of income and is directing the Department of Education to increase efforts to reach out to students struggling with their loans to make sure that they understand their repayment options. Eligible Direct loans are the subsidized, unsubsidized, PLUS (to graduate or professional students), and consolidation loans (without underlying PLUS loans made to parents).

Loans that are ineligible include Direct PLUS Loans (made to parents), Direct Consolidation Loans that repaid PLUS loans (Direct or FFEL) made to parents, FFEL Program loans, and private education loans.

Income-Contingent Repayment Plan (ICR): Payments are calculated each year and are based on adjusted gross income, family size, and the total amount of Direct Loans. Payments change as income changes. The maturity is up to 25 years. If students do not repay this loan in full after making the equivalent of 25 years of qualifying monthly payments, the unpaid portion will be forgiven under the current rules. The amount forgiven may then be taxed as income during the year the loan is discharged. The loans eligible for the ICR plan are Direct Subsidized, Direct Unsubsidized, Direct PLUS (to graduate or professional students), and Direct Consolidation (except Direct PLUS Consolidation Loans). The FFEL Program loans are not eligible. Also, Parent PLUS Loans are ineligible unless they are consolidated into a Direct Consolidation Loan on or after July 1, 2006.

Income-Sensitive Repayment Plan: Monthly payment is based on annual income. Payments change as income changes. The maturity is up to 10 years. This plan is not available for Direct Loans. It is available for the FFEL Stafford, PLUS, and consolidation loans.

Standard Repayment Plan: Payments are a fixed amount of at least $50 per month and last up to 10 years when the loan matures.

Here is a simple interest example of a standard repayment plan for 10 years and an extended repayment plan for 25 years, with a 6.80 percent fixed interest rate on a $31,000 loan.

Loan Amount	Interest Rate	Monthly Payments	Interest after 10 Years	Interest after 25 Years	Total Payments of Principal Plus Interest
$31,000	6.80%	$356.83	$11,819.60	Not applicable	$42,819.60
$31,000	6.80%	$215.26	Not applicable	$33,578.00	$64,578.00

Monthly payments of $215.26 are lower in the 25-year extended repayment plan when compared with the $356.83 monthly payments required in the 10-year standard repayment plan. However, the total amount of interest is $21,758.40 greater in the 25-year extended repayment plan than in the 10-year standard plan (total payments of $64,578.00 minus $42,819.60 or interest payments of $33,578.00 minus $11,819.60).

Additional details of the various loan repayment plans can be found at http://studentaid.ed.gov/repay-loans/understand/plans.

The federal government does not typically consolidate federal student loans with private student loans, although many college students and families continue to turn to private student loans to fill the financial gap between the COA and federal student loan limits in order to pay their EFC. There are many loan variables for borrowers to consider before selecting a credit-based private student loan over federal student loans; there are many private loan options and private lenders to research. The private loan process begins with the lender obtaining a credit report for each person applying for the loan; it is available from credit bureau agencies by using the personal information provided by the students, parents, and creditworthy cosigners during the time of application.

The Credit Report: A Report Card for Life

> *Counseling needs to provide upfront what a credit-based loan is, what it means to them in their future, in getting a car loan, or a house loan, or anything like that. I think the more information we could provide to them upfront about that, the better off they'll be financially, you know, when they graduate and look at getting a mortgage, and getting a car loan, and things like that, because by having that much debt, it's really hindering them on doing things otherwise that aren't related to education in the future.*
>
> —Financial aid counselor, 2008

A CREDIT REPORT contains detailed information on a person's credit history, including personal identifying information, credit accounts and loans, bankruptcies, late payments, collections, and recent inquiries. Prospective lenders can obtain a credit report to determine an applicant's creditworthiness. Most private lenders rely on credit scoring and repayment ratios based on proven income to determine eligibility for private student loans. A credit score will influence the interest rates and fees available on loans to borrowers; the better the score, the lower the fees and the lower the stated interest rates. Federal student loans are limited to borrowers having no adverse credit for PLUS loans; private student loan decisions include unlimited amounts of information obtained from an applicant's credit report.

Because credit scores are used for much more than consumer loan decisions, it is best for students to show financial responsibility and begin establishing good credit as soon as possible, very soon after they are 18 years old and of legal age. One of the safest credit card options for an 18-year-old who wants to establish credit is a secured credit card. In order to receive a secured credit card, the applicant must make a security deposit with the creditor. With a secured card, the credit limit will be equal to the amount of money paid as a security deposit. The credit card company can then use that deposit as the payment if a payment is ever missed. It is beneficial for consumers to earn an excellent credit rating as soon as possible; it is a gateway to many other financial opportunities and consumer transactions. It is best for students to start establishing good credit while they are in college, as those four or five years of credit history allow for more financial opportunities once students exit college, such as the independent ability to do the following:

- Get a job
- Buy insurance (credit scores are used in insurance scoring)
- Rent an apartment or house
- Qualify for credit to borrow money for consumer purchases, such as college, a car, or a house

If a college student accepts responsibility for the cable connection or utilities of a shared house under their own name and there is an unpaid balance that goes to collection, it will negatively affect their own credit report. In that case, it is best for the student to pay the bill when it is due (long before it goes to collection) and then attempt to collect from their college roommates after the payment has been made. It is not unusual for this to happen to the most financially responsible roommate, the one who coordinates services and joint payments for all of the other roommates. College students should notify all service providers of any change in their address or phone number. College students should also guard their personal identifying information and Social Security numbers from peers while attending college to avoid identity theft, to deter the illegal use of their personal information, and to protect their own credit rating. A low credit rating could negatively affect many financial opportunities, including future job offers after a preemployment background check (SBA.gov n.d.).

> **Opportunities for financial independence in the United States improve for consumers who have a college degree and an excellent credit score.**

Credit Scores

A credit score is an objective measure of credit risk. It summarizes the information from an individual's credit history into a single number. The basis for credit scoring is that the lower a person's credit score is, the greater the probability that the person will default on a loan. Borrowers with higher credit scores represent lower risks to the lender.

The most popular credit score is the FICO score, developed by the Fair Isaac Corporation, which now uses FICO as its trademark and corporate identity. More information about the Fair Isaac Corporation Consumer Division can be found at http://www.myfico.com. FICO scores range from 300 to 850; 850 is the best possible FICO score. Generally, the FICO score depends on the following factors (FinAid n.d.-a):

Score Component	Weight
Payment History	35 percent
Amounts Owed	30 percent
Length of Credit History	15 percent
New Credit	10 percent
Types of Credit Used	10 percent

The Stafford, Perkins, and PLUS loans do not depend on an applicant's credit score when obtaining the loans. The Stafford and Perkins loans are available entirely without regard to an applicant's credit history. The PLUS loan, however, requires that the borrower not have an adverse credit history, which is defined as being more than 90 days late on any debt or having had any Title IV debt within the past five years that is subject to default determination, bankruptcy discharge, foreclosure, repossession, tax lien, wage garnishment, unpaid collection account, or write-off. A full listing of categories considered in an adverse credit history for a PLUS loan can be found at http://studentaid.ed.gov/glossary#Adverse_Credit_History. The PLUS loan does not otherwise involve an applicant's credit score (Federal Student Aid n.d.-b).

Students and parents need to be aware of a recent trend in debt collections, especially as it pertains to medical collections and adverse credit for Graduate PLUS and Parent PLUS Loans. Parents may have unpaid medical collections from medical services for their children back to a time in history when the children were minors. Once the minor is of legal age, on their 18th birthday, the unpaid collection amounts specific to the child's medical services will then be added to the child's credit report upon legal age. The collection will also remain on the parents' credit report, as they are the insured. The medical provider has the patient's Social Security number, date of birth, and previous mailing address, and that is all that is needed to add the collection to the child's (the patient's) credit report. The patient will then have a medical collection on their own credit report, and their credit history will begin negatively with an unpaid collection. If the student tries to qualify for a Graduate PLUS Loan, they will have adverse credit because of an unpaid medical expense incurred when they were a minor. They may not be eligible for a Graduate PLUS Loan due to an unpaid medical collection, under the current rules.

Private education lenders generally use the FICO score in combination with other factors to determine eligibility for private student loans. The other criteria typically involve debt-to-income ratios and recent bankruptcies. In most cases, an applicant will not be able to obtain a private student loan with a FICO score below about 630–650. The average FICO score for all people obtaining all forms of credit is around 710. Lenders will often consider alternate criteria, such as the college major, grade point average (GPA), or college reputation, in addition to an applicant's credit score (FinAid n.d.-a).

If a student has a credit score that is too low, a cosigner with a good credit score can be required by the lender in order to qualify for a loan. A cosigner with a better credit score can potentially lead to a reduced interest rate and fewer fees charged on a loan. Maintaining a good credit score can save a borrower thousands of dollars in interest on private student loans. Some lenders average the two credit scores (the student's and the cosigner's credit scores), while other lenders use the better of the two credit scores to determine eligibility and the cost of credit. Some lenders may use the lower of the two credit scores when determining interest rates and fees. College students and parents should check with the private lender on how their credit scores are analyzed for loan approval.

A low credit score can significantly affect the ability of applicants to obtain private student loans and the cost of those loans. Abusing credit cards, for example, can negatively affect the interest rates and fees charged on future private student loans. Failure to repay on college loans negatively affects the credit ratings for everyone who has signed on the loans. Some cosigners, for example, once thought they would never have to repay on cosigned student loans and later found that they needed to pay the monthly loan amounts in order to protect their own credit rating for future credit needs.

There are times when an individual will not have a credit score because of insufficient credit history or lack of credit use. This is typical for many college-age students, and that is one of the reasons why the need for cosigners exists. The other major reason for needing a cosigner is that college students may not earn enough income while attending college to be able to make sufficient payments on loans.

Every loan application or credit inquiry has the potential to reduce an individual's credit score. According to the Fair Isaac Corporation, the company that produces the FICO score used by most education lenders, one inquiry will generally result in a 5-point reduction in the FICO score. Under that assumption, 10 credit inquiries authorized by a college student in order for them to receive 10 free T-shirts could reduce their FICO score by 50 points. The credit reporting agencies do account more for "shopping around" for auto loans and mortgages, but it is somewhat limited for education loans. This is partly because private student loans are relatively new and partly because lenders have not been distinguishing private student loans from other forms of unsecured credit. FinAid, the SmartStudent Guide to Financial Aid, recommends limiting private loan applications to one bank, one nonbank specialty lender, and the nonprofit loan agencies in the state where the applicant resides and in the state where the college is located (FinAid n.d.-a).

Credit bureaus are liaisons between credit granters and consumers. Credit bureaus maintain credit files on individuals. Each person's credit report is separate and unique from all others (such as a spouse's). All Title IV lenders report education loans to the three major credit reporting agencies: Equifax, Experian, and TransUnion.

Equifax Credit Information Services, Inc.
P.O. Box 740241
Atlanta, GA 30374
http://www.equifax.com
1-800-685-1111

Experian
475 Anton Boulevard
Costa Mesa, CA 92626
http://www.experian.com
1-888-397-3742

TransUnion
P.O. Box 2000
Chester, PA 19022-2000
http://www.transunion.com
1-800-888-4213, 1-800-916-8800

A good payment history will help borrowers of student loans qualify for other forms of credit, such as home mortgages. However, the credit reporting agencies will sell contact information to other education lenders that wish to consolidate student loans. Applicants who do not wish to be inundated with consolidation loan marketing materials can opt out by visiting http://www.OptOutPrescreen.com. This allows an individual to opt out for up to five years via the online process. Individuals who wish to opt out permanently can complete a form available on the website and send it by United States Postal Service (USPS) mail.

With the shift to more credit-based financing to pay for college, parents are finding out that there is a cost for not protecting their own credit scores when they are either unable to obtain a loan for their college students or paying higher interest rates and fees for having a less-than-desirable credit score. College students are becoming more involved in knowing their parents' credit ratings when parents are involved in their credit-based private student loans. A credit report is one report card that will follow an individual their entire life.

Consumers, including college students, their parents, and their creditworthy cosigners, are entitled to a free copy of their individual credit report from each of the three major credit reporting agencies once a year. A free credit report can be obtained at http://www.annualcreditreport.com (or by calling the central source at 1-877-322-8228 [877-FACTACT]). This free report does not include a credit score; however, a credit score can be obtained for a nominal fee. There are credit sites with similar names that may charge consumers a fee for the actual credit report. There will be slight variations in FICO scores at each credit reporting bureau because the credit history reported to each agency and the analysis of that history may be slightly different (AnnualCreditReport.com n.d.).

Students and parents can benefit from obtaining copies of their credit reports and credit scores before applying for credit-based private student loans. It does not affect a person's credit score when a copy of their own credit report is requested no more than once a year. The credit score focuses on consumer-initiated inquiries that involve applying for new credit. A credit report differentiates between federal student loans (the lender shows as US DEPT ED) and student loans that were obtained from private lenders. It will show who is responsible for the student loan—the student, the parent, or both.

For borrowers who are unsure of whether their college loans are federal or private (nonfederal), a list of federal student loans is available on the National Student Loan Database System (http://www.nslds.ed.gov/nslda_SA/) (Consumer Financial Protection Bureau n.d.). Student loan lenders may also use loan servicers, and borrowers will need to send their payments to these servicers. Sometimes the original lender will be the one collecting payments; however, a loan servicer is often chosen by the lender to service the loan and collect payments from borrowers (Chopra 2013a). Federal student loans managed by loan servicers whose names are different than the original federal lender will continue to be considered federal student loans on the National Student Loan Database System. Loans excluded from this listing are considered private student loans.

Credit reports are specific to an individual. A credit report typically can include this personal information:

- Name (current name, previous names, incorrect spelling of a name, and even some nicknames)
- Address (current address and previous addresses)
- Social Security number
- Date of birth
- Phone number
- Employer (current employer and previous employers)

There are many purposes for a credit report. It can verify the following:

- Customer names(s)
- Social Security number(s)
- Employment
- Repayment history
- Available credit
- Credit inquiries
- Length of current loans
- Expected monthly payments
- College loans (including cosigned loans)

- Medical expenses in collection
- Liens, judgments, and bankruptcy
- Collection accounts
- Balances on revolving accounts
- Balances on installment loans (such as a home, car, camper, boat, motorcycle, equipment, truck, or machinery)

Improving a Credit Score

More parents have not qualified for credit-based loans over the last few years because of low credit scores due to increased medical collections (even while insured), late payments (some being the result of the recent housing crisis), and loss of income that would have been used to repay debts. Much of this is due to increased unemployment in the United States. Parents can still work to strengthen their credit scores, one payment at a time. Parents should not agree to cosign a loan thinking they will never have to make payments. Parents certainly can end up having to make the payments of any credit-based loan on which they have signed. Many college students may not have a credit score or may not have started building good credit.

There are no quick fixes for improving a credit score. If a credit report contains inaccurate information, those errors should be disputed in writing. Disputing all negative information on a credit report will not automatically improve an individual's credit score. Negative but accurate information will not be removed. It is very easy to ruin a credit score, but it takes a long time to improve a low credit score.

Here are some tips for improving a credit score (FinAid n.d.-a):

1. Pay bills on time. The number of accounts that are current and the length of time during which they are paid on time has a big impact on a credit score.

2. Paying off an account with negative information does not remove that information from an individual's credit history. Only time can reduce the impact of negative information. Older credit history does not count as much as more recent information.
3. Do not close accounts that are current. It is more important to have accounts with positive history than to have no history because there are no accounts.
4. Minimize the use of revolving credit, such as credit cards and department store cards. Ignore free gifts offered on college campuses and given in exchange for applying for a new credit card.
5. Keep credit card balances low, preferably no more than 50 percent of the maximum allowable credit. For example, if a credit card limit is $1,000, then the balance should not exceed $500. Do not "max out" credit cards.
6. Pay down installment loans. The ratio of the current balance compared with the original highest balance is a measurement of a borrower's ability to repay debt. (Examples of installment loans are college, car, and home loans.)
7. Avoid opening new accounts that are not needed. Opening too many accounts can negatively affect a credit score.
8. Do not file for bankruptcy unless absolutely necessary. A bankruptcy will negatively affect an individual's credit for 7 to 10 years.

The Fair Isaac Corporation announced in 2007 that it would no longer allow authorized users to inherit the credit history of an account. Various credit reporting agencies implemented these changes in fall 2007 and spring and summer 2008. This had the effect of preventing parents from giving children a good credit score by adding them as authorized users on one of their credit cards (FinAid n.d.-a). The net impact of this is that fewer students will be able to qualify for private student loans on their own and will need to apply with a creditworthy cosigner.

Private Student Loans

When they're filling a gap utilizing the Parent PLUS Loan or they use the private student loan, overwhelmingly students chose the private student loan for a variety of reasons: [repayment on] private loans could be deferred until after the student graduates, interest rates were more favorable. We found that many parents were unwilling and unable to borrow the PLUS loan on behalf of their students; they did not want to take on more debt in their own names, impact their credit histories. The fact that the private loan was in the student's name seemed to be quite attractive. —Financial aid counselor, 2008

PRIVATE LOANS are nonfederal higher education loans that can either supplement or replace federal guaranteed loans such as Stafford Loans, Perkins Loans, and PLUS loans. A private student loan, sometimes referred to as an alternative loan, is based on the applicant's credit rating and repayment capacity. Private student loans are typically unsecured loans whereby the private lender has no guarantee of collection during times of default and nothing to repossess. Loan rates and fees are determined based on those repayment risks.

Parents of college students may remember a time when college students could qualify for unsecured private student loans on their own. During that time in financial aid history, colleges felt free to assist students in finding private lenders and relied on private student loans to fill the financial gap. Some college financial aid award letters included private student loans for students that were packaged next to their scholarships and grants; some included loan papers that were ready for borrowers' signatures. According to the 2007 preferred lender investigation leading to the SLATE Act, there were times when private lenders met directly with students on college campuses to complete their private student loan transactions. Students wanted to be able to pay increasing college costs, like today's college students; however, they were able to stay enrolled by combining the funds they could get through scholarships, work-study, and the Pell Grant, and then sign their own federal and private student loans. They did not have to involve their parents beyond the FAFSA application in order to qualify for federal financial aid.

> *Parents will fill out the FAFSA form, but students say they aren't helping financially—not sure how valid that assessment is. Bills may be getting paid by parents or by private loans. Private loans do not involve the parents because it is just more convenient for the student to not involve the parents or the parents are unwilling or unable.* —Financial aid counselor, 2008

> *It's really taken off...jumped considerably, due to the rising costs of tuition, room, and board.* —Financial aid counselor, 2008

In order for students to pay for their increasing college costs without involving their parents, use of private (alternative) student loans instead of Parent PLUS Loans was increasing by 2001. By 2005 there was $13.8 billion in private loans, compared with $8.2 billion in Parent PLUS Loans (Lederman 2006). A Parent PLUS Loan requires both dependent students and parents to complete the FAFSA annually, which contains over 100 questions. Financial aid counselors stated that college students and families viewed the FAFSA as a long, complicated process that was financially invasive. Parents preferred to have their child sign their own student loans and finance their own education. More families did not accept the Parent PLUS Loan as an option, leaving many students to seek private loan sources.

This resulted in more college students accepting financial responsibility to repay all of their college loans (both federal and private loans) and fewer parents accepting financial responsibility to sign on college loans to pay for their children's college. Some students opted to exclude their parents and did not complete the FAFSA process, as they could obtain up to 100 percent of COA from private lenders to pay for college. Here are some of the reasons that students elected their own private loans over Parent PLUS Loans, which are still true today:

- Monthly payments on private student loans can be delayed until the student exits college; Parent PLUS Loan payments begin soon after the student enters college and 60 days after final loan funds are disbursed (unless deferred payments are applied for and approved).
- The loan application process is easier for private student loans, significantly easier than completing the FAFSA, which is required for students and parents for all federal student loans, including Parent PLUS Loans.
- Approvals for private student loans are often quicker (some are within minutes) than those for federal student loans (which can take weeks or months).

- Private lenders use FICO credit scoring in their underwriting standards. Borrowers view this as being comparable to the underwriting requirements for a Parent PLUS Loan which requires that only one parent apply, who does not have an adverse credit history.

- Lenders advertise comparable stated interest rates, and many borrowers see no great differences between a variable-rate loan, when the rate increases and decreases with the market, and a fixed-rate loan. When there is a 7.90 percent fixed-rate loan and a 7.90 percent variable-rate loan, borrowers tend to give them equal value as 7.90 percent loans and may not consider the additional risks of a variable-rate loan being able to increase up to a 10.50 percent cap rate, for example, or a variable-rate loan being able to increase to any interest rate because it does not have a cap limit.

The decline in the economy and the increase in private student loan defaults led private lenders to reassess their underwriting standards and whether or not to stay in the business of private student loans. Lenders that remained in the private student loan business tightened their credit underwriting standards. Private lenders began offering very few student loans solely to college students. Private lenders determined that they could have fewer defaults on their private student loans due to creditworthy cosigners than when they had the student sign alone.

> *The availability of private loans without a cosigner for a student is next to impossible. They now have to find cosigners.*
> —Financial aid counselor, 2008

A typical college student has not had enough time or enough credit transactions to build good credit, through no fault of their own. Few college students own unencumbered collateral to be able to qualify for private student loans on their own. College students who were once able to obtain private loan funds on their own now need creditworthy cosigners. The underwriting decision is complicated by the fact that college students often do not have a good credit history, or any history that would indicate creditworthiness.

In August 2012, the CFPB completed a report on private student loans. They reported that consumers owe more than $150 billion in outstanding private student loan debt. In July 2013, the amount of private student loan debt estimated by CFPB was $165 billion (Chopra 2013b). Students may find themselves resorting to private student loans because federal student loan limits are not high enough to cover college costs or because the application process is easier if they have a creditworthy and willing cosigner. There could be times when a parent would not qualify for a federal PLUS Loan due to adverse credit but may qualify as a cosigner for a private loan. A United States government shutdown could steer students and parents away from federal student loans and toward private student loans. Private loans with fixed interest rates may appear superior to variable-rate federal student loans during market rate increases.

> I've been a counselor for nine years, and when I first started, we did very, very few alternative loans. Now, it seems like it's more the norm than abnorm[al]. The biggest reason, I think, is that the education costs have increased so much and living expenses have increased so much and other forms of aid have not. —Financial aid counselor, 2008

> There is definitely more private loan volume than there was five years ago. That is for certain. I think [the reason is] that it's marketed more through the media and through these private loan companies. We'd never, ever until last year seen

> them advertised on TV. We used to see little advertising on private student loans. But, we certainly give students the opportunity to pick any lender that they choose. —Financial aid counselor, 2008

> The volume has increased dramatically. It has consistently, of course, gone up over the last years. We're averaging anywhere, if I go back to 2003, 2004, we're up about 15 percent at that point. The next year was about 17 percent, the next year at 19 percent, and 2006–2007 was about 20 percent up. —Financial aid counselor, 2008

> The student is forced to go and get private loans, cosigned often by those parents who are refusing to do PLUS loans. —Financial aid counselor, 2008

> I've worked here in our financial aid office going on nine years, and as of eight years ago we had 25 students. As of today, we have about 195 students processing an alternative [private] loan. —Financial aid counselor, 2008

The shift in requiring cosigners seemed simple enough until an increasing number of parents could not qualify for credit-based financing and a growing number of parents refused to cosign private loans for their child to be able to go to college. There were also those college students who did not want to have to involve their parents.

> They're choosing not to complete the full financial aid process to seek the federal loans first [the other option, then, is private loans]. The reasons: not going to be approved for any loan anyway, don't want parents involved, we can't do PLUS loans, we won't do PLUS loans.
> —Financial aid counselor, 2008

> *Some say, "Well, I'm not going to be approved for any loan anyway."* —Financial aid counselor, 2008

Although counselors stated that they encouraged Parent PLUS Loans over private student loans, some parents refused to complete the FAFSA for various reasons:

- The application questions are financially invasive.
- They will not qualify.
- They did not want to.
- They should not have to.
- The process is long and complicated.

> *We do counsel families, pretty strenuously, that they should pursue the PLUS loan before private loans, but many families still opt to go the private loan route.* —Financial aid counselor, 2008

Also, counselors highlight the protection provided with federal loans, as they can be forgiven if the student dies or if the parent who signed on a federal Parent PLUS Loan dies or becomes totally or permanently disabled. Although counselors did not acknowledge this during the interviews, it is important for borrowers to realize that loan forgiveness due to death and disability is taxable income during the year in which the debt is erased, with few exceptions. The same tax rules would be applied if a private lender forgave student loan debt, which is less unlikely. The taxes are subject to IRS collection rules.

> *The federal loans are guaranteed...if permanently disabled or they die, their family is not responsible for that federal loan. Where, if they have a cosigner on a private loan, too bad, you still have to pay it.* —Financial aid counselor, 2008

Most college students cannot qualify for unsecured credit on their own. Their credit scores and income are both too low to qualify for credit-based financing. College students are left to seek out possibilities from a full range of private loan options and compare interest rates, upfront fees, back-end fees, prepayment penalties, repayment terms, and costs of defaulting. Although both are student loans requiring principal and interest to be repaid monthly, the options for private student loans vary considerably, and private student loans vary from federal student loan options.

> *Students must compare options...whether it is in the front end in origination fees, interest rates, timely repayment incentives, rebates on the back end, or penalties for late payment.*
> —Financial aid counselor, 2008

Many students have been able to find willing cosigners. Cosigners help keep students in school and help colleges meet their enrollment goals even during times of increasing tuition costs. The financial probability of private lenders receiving full student loan repayment increases with creditworthy cosigners.

Choosing a Private Lender

Private student loans can be riskier than federal student loans mainly due to variable interest rates without cap rates; however, financial aid counselors stated that many students disregard the differences in financial risks and continue to obtain private student loans. Although federal student loans now have variable rates, with the exception of the Perkins Loans and consolidation loans, there are caps on the federal Stafford and PLUS variable-rate loans that offer more protection than private variable-rate loans with higher cap rates or private loans without any cap rates. Here are some of the areas for consideration when students compare private lenders and private student loan options:

- Is a cosigner required? If yes, what are the cosigner requirements? Are there options to be able to release a cosigner prior to the loan's maturity?
- What is the stated interest rate? What is the annual percentage rate (APR)?
- What is the stated interest rate for the in-school and grace periods? What is the stated interest rate when the loan enters repayment?
- Is the interest rate fixed or variable? If variable, how often and how much can the interest rate change? If variable, is there a limit to how low the interest rate can decline (a floor rate)? If variable, is there a maximum cap rate? If yes, what is the cap rate?
- When do payments begin? Do payments need to be made while the student is in school?
- What are the loan fees, and when are they charged?
- What is the minimum amount that can be borrowed?
- What is the maximum amount that can be borrowed?
- Does the lender capitalize interest (i.e., add any unpaid interest to the principal loan balance, which increases the amount of money that needs to be repaid)? Is yes, how often is interest capitalized: monthly, quarterly, semiannually, or annually?
- Will the lender consolidate multiple private loans so that there is only one monthly payment? If yes, what is the consolidation fee? Do any fee rebates and loan discounts need to be repaid on the loans being consolidated?
- Does the lender offer electronic payments? Will setting up automatic electronic payments reduce the interest rate?

- Can the loan be used to cover an unpaid balance from a previous school term?
- Does the lender offer interest rate reductions or other borrower incentives?
- Can the loan be consolidated with federal student loan amounts?
- Does the lender offer forbearance or deferment in certain situations? If yes, what are those circumstances?
- What is the lender's reputation?
- How is the lender's customer service?
- What satisfies the proof of college enrollment when it is required to be able to apply for a student loan?
- How much can be borrowed based on the college's COA?
- What is the loan's maturity date?
- What is the in-school interest rate?
- What is the interest rate during the grace period?
- What is the interest rate when the loan enters repayment?
- When does the loan enter repayment?

Many financial aid offices provide limited, if any, information to college students on private student loans and refrain from endorsing any particular private lender. When asked, financial aid counselors may offer very general information and suggest that the student begin their own research and look online for private (alternative) lenders who offer private student loans.

> *If the student comes in inquiring for additional sources of borrowing on their behalf, we do provide them with the lenders, the Web addresses, and the 800 numbers.*
> —Financial aid counselor, 2008

Students may find some information on private loans using a college's website and searching under "alternative student loans" or "private alternative loans." Students can also contact their local lending institution for private loan options, or they can search online under "private student loans." Students can also locate their state's student assistance agency for any state loan programs that may be available at the National Association of State Student Grant & Aid Programs (http://www.nassgap.org/links.aspx). It is then up to each student to compare lenders and the various loan options such as interest rates, fees, repayment terms, repayment options, collateral requirements, and any other variables they want to compare.

Private Student Loan Lenders

In July 2013, the following private lenders were found when searching private student loans online. These lenders offered both undergraduate and graduate student loans at the time. This private lender list provides no endorsement for any of the lenders. Their advertised variable-interest rates (typically the lender's best rates) were stated from 2.25 percent to 9.86 percent, the indexes were either the one-month LIBOR (London Interbank Offered Rate) or the prime rate, loan maturity dates ranged from 5 to 25 years, and lenders quoted interest rate caps ranging from 18 percent to 21 percent; some loans had no cap rates. These private lenders had automatic-payment discounts from .25 percent to .50 percent, and no origination fees were advertised. The stated fixed-interest rates for the private student loans ranged from 4.50 percent to 11.75 percent. It is not uncommon for lenders to advertise a lower rate for the in-school and grace periods, with a higher rate in effect when the loan enters repayment. The private lenders are listed at random, and no significance should be inferred from the order in which the lenders are listed (Student Lending Analytics 2012):

Private Lenders

Wells Fargo	https://wellsfargo.com/student/index 800-378-5526
Sallie Mae	https://www.salliemae.com/student-loans/ 877-279-7172
Charter One	http://charterone.com/student-services/ 800-721-3969
SunTrust	https://www.suntrust.com/personalbanking/loans/educationloans 866-232-3889
PNC Bank	http://www.pnconcampus.com/studentloanguide/privateloans/undergraduates/index.html 800-762-1001
Citizens Bank	http://www.citizensbank.com/student-services/ 800-708-6684
Discover	https://www.discover.com/student-loans/ 877-728-3030

As an example for July 2013, Wells Fargo offered credit-based private student loans with variable interest rates ranging from 3.50 to 9.00 percent; fixed interest rates ranged from 6.74 to 12 percent. Both the variable-rate and fixed-rate private loan options had a 15-year loan maturity. Lenders may elect to advertise only the lowest interest rate they charge for good credit borrowers. Borrowers with bad credit can expect interest rates that are as much as 6 percent higher, loan fees that are as much as 9 percent higher, and loan limits that are two-thirds lower than the advertised figures. The quoted and advertised interest rates will include disclaimers that they are subject to change.

Choosing a Cosigner

An eligible cosigner affects loan eligibility and approval, so borrowers should select their cosigner(s) wisely. Here are some cosigner strengths to look for:

- No serious derogatory items exist on the cosigner's credit report.
- All credit obligations are maintained as agreed.
- Credit is not overextended.
- A majority of revolving credit lines remain unused.
- The cosigner has at least four to five years of credit history.
- The cosigner has steady employment with income sufficient to meet current debt obligations.

Comparing Loan Options

Interest Rates

Interest rates can vary greatly and can be influenced by the applicant's credit history. Lenders typically offer applicants loan choices for both fixed interest rates (the interest rate never changes) and variable interest rates (interest rates can fluctuate and will likely change over time). If all other things are equal, a higher interest rate is expected on a loan having a fixed rate versus one with a variable rate. The offset to that risk is that a fixed interest rate will not change until maturity, assuming that the loan is being repaid as agreed.

Private lenders score their loans using various variable-rate indexes, such as the prime lending rate (prime), the 91-day Treasury bill, and the LIBOR for one month, three months, and six months (FinAid n.d.-h). Lenders predetermine the spread that is to be added or subtracted from these variable-rate indexes, and that is disclosed in the loan documents. Private lenders can also amend an interest rate index when borrowers sign and agree to the change. Each index can be found in the Federal Reserve's Statistical Release (http://www.federalreserve.gov/releases/H15/current/h15.pdf). The LIBOR rate appears in the Eurodollar Deposits (London) line on this website (Federal Reserve 2013).

When shopping for private college loans, while it is tempting for students to choose one based on stated interest rates alone, it is best to compare rates by the APR. Unlike stated interest rates, which may not represent the true cost of the loan, the APR takes into account all associated loan costs such as finance charges and loan fees (except penalty charges such as late payment fees). The formula used for calculating the APR also takes into account deferment periods and repayment terms. Each of these factors can have a significant impact on the cost of a student loan. The APR adjusts for each of these items, illustrating the true cost of borrowing for college costs over the entire life of the loan. Be wary of comparing APRs on loans having different maturities, as a longer-term loan reduces the APR even though it increases the total amount of interest paid. According to a financial aid counselor, federal student loans do not disclose APRs for the true borrowing costs. Private lenders are required to disclose APRs to consumers.

Additionally, private lenders may not be able to disclose what the actual interest rate will be until after a completed application is submitted and they are able to evaluate each applicant's credit history, credit scores (from all three credit bureaus), and repayment ability. This differs from federal student loans, as the application process does not require repayment ability and credit scores. The APR examples help applicants understand the lowest and highest interest rates that are available. Private lenders provide applicants this type of information on their loan disclosures soon after an application for financing is completed.

Fees

The fees charged by some lenders can significantly increase the cost of the loan. A loan with a relatively low interest rate but high fees can cost more than a loan with a higher interest rate and no fees. When fees are high enough, they can offset the benefit of a lower interest rate. The lenders that do not charge fees often roll the difference into the interest rate. A good rule of thumb is that 3 to 4 percent in fees is about the same as a 1 percent higher interest rate.

Repayment Terms

There are two time-sensitive questions that applicants can ask: First, when do payments start? Some loans offer a grace period after the student graduates, during which no payments need to be made. A grace period allows time for students to find a job after exiting college and before repayment terms begin. Some loans require immediate repayment, even while the student is in school.

Second, for how long are payments expected to be made (or what is the maturity date of the loan)? A longer repayment period means lower payments and a larger amount of total interest being paid. With all things being equal, a longer repayment term will have a lower APR even though the borrower will pay more in interest over that longer timeframe (the fee can be spread over more years when the APR is calculated on longer maturities).

Repayment Options

There may be options for temporarily suspending loan payments, such as forbearances or deferments. When in forbearance, borrowers who cannot make scheduled loan payments may be able to stop making payments or reduce monthly payments for a predetermined amount of time. Borrowers who are granted forbearance should follow these steps:

- Contact the lender or servicer to obtain the necessary forms.
- Complete the forms, follow their directions, and return the forms to the lender or servicer.
- Continue to make the scheduled payments until a confirmation is received from the lender or servicer that the forbearance has been processed and approved.

Truth in Lending

Students, parents, and cosigners have the opportunity to review interest rates, loan fees, maturity dates, repayment terms, and deferral options when applying for a private student loan, subject to the Truth in Lending (TIL) Act and prior to agreeing to a private student loan. Subpart F of the TIL Act includes disclosure requirements that apply to creditors making private education loans. It also requires that creditors obtain a self-certification form signed by the consumer before advancing loan funds. For private education loans subject to Subpart F, TIL ensures that the required disclosures are accurate and timely. This is a listing of minimal information that applicants should expect to receive before signing a private student loan:

- Interest rate, whether fixed or variable.
- Whether the interest rate can increase and any rate limitations.
- Whether the rate will typically be higher if the loan is not co-signed or guaranteed.
- Fees and default or late payment costs.
- Repayment terms—principal amount, maturity date, payment amount.

- The period during which regularly scheduled payments of principal and interest will be due.
- Deferral options or a statement that the consumer does not have the option to defer payments.
- If deferral is an option, the interest that will accrue during deferral.
- If the consumer files for bankruptcy, the statement that they may still be required to repay the loan.
- Cost estimates using the highest interest rate and all applicable finance charges. If a maximum rate cannot be determined, a rate of 25 percent will be used.
- Eligibility (such as any age or school enrollment eligibility requirements).
- Alternatives to private education loans, including a statement that the consumer may qualify for federal student loans.
- A statement that before loan proceeds are advanced, the borrower must complete a self-certification form obtained from the student's institution of higher education.

When a private loan is first received, borrowers have the right to cancel, and there will be information on the methods for cancellation, without penalty, and the allowable timeframe. It will include a statement that the loan amount will not be disbursed until the cancellation period expires (after a three-day right of rescission, for example).

Private Student Loan Consolidation

The main benefit of loan consolidation is to combine several loans into one loan in order to obtain a single monthly payment. Federal student loan lenders generally do not consolidate federal student loans with private student loans. However, some private lenders may agree to consolidate private student loans with any remaining federal student loans. When this happens, students lose the benefits of their federal student loans.

Some private lenders will consolidate all of a student's private student loans originated by any number of private lenders for those applicants who qualify. The private lender determines the interest rate and the ability to consolidate based on the credit scores and the income of the applicant(s). A student may be able to obtain a lower rate through a private consolidation if their credit score has improved significantly (50 to 100 points) between the time when the loan was first obtained and the time of the consolidation application. On private student loan consolidations, the interest rate is based on the credit score and repayment capacity; the private lender dictates the interest rates. Additional fees may be charged for consolidating private student loans. When evaluating a private consolidation loan, students should ask what the interest rate is and whether the interest rate is fixed or variable, what the fees are, when fees will be charged, and whether there are prepayment penalties on consolidated loans (FinAid n.d.-a).

In August 2013, SunTrust offered fixed interest rate loans from 7 percent to 10.25 percent when college graduates consolidated their private student loans. They recently reentered the private loan consolidation market and were very specific that they do not consolidate unless the applicant has at least a four-year degree. The maturities on the consolidated loans were 15, 20, and 25 years. Their variable interest rates, based on the one-month LIBOR, ranged from stated rates of 4.85 percent to 7.96 percent with no cap rate, with the exception of the state of Texas having an 18 percent cap rate. There was a .25 percent discount for an automatic monthly payment from any checking account and a .50 percent discount for an automatic monthly payment from a SunTrust checking or savings account. There were no origination fees (SunTrust telephone inquiry 2013).

In June 2013, Wells Fargo offered fixed interest rate loans from 7.49 percent to 12.29 percent when consolidating private student loans. The maturity on the consolidated loans varied from 15 to 20 years. Their variable interest rates, based on the prime rate, ranged from stated rates of 4.00 percent to 8.75 percent. Both the fixed-rate and variable-rate quotes had relational discounts available, meaning that a discounted rate is possible when a borrower also has a Wells Fargo checking or savings account. There were no origination fees at the time (Wells Fargo telephone inquiry 2013).

Variable Prime Rate Index	Added Spread	Stated Interest Rate (without fees included)
3.25%	.25%	4.00%
3.25%	5.50%	8.75%

Financial Aid Certification Requirements

Financial aid counselors are required to certify that all sources of financial aid do not total an amount that exceeds 100 percent of a college's COA. This includes, but is not limited to, federal student loans, grants, scholarships (including college scholarships awarded to students while in high school), family loans and gifts, and private student loans. Although counselors are not required to counsel students on private student loans, they are still required to certify the amount and the purpose of each private loan.

Certification is basically a borrower protection put in place to make sure that correct loan amounts are being distributed to students. Certification requires counselors to confirm each student's registration status and financial aid eligibility and to verify that the student's total financial aid does not exceed the college's COA or budget. Colleges invest time and money in training their financial aid counselors to resolve conflicting information and give serious attention to determine whether or not sources of financial aid are within a college's COA. If excess is verified during the certification process, federal financial aid may be reduced or canceled. That could mean that a Pell Grant or a federal loan is forfeited if private loan funds are already obtained and combining all aid exceeds the college's total COA. If students mistakenly receive too much aid and it is discovered during certification, the excess amount must be repaid.

> *The biggest thing that has to happen is that legislation has to come out that says they have to tie these direct-to-student loans to the current federal rules. And that is, look, if it's a school loan, and it's for tuition, fees, room and board, personal transportation, or anything else that is in the budget, it has to fit within that budget.* —Financial aid counselor, 2008

Financial aid counselors are not privy to all private student loan information, especially information about direct-to-student (DTS) loans. These private loans are also called direct-to-consumer loans. This is when private lenders work directly with the college student and their cosigner(s) and bypass the college financial aid office.

> *There are private loans that exist where it's just an agreement between the student and the lender. The lender never contacts the school; the student probably has to show proof that they're enrolled by showing them their schedule or their registration or maybe their bill. They don't necessarily contact the school to find out if the student really needs this, if they need this to cover their costs.* —Financial aid counselor, 2008

> *There is a limit to what we can offer in the way of counseling. We won't know what the terms of the loan are until after the student's been approved.* —Financial aid counselor, 2008

Loan funds from a private DTS loan are sent straight to the borrower(s) and bypass the financial aid office. Schools are often unaware of funds from DTS loans. These lenders cap the annual loan amount at up to 100 percent of the COA without regard to any of the other amounts that students received from any other aid sources. If those same applicants also obtain grants, scholarships, or federal loans, then their combined amount of aid could exceed the college's total COA. The financial risk in having students and parents obtain total financial aid in excess of the COA has also increased since private student loan volume and the use of DTS lenders has increased; it can lead to devastating financial results.

> *They will do the loan, and it requires no school certification. They can have regular student loans that have to be certified by the school. Then they have these direct-to-student loans, too.... So this student can have a budget [limit] of $27,000, they could have $3,500 in Stafford, $1,500 in Perkins, $10,000 in a Partnership Loan, and they could turn right around and they could borrow [the full $27,000] from another [private] lender.* —Financial aid counselor, 2008

The CFPB found that from 2005 to 2007, private lenders increasingly marketed and disbursed loans directly to students, reducing the involvement of schools in the process. The percentage of loans to undergraduates made without school involvement or certification of need grew from 18 percent to over 31 percent during that period. As a result, many students borrowed more than they needed to finance their education and more than 100 percent of the college's COA (Consumer Financial Protection Bureau 2012).

> *I am required to resolve conflicting information. If I discover there is a direct-to-student loan, then it needs to come out*

> of the other funding. The total amount cannot be more than
> budget. So the student comes in and he's talking, "Yeah,
> I did a loan with Astrive." [I say], "So, do you want me to
> send back your state tuition grant? Do you want me to send
> back your college grant? Do you want me to send back
> your athletic scholarship? Where do we want to fit that in?"
> But, maybe I can back him out of some of those loans.
> —Financial aid counselor, 2008

Private lenders of DTS loans have consumer compliance and privacy rights of their own that they follow, and those lenders do not voluntarily disclose information directly to the college even when asked by a counselor. Private loans are consumer transactions between the borrower and the lender. Students are expected to accept sole responsibility to disclose DTS loans through self-certification. Falsifying certification could lead to government penalties, including fines, being sent to prison, or both.

> We make it very clear to students that if that's the process
> they're going to go through, especially since it's direct to
> consumer, it's very important that they contact us to let
> us know who the lender is, how much they're planning
> to borrow. —Financial aid counselor, 2008

There are also private student loans called *school-channeled loans*. Counselors are better able to comply with certification requirements for school-channeled loans because the money from these loans is transferred directly to the student's college of choice and the financial aid office is notified of the amount at that time. These lenders will also cap the annual loan amount at the COA minus the financial aid received (COA–Aid).

In 2010, a Sallie Mae spokeswoman stated that 16 percent of students receive money from relatives who are not their parents. Also, one out of five students receives financial assistance from grandpa and grandma and other relatives and friends. Financial assistance from grandparents could include both cash gifts and loans. Students are not asked if they expect help from grandparents on forms like the FAFSA, although one question asks students if they received cash support from someone other than their parents in the previous year (Post 2010).

Students may hesitate to report, to their college and to the government, how much money their grandparents are giving them. That amount would not be included in the EFC. Gifts from grandparents for college are viewed much like scholarships and grants and need to be reported to meet federal financial aid certification requirements. In addition, self-certification should include the amount in high school scholarships that students receive for college if that amount is not being reported by their high school counselors. A Private Education Loan Applicant Self-Certification form is included in Appendix D.

It is up to college students to report all sources of financial aid to their college financial aid offices. Cash gifts may be difficult to track; however, student loan amounts and the lender information for both federal and private student loans that are reported to credit bureau agencies will appear on the credit reports of all of the parties signed on each loan, such as college students, parents, and cosigners. Once the grace period or a deferment period has expired on each loan, the monthly repayment terms are shown on credit reports (the stated interest rate does not appear on a credit report). These numbers then become the monthly repayment amounts used by lenders when determining debt-to-income ratios for future credit-based loans, such as car and house loans.

In order for students to ensure their own financial security and ability to buy a house or a car in the future, it is important that they make responsible borrowing decisions while in college. To improve their chances for financial independence, college students should graduate with a college degree, borrow no more than *half* of their anticipated wages the first year out of college, pay the accrued interest on their student loans to avoid any capitalized interest (subsidized loans for undergraduates are paid by the government), and agree to repayment amortizations where the monthly payment amounts are no more than 7 percent of their gross monthly income.

Hypothetically Speaking

One would think with so many entities and individuals (Department of Education, lenders, guarantors, high school counselors, financial aid counselors, parents, students themselves) assisting students with applying to and choosing a college, program of study, completing scholarship applications and the FAFSA application, all parties could work together on educating students on student loans and debt.
—College graduate student and financial aid employee, 2012

TUITION IS RISING, the job market is weak, and everyone seems to be debating the value of a college degree (Supiano 2011). Nearly 7 in 10 U.S. adults (69 percent) strongly agree or agree that having a college degree is essential for getting a good job in this country, according to a study by the Gallup and Lumina Foundation for Education (English 2011). A report, titled *The Big Payoff: Educational Attainment and Synthetic Estimates of Work-Life Earnings*, reveals that over an adult's working life, high school graduates can expect, on average, to earn $1.2 million; those with a bachelor's degree, $2.1 million; and people with a master's degree, $2.5 million (Day and Newburger 2002). A college degree remains the nation's central economic credential (Meacham, Gray, and Rhodan 2013).

The American Dream 2.0 report suggests that anyone who does not get a college credential will remain in a cycle of poverty (HCM Strategists 2012). Consistent with these perceptions, Gallup Daily's tracking of unemployment and underemployment in the United States finds that college-educated Americans fare better in the workforce than U.S. adults without a college degree. Unemployment and underemployment rates for college-educated individuals in 2011 are lower than those rates for Americans with less education and are also well below the national averages.

The number of students who are applying to attend college is increasing, and more Americans are staying in school longer than ever before (Longley 2010); individuals who want to improve their job skills in order to compete in a declining job market are returning to school. While colleges have steadily increased tuition costs, they have kept up with the demand for college enrollments and have supplied college students with state-of-the-art campuses, a large variety of degree programs, and many of the student services that college students have come to expect.

A Pew report dated March 2012 supports the fact that 39 percent of 18-to-24-year-olds were enrolled in college. Among 18-to-24-year-olds, those enrolled in college were much more likely than those not in college to be living at home—66 percent versus 50 percent. The steady rise in the share of young adults who live in their parents' home, according to Pew, appears to be driven by a combination of economic, educational, and cultural factors. Among the reasons are declining employment and rising college enrollment (Fry 2013). *The American Dream 2.0* states that 38 percent of students are enrolled in college part-time, 15 percent of college students live on campus, and 25 percent of college students have children (HCM Strategists 2012).

In order to attain a college degree, students will need to continually look for ways to save their financial future by approaching college in more nontraditional ways. Students will need to limit borrowing to an amount much less than 100 percent of a college's COA even if they are able to borrow that much. Colleges offer a variety of course deliveries that allow students to work a full-time job and still attend college either part-time or full time, for example. Some colleges refer to this as *distance learning*, where most or all of the work can be done at home or away from a campus classroom (Hacker and Dreifus 2011). Students may also find benefits in saving on their room and board costs and elect to live at home while attending college versus needing to come home to live after college—a pay-now-versus-pay-later alternative for their parents. This could mean attending classes on a campus within commuting distance from home or attending online classes. By 2025, it is projected that the average four-year college tuition cost (without fees, room, and board) at private colleges will be $160,000, and $97,000 for tuition at public colleges (Meacham, Gray, and Rhodan 2013).

In the current economy, a greater share of parents can no longer help their children pay for the rising costs of college. According to the financial aid counselors, more parents are also unwilling to help their children pay for college. For those stakeholders who see benefits in shifting back to a time when college students could qualify on their own to finance college costs and make all financial decisions, two counselors shared similar solutions; both suggestions are noteworthy.

> *Schools are going to have to step up and help students. It's going to be up to the institutions to either make access and affordability easier, or they're going to look at a different population of students.* —Financial aid counselor, 2008
>
> *We may even see institutions going out and creating their own institutional loans. So, they're controlling where*

> *students are borrowing and can lend to students at a much cheaper rate than private loans from a bank.* —Financial aid counselor, 2008

Some colleges already have an unofficial lender role when offering payment plans that allow students to pay monthly on their college account during an academic year. It is anyone's guess what interest rates would be, whether rates would be variable or fixed, and what the loan terms and fees would be if colleges created their own loans to help students stay in their schools. This idea of shifting the responsibility for financing college from federal and private lenders that require signatures from parents, grandparents, and other creditworthy cosigners to colleges that would offer loans signed only by the students opens up some new possibilities in higher education.

- Would having colleges as lenders be an opportunity for them to generate enough revenue from interest income to be able to lower tuition costs for their students?
- What would happen to student loan default rates in the United States if colleges provided loans that were the sole repayment responsibility of the college student?
- Would the U.S. government gradually reduce its federal student loan limits if colleges filled the gap and loaned money to their own college students?
- Would colleges replace the FAFSA and develop their own loan application process?
- What would happen to college enrollment numbers and student demographics if colleges loaned their own money to students?
- Would degree options change and would colleges determine borrowing limits on their loans based on a student's college major?

- Would more students graduate from college if colleges financed their own students' education?
- Would the ease of college transfers change when unpaid loans to colleges were involved in the transfer?
- With colleges as lenders, would student borrowers be required to complete any loan counseling?
- Would colleges withhold loan proceeds until students satisfactorily complete each college course?
- Would having colleges as lenders simplify the current financial aid process?

As far as getting repaid on loans, colleges hold a strategic position that no one else shares. They are the only entities that can offset some of the risks in offering their own institutional loans by directly benefiting from additional student enrollments. Colleges also have the unique ability to erase unpaid college credits and unpaid college degrees from the academic records of any nonpaying students. The loss of a college degree is a serious repayment incentive that could affect a student's future earning power.

There is an immediate need for borrowers to consciously limit the amount of money that they borrow for college to something much less than 100 percent of costs and to an amount they can likely afford to repay, borrowing no more than *half* of their anticipated first-year wages, paying interest on loans while in college, and structuring student loan payments to where the combined monthly amounts do not exceed 7 percent of their monthly gross income. This is possible for a college graduate with annual wages of $31,000, a maximum loan amount of $15,500, an interest rate no greater than 7 percent, and 120 monthly payments (10 years), or for a parent earning $50,000, with a maximum loan amount of $25,000, a 7 percent interest rate, and 120 monthly payments (10 years); these financial limitations may require joint efforts and personal sacrifices.

Earning a college degree and limiting college debt to an affordable amount will help borrowers build a financial foundation that will allow them to meet a lifetime of repayment obligations and personal goals. There are federal lenders, private lenders, grant and scholarship donors, college students, college alums, employers, parents, and grandparents who are independently helping students stay in school. Students want and value a college degree, and the current college landscape will likely continue as is as long as there are all of these willing investors and there are employers who place a higher value on a job applicant with a college degree over one without a degree.

The amount of money that college students can borrow to attend college has proven to be too much for many of them to be able to repay and still maintain their financial independence. It has delayed their ability to buy a home, invest in a business, or save for their own retirement. Defaulting on these loans can eventually ruin a borrower's credit rating for future job offers and consumer purchases; it can be a life-changing experience. Borrowing too much money for college is a financial problem that can begin to be solved with the help of the financial guidelines offered in this book. College students should not expect the individuals and entities of the current financial aid structure to work together in an effort to financially protect and guide them; they will need to accomplish all of that on their own.

APPENDIX A: Financial Aid Shopping Sheet

University of the United States (UUS)
Student Name, Identifier

MM / DD / YYYY

Costs in the 2013-14 year

Estimated Cost of Attendance .... $ X,XXX / yr
Tuition and fees .... $ X,XXX
Housing and meals .... X,XXX
Books and supplies .... X,XXX
Transportation .... X,XXX
Other educational costs .... X,XXX

Grants and scholarships to pay for college

Total Grants and Scholarships ("Gift" Aid; no repayment needed) ... $ X,XXX / yr
Grants from your school .... $ X,XXX
Federal Pell Grant .... X,XXX
Grants from your state .... X,XXX
Other scholarships you can use .... X,XXX

What will you pay for college

Net Costs .... $ X,XXX / yr
(Cost of attendance minus total grants and scholarships)

Options to pay net costs

Work options
Work-Study (Federal, state, or institutional) .... $ X,XXX

Loan options*
Federal Perkins Loans .... $ X,XXX
Federal Direct Subsidized Loan .... X,XXX
Federal Direct Unsubsidized Loan .... X,XXX

*Recommended amounts shown here. You may be eligible for a different amount. Contact your financial aid office.

Other options

Family Contribution .... $ X,XXX / yr
(As calculated by the institution using information reported on the FAFSA or to your institution.)

• Payment plan offered by the institution   • Military and/or National Service benefits
• Parent PLUS Loan   • Non-Federal private education loan

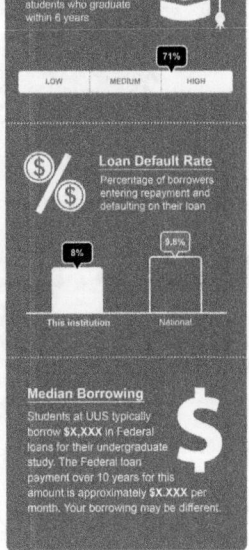

Graduation Rate
Percentage of full-time students who graduate within 6 years

71%
LOW   MEDIUM   HIGH

Loan Default Rate
Percentage of borrowers entering repayment and defaulting on their loan

8%   9.8%
This institution   National

Median Borrowing
Students at UUS typically borrow $X,XXX in Federal loans for their undergraduate study. The Federal loan payment over 10 years for this amount is approximately $X.XXX per month. Your borrowing may be different.

Repaying your loans
To learn about loan repayment choices and work out your Federal Loan monthly payment, go to: http://studentaid.ed.gov/repay-loans/understand/plans

For more information and next steps:
University of the United States (UUS)
Financial Aid Office
123 Main Street
Anytown, ST 12345
Telephone: (123) 456-7890
E-mail: financialaid@uus.edu

Customized Information from UUS

213

APPENDIX B: FAFSA Form—English Version

FAFSA℠
FREE APPLICATION for FEDERAL STUDENT AID

July 1, 2013 – June 30, 2014

Federal Student Aid | PROUD SPONSOR of the AMERICAN MIND℠
An OFFICE of the U.S. DEPARTMENT of EDUCATION

Use this form to apply free for federal and state student grants, work-study and loans.

Or apply free online at **www.fafsa.gov**.

Applying by the Deadlines
For federal aid, submit your application as early as possible, but no earlier than January 1, 2013. We must receive your application no later than June 30, 2014. Your college must have your correct, complete information by your last day of enrollment in the 2013-2014 school year.

For state or college aid, the deadline may be as early as January 2013. See the table to the right for state deadlines. You may also need to complete additional forms.

Check with your high school guidance counselor or a financial aid administrator at your college about state and college sources of student aid and deadlines.

If you are filing close to one of these deadlines, we recommend you file online at www.fafsa.gov. This is the fastest and easiest way to apply for aid.

Using Your Tax Return
If you (or your parents) need to file a 2012 income tax return with the Internal Revenue Service (IRS), we recommend that you complete it before filling out the FAFSA. If you have not completed your return yet, you can submit your FAFSA now using estimated tax information, and then correct that information after you file your return.

The easiest way to complete or correct your FAFSA with accurate tax information is by using the IRS Data Retrieval Tool through **www.fafsa.gov**. In a few simple steps, you may be able to view your tax return information and transfer it directly into your FAFSA.

Filling Out the FAFSA℠
If you or your family has unusual circumstances that might affect your financial situation (such as loss of employment), complete this portion to the extent you can, then submit it as instructed and consult with the financial aid office at the college you plan to attend.

For help in filling out the FAFSA, go to **www.studentaid.gov/completefafsa** or call 1-800-4-FED-AID (1-800-433-3243). TTY users (for the hearing impaired) may call 1-800-730-8913.

Fill the answer fields directly on your screen or print the form and complete it by hand. Your answers will be read electronically; therefore if you complete the form by hand:

- use black ink and fill in circles completely: Correct ● Incorrect ⊗ ⊘
- print clearly in CAPITAL letters and skip a box between words: `|1|5| |E|L|M| |S|T|`
- report dollar amounts (such as $12,356.41) like this: `$ |1|2|3|5|6| no cents`

Green is for student information and purple is for parent information.

Mailing Your FAFSA℠
After you complete this application, make a copy of pages 3 through 8 for your records. Then mail the original of pages 3 through 8 to:

Federal Student Aid Programs, P.O. Box 7002, Mt. Vernon, IL 62864-0072.

After your application is processed, you will receive a summary of your information in your *Student Aid Report* (SAR). If you provide an e-mail address, your SAR will be sent by e-mail within 3-5 days. If you do not provide an e-mail address, your SAR will be mailed to you within three weeks. If you would like to check the status of your FAFSA, go to **www.fafsa.gov** or call 1-800-4-FED-AID.

Let's Get Started!
Now go to page 3 of the application form and begin filling it out. Refer to the notes as instructed.

APPLICATION DEADLINES
Federal Aid Deadline - June 30, 2014
State Aid Deadlines - See below.

Check with your financial aid administrator for these states and territories:
AL, AS *, AZ, CO, FM *, GA, GU *, HI *, MH *, MP *, NE, NM, NV *, PR, PW *, SD *, TX, UT, VA *, VI *, WI and WY *.

Pay attention to the symbols that may be listed after your state deadline.

AK AK Education Grant and AK Performance Scholarship - June 30, 2013 *(date received)*
AR Academic Challenge - June 1, 2013 *(date received)*
    Workforce Grant - Contact the financial aid office.
    Higher Education Opportunity Grant - June 1, 2013 *(date received)*
CA Initial awards - March 2, 2013 + *
    Additional community college awards - September 2, 2013 *(date postmarked)* + *
CT February 15, 2013 *(date received)* # *
DC May 31, 2013 *(date received)* * For priority consideration, submit application by April 30, 2013.
DE April 15, 2013 *(date received)*
FL May 15, 2013 *(date processed)*
IA July 1, 2013 *(date received)*; earlier priority deadlines may exist for certain programs. *
ID Opportunity Grant - March 1, 2013 *(date received)* # *
IL As soon as possible after January 1, 2013. Awards made until funds are depleted.
IN March 10, 2013 *(date received)*
KS April 1, 2013 *(date received)* # *
KY As soon as possible after January 1, 2013. Awards made until funds are depleted.
LA June 30, 2014 (July 1, 2013 highly recommended)
MA May 1, 2013 *(date received)* #
MD March 1, 2013 *(date received)*
ME May 1, 2013 *(date received)*
MI March 1, 2013 *(date received)*
MN 30 days after term starts *(date received)*
MO April 1, 2013 *(date received)*
MS MTAG and MESG Grants - September 15, 2013 *(date received)*
    HELP Scholarship - March 31, 2013 *(date received)*
MT March 1, 2013 *(date received)* #
NC As soon as possible after January 1, 2013. Awards made until funds are depleted.
ND April 15, 2013 *(date received)* # Early priority deadlines may exist for institutional programs.
NH NH is not offering a state grant this year.
NJ 2012-2013 Tuition Aid Grant recipients - June 1, 2013 *(date received)*
    All other applicants
    - October 1, 2013, fall & spring terms *(date received)*
    - March 1, 2014, spring term only *(date received)*
NY June 30, 2014 *(date received)* *
OH October 1, 2013 *(date received)*
OK March 1, 2013 *(date received)* # *
OR OSAC Private Scholarships - March 1, 2013 *(date received)*
    Oregon Opportunity Grant - February 1, 2013 *(date received)*
PA All first-time applicants at a community college; a business/trade/technical school; a hospital school of nursing; or enrolled in a non-transferable two-year program - August 1, 2013 *(date received)*
    All other applicants - May 1, 2013 *(date received)* #
RI March 1, 2013 *(date received)* #
SC Tuition Grants - June 30, 2013 *(date received)*
    SC Commission on Higher Education - As soon as possible after January 1, 2013. Awards made until funds are depleted.
TN State Grant - As soon as possible after January 1, 2013. Awards made until funds are depleted.
    State Lottery - September 1, 2013 *(date received)* #
VT As soon as possible after January 1, 2013. Awards made until funds are depleted. *
WA As soon as possible after January 1, 2013. Awards made until funds are depleted.
WV Promise Scholarship - March 1, 2013 *(date received)* # *
    WV Higher Education Grant Program - April 15, 2013 *(date received)* #

\# For priority consideration, submit application by date specified.
+ Applicants encouraged to obtain proof of mailing.
* Additional form may be required.

STATE AID DEADLINES

Federal Student Aid logo and FAFSA are service marks or registered service marks of Federal Student Aid, U.S. Department of Education.

Notes for questions 14 and 15 (page 3)
If you are an eligible noncitizen, write in your eight- or nine-digit Alien Registration Number. Generally, you are an eligible noncitizen if you are (1) a permanent U.S. resident with a Permanent Resident Card (I-551); (2) a conditional permanent resident with a Conditional Green Card (I-551C); (3) the holder of an Arrival-Departure Record (I-94) from the Department of Homeland Security showing any one of the following designations: "Refugee," "Asylum Granted," "Parolee" (I-94 confirms that you were paroled for a minimum of one year and status has not expired), T-Visa holder (T-1, T-2, T-3, etc.) or "Cuban-Haitian Entrant;" or (4) the holder of a valid certification or eligibility letter from the Department of Health and Human Services showing a designation of "Victim of human trafficking."

If you are in the U.S. on an F1 or F2 student visa, a J1 or J2 exchange visitor visa, or a G series visa (pertaining to international organizations), select "No, I am not a citizen or eligible noncitizen." You will not be eligible for federal student aid; however, you should still complete the application because you may be eligible for state or college aid.

Notes for questions 16 and 17 (page 3)
Report your marital status as of the date you sign your FAFSA. If your marital status changes after you sign your FAFSA, check with the **financial aid office at the college**. According to the Defense of Marriage Act (1996), "...the word 'marriage' means a legal union between one man and one woman as husband and wife, and the word 'spouse' refers to a person of the opposite sex who is a husband or a wife." Therefore, same-sex unions are not considered marriages for federal purposes, including the FAFSA.

Notes for question 22 (page 3)
The Selective Service System, and the registration requirement for young men, preserves America's ability to provide manpower in an emergency to the U.S. Armed Forces (Army, Navy, Air Force, Marines or Coast Guard). Almost all men—ages 18 through 25—must register. For more information about Selective Service, visit **www.sss.gov**.

Notes for questions 33 (page 4) and 80 (page 6)
If you filed or will file a foreign tax return, a tax return with Puerto Rico, another U.S. territory (e.g., Guam, American Samoa, the U.S. Virgin Islands, Swain's Island or the Northern Marianas Islands) or one of the Freely Associated States (i.e., the Republic of Palau, the Republic of the Marshall Islands or the Federated States of Micronesia), use the information from that return to fill out this form. If you filed a foreign return, convert all monetary units to U.S. dollars, using the exchange rate that is in effect today. To view the daily exchange rate, go to **www.federalreserve.gov/releases/h10/current**.

Notes for questions 34 (page 4) and 81 (page 6)
In general, a person is eligible to file a 1040A or 1040EZ if he or she makes less than $100,000, does not itemize deductions, does not receive income from his or her own business or farm and does not receive alimony. A person is not eligible to file a 1040A or 1040EZ if he or she makes $100,000 or more, itemizes deductions, receives income from his or her own business or farm, is self-employed, receives alimony or is required to file Schedule D for capital gains. If you filed a 1040 only to claim American Opportunity, Hope or Lifetime Learning credits, and you would have otherwise been eligible for a 1040A or 1040EZ, answer "**Yes**" to this question. If you filed a 1040 and were not required to file a tax return, answer "**Yes**" to this question.

Notes for questions 37 (page 4) and 85 (page 7) — Notes for those who filed a 1040EZ
On the 1040EZ, if a person didn't check either box on line 5, enter 01 if he or she is single, or 02 if he or she is married. If a person checked either the "you" or "spouse" box on line 5, use 1040EZ worksheet line F to determine the number of exemptions ($3,800 equals one exemption).

Notes for questions 41 and 42 (page 4) and 89 and 90 (page 7)
Net worth means current value minus debt. If net worth is negative, enter 0.

Investments include real estate (do not include the home you live in), trust funds, UGMA and UTMA accounts, money market funds, mutual funds, certificates of deposit, stocks, stock options, bonds, other securities, installment and land sale contracts (including mortgages held), commodities, etc.

Investments also include qualified educational benefits or education savings accounts (e.g., Coverdell savings accounts, 529 college savings plans and the refund value of 529 prepaid tuition plans). For a student who does not report parental information, the accounts owned by the student (and/or the student's spouse) are reported as student investments in question 41. For a student who must report parental information, the accounts are reported as parental investments in question 89, including all accounts owned by the student and all accounts owned by the parents for any member of the household.

Investments do not include the home you live in, the value of life insurance, retirement plans (401[k] plans, pension funds, annuities, non-education IRAs, Keogh plans, etc.) or cash, savings and checking accounts already reported in questions 40 and 88.

Investments also do not include UGMA and UTMA accounts for which you are the custodian, but not the owner.

Investment value means the current balance or market value of these investments as of today. Investment debt means only those debts that are related to the investments.

Business and/or investment farm value includes the market value of land, buildings, machinery, equipment, inventory, etc. Business and/or investment farm debt means only those debts for which the business or investment farm was used as collateral.

Business value does not include the value of a small business if your family owns and controls more than 50 percent of the business and the business has 100 or fewer full-time or full-time equivalent employees. For small business value, your family includes (1) persons directly related to you, such as a parent, sister or cousin, or (2) persons who are or were related to you by marriage, such as a spouse, stepparent or sister-in-law.

Investment farm value does not include the value of a family farm that you (your spouse and/or your parents) live on and operate.

Notes for question 48 (page 5)
Answer "**Yes**" if you are currently serving in the U.S. Armed Forces or are a National Guard or Reserves enlistee who is on active duty for other than state or training purposes.

Answer "**No**" if you are a National Guard or Reserves enlistee who is on active duty for state or training purposes.

Notes for question 49 (page 5)
Answer "**Yes**" (you are a veteran) if you (1) have engaged in active duty in the U.S. Armed Forces or are a National Guard or Reserves enlistee who was called to active duty for other than state or training purposes, or were a cadet or midshipman at one of the service academies, **and** (2) were released under a condition other than dishonorable. Also answer "**Yes**" if you are not a veteran now but will be one by June 30, 2014.

Answer "**No**" (you are not a veteran) if you (1) have never engaged in active duty in the U.S. Armed Forces, (2) are currently an ROTC student or a cadet or midshipman at a service academy, (3) are a National Guard or Reserves enlistee activated only for state or training purposes, or (4) were engaged in active duty in the U.S. Armed Forces but released under dishonorable conditions.

Also answer "**No**" if you are currently serving in the U.S. Armed Forces and will continue to serve through June 30, 2014.

Page 2   Notes continued on page 9.

FAFSA℠
FREE APPLICATION *for* FEDERAL STUDENT AID

July 1, 2013 – June 30, 2014

Federal Student Aid
An OFFICE of the U.S. DEPARTMENT of EDUCATION
PROUD SPONSOR of the AMERICAN MIND℠

Step One (Student): For questions 1-31, leave blank any questions that do not apply to you (the student).

OMB # 1845-0001

Your full name (**exactly as it appears on your Social Security card**) If your name has a suffix, such as Jr. or III, include a space between your last name and suffix.

1. Last name
2. First name
3. Middle initial

Your mailing address
4. Number and street (include apt. number)
5. City (and country if not U.S.)
6. State
7. ZIP code

8. Your Social Security Number
9. Your date of birth   MONTH   DAY   YEAR
10. Your permanent telephone number

Your driver's license number and driver's license state (if you have one)
11. Driver's license number
12. Driver's license state

13. Your e-mail address. If you provide your e-mail address, we will communicate with you electronically. For example, when your FAFSA has been processed, you will be notified by e-mail. Your e-mail address will also be shared with your state and the colleges listed on your FAFSA to allow them to communicate with you. If you do not have an e-mail address, leave this field blank.

14. Are you a U.S. citizen? Mark only one. See Notes page 2.
  - Yes, I am a U.S. citizen (U.S. national). **Skip to question 16.** ○ 1
  - No, but I am an eligible noncitizen. **Fill in question 15.** ○ 2
  - No, I am not a citizen or eligible noncitizen. **Skip to question 16.** ○ 3

15. Alien Registration Number
A

16. What is your marital status as of today? See Notes page 2.
  - I am single ○ 1
  - I am separated ○ 3
  - I am married/remarried ○ 2
  - I am divorced or widowed ○ 4

17. Month and year you were married, remarried, separated, divorced or widowed. See Notes page 2.
MONTH   YEAR

18. What is your state of legal residence?   STATE

19. Did you become a legal resident of this state before January 1, 2008?
  - Yes ○ 1
  - No ○ 2

20. If the answer to question 19 is "No," give month and year you became a legal resident.
MONTH   YEAR

21. Are you male or female?
  - Male ○ 1
  - Female ○ 2

22. **If female, skip to question 23.** Most male students must register with Selective Service to receive federal aid. If you are male, age 18-25 and not registered, fill in the circle and we will register you. **See Notes page 2.**
Register me ○ 1

23. Have you been convicted for the possession or sale of illegal drugs for an offense that occurred while you were receiving federal student aid (such as grants, loans or work-study)?
Answer "No" if you have never received federal student aid or if you have never had a drug conviction while receiving federal student aid. If you have a drug conviction for an offense that occurred while you were receiving federal student aid, answer "Yes," but complete and submit this application, and we will mail you a worksheet to help you determine if your conviction affects your eligibility for aid. If you are unsure how to answer this question, call 1-800-433-3243 for help.
  - No ○ 1
  - Yes ○ 3

Some states and colleges offer aid based on the level of schooling your parents completed.

24. Highest school your father completed
  - Middle school/Jr. high ○ 1
  - High school ○ 2
  - College or beyond ○ 3
  - Other/unknown ○ 4

25. Highest school your mother completed
  - Middle school/Jr. high ○ 1
  - High school ○ 2
  - College or beyond ○ 3
  - Other/unknown ○ 4

26. When you begin college in the 2013-2014 school year, what will be your high school completion status?
  - High school diploma. **Answer question 27.** ○ 1
  - Homeschooled. **Skip to question 28.** ○ 3
  - General Educational Development (GED) certificate. **Skip to question 28.** ○ 2
  - None of the above. **Skip to question 28.** ○ 4

For Help — www.studentaid.gov/completefafsa   Step One CONTINUED on page 4

218 *College Financial Aid*

Step One CONTINUED from page 3

27. What is the name of the high school where you received or will receive your high school diploma? Enter the complete high school name, and the city and state where the high school is located.

High School Name [   ]
High School City [   ]   STATE [ ]

28. Will you have your first bachelor's degree before July 1, 2013?

Yes ○ 1   No ○ 2

29. When you begin the 2013-2014 school year, what will be your grade level?

Never attended college and 1st year undergraduate .... ○ 0
Attended college before and 1st year undergraduate .... ○ 1
2nd year undergraduate/sophomore .... ○ 2
3rd year undergraduate/junior .... ○ 3
4th year undergraduate/senior .... ○ 4
5th year/other undergraduate .... ○ 5
1st year graduate/professional .... ○ 6
Continuing graduate/professional or beyond .... ○ 7

30. When you begin the 2013-2014 school year, what degree or certificate will you be working on?

1st bachelor's degree .... ○ 1
2nd bachelor's degree .... ○ 2
Associate degree (occupational or technical program) .... ○ 3
Associate degree (general education or transfer program) ..... ○ 4
Certificate or diploma (occupational, technical or education program of less than two years) .... ○ 5
Certificate or diploma (occupational, technical or education program of two or more years) .... ○ 6
Teaching credential (nondegree program) .... ○ 7
Graduate or professional degree .... ○ 8
Other/undecided .... ○ 9

31. Are you interested in being considered for work-study?   Yes ○ 1   No ○ 2   Don't know ○ 3

Step Two (Student): Answer questions 32–57 about yourself (the student). If you are single, separated, divorced or widowed, answer only about yourself. If you are married or remarried as of today, include information about your spouse (husband or wife).

32. For 2012, have you (the student) completed your IRS income tax return or another tax return listed in question 33?

I have already completed my return .... ○ 1
I will file but have not yet completed my return .... ○ 2
I'm not going to file. **Skip to question 38.** .... ○ 3

33. What income tax return did you file or will you file for 2012?

IRS 1040 .... ○ 1
IRS 1040A or 1040EZ .... ○ 2
A foreign tax return. **See Notes page 2.** .... ○ 3
A tax return with Puerto Rico, another U.S. territory, or Freely Associated State. **See Notes page 2.** .... ○ 4

34. If you have filed or will file a 1040, were you eligible to file a 1040A or 1040EZ? **See Notes page 2.**   Yes ○ 1   No ○ 2   Don't know ○ 3

For questions 35–44, if the answer is zero or the question does not apply to you, enter 0. Report whole dollar amounts with no cents.

35. What was your (and spouse's) adjusted gross income for 2012? Adjusted gross income is on IRS Form 1040—line 37; 1040A—line 21; or 1040EZ—line 4. $[   ]

36. Enter your (and spouse's) income tax for 2012. Income tax amount is on IRS Form 1040—line 55; 1040A—line 35; or 1040EZ—line 10. $[   ]

37. Enter your (and spouse's) exemptions for 2012. Exemptions are on IRS Form 1040—line 6d or Form 1040A—line 6d. For Form 1040EZ, **see Notes page 2.**   [   ]

Questions 38 and 39 ask about earnings (wages, salaries, tips, etc.) in 2012. Answer the questions whether or not a tax return was filed. This information may be on the W-2 forms, or on IRS Form 1040—lines 7 + 12 + 18 + Box 14 (Code A) of IRS Schedule K-1 (Form 1065); on 1040A—line 7; or on 1040EZ—line 1. If any individual earning item is negative, do not include that item in your calculation.

38. How much did you earn from working in 2012? $[   ]

39. How much did your spouse earn from working in 2012? $[   ]

40. As of today, what is your (and spouse's) total current balance of cash, savings and checking accounts? **Don't include** student financial aid. $[   ]

41. As of today, what is the net worth of your (and spouse's) investments, including real estate? **Don't include** the home you live in. Net worth means current value minus debt. **See Notes page 2.** $[   ]

42. As of today, what is the net worth of your (and spouse's) current businesses and/or investment farms? **Don't include** a family farm or family business with 100 or fewer full-time or full-time equivalent employees. **See Notes page 2.** $[   ]

For Help — 1-800-433-3243   Page 4   Step Two CONTINUED on page 5

Step Two CONTINUED from page 4

43. **Student's 2012 Additional Financial Information** (Enter the combined amounts for you and your spouse.)

   a. Education credits (American Opportunity, Hope or Lifetime Learning tax credits) from IRS Form 1040—line 49 or 1040A—line 31. $ ____

   b. Child support paid because of divorce or separation or as a result of a legal requirement. **Don't include** support for children in your household, as reported in question 93. $ ____

   c. Taxable earnings from need-based employment programs, such as Federal Work-Study and need-based employment portions of fellowships and assistantships. $ ____

   d. Taxable student grant and scholarship aid **reported to the IRS in your adjusted gross income**. Includes AmeriCorps benefits (awards, living allowances and interest accrual payments), as well as grant and scholarship portions of fellowships and assistantships. $ ____

   e. Combat pay or special combat pay. Only enter the amount that was taxable and included in your adjusted gross income. **Don't include** untaxed combat pay. $ ____

   f. Earnings from work under a cooperative education program offered by a college. $ ____

44. **Student's 2012 Untaxed Income** (Enter the combined amounts for you and your spouse.)

   a. Payments to tax-deferred pension and savings plans (paid directly or withheld from earnings), including, but not limited to, amounts reported on the W-2 forms in Boxes 12a through 12d, codes D, E, F, G, H and S. $ ____

   b. IRA deductions and payments to self-employed SEP, SIMPLE, Keogh and other qualified plans from IRS Form 1040—line 28 + line 32 or 1040A—line 17. $ ____

   c. Child support received for any of your children. **Don't include** foster care or adoption payments. $ ____

   d. Tax exempt interest income from IRS Form 1040—line 8b or 1040A—line 8b. $ ____

   e. Untaxed portions of IRA distributions from IRS Form 1040—lines (15a minus 15b) or 1040A—lines (11a minus 11b). Exclude rollovers. If negative, enter a zero here. $ ____

   f. Untaxed portions of pensions from IRS Form 1040—lines (16a minus 16b) or 1040A—lines (12a minus 12b). Exclude rollovers. If negative, enter a zero here. $ ____

   g. Housing, food and other living allowances paid to members of the military, clergy and others (including cash payments and cash value of benefits). **Don't include** the value of on-base military housing or the value of a basic military allowance for housing. $ ____

   h. Veterans noneducation benefits, such as Disability, Death Pension, or Dependency & Indemnity Compensation (DIC) and/or VA Educational Work-Study allowances. $ ____

   i. Other untaxed income not reported in items 44a through 44h, such as workers' compensation, disability, etc. Also include the first-time homebuyer tax credit from IRS Form 1040—line 67. **Don't include** student aid, earned income credit, additional child tax credit, welfare payments, untaxed Social Security benefits, Supplemental Security Income, Workforce Investment Act educational benefits, on-base military housing or a military housing allowance, combat pay, benefits from flexible spending arrangements (e.g., cafeteria plans), foreign income exclusion or credit for federal tax on special fuels. $ ____

   j. Money received, or paid on your behalf (e.g., bills), not reported elsewhere on this form. $ ____

Step Three (Student): Answer the questions in this step to determine if you will need to provide parental information. Once you answer "Yes" to any of the questions in this step, skip Step Four and go to Step Five on page 8.

45. Were you born before January 1, 1990? .... Yes ○₁   No ○₂
46. As of today, are you married? (Also answer "Yes" if you are separated but not divorced.) .... Yes ○₁   No ○₂
47. At the beginning of the 2013-2014 school year, will you be working on a master's or doctorate program (such as an MA, MBA, MD, JD, PhD, EdD, graduate certificate, etc.)? .... Yes ○₁   No ○₂
48. Are you currently serving on active duty in the U.S. Armed Forces for purposes other than training? **See Notes page 2**. .... Yes ○₁   No ○₂
49. Are you a veteran of the U.S. Armed Forces? **See Notes page 2**. .... Yes ○₁   No ○₂
50. Do you have children who will receive more than half of their support from you between July 1, 2013 and June 30, 2014?... Yes ○₁   No ○₂
51. Do you have dependents (other than your children or spouse) who live with you and who receive more than half of their support from you, now and through June 30, 2014? .... Yes ○₁   No ○₂
52. At any time since you turned age 13, were both your parents deceased, were you in foster care or were you a dependent or ward of the court? **See Notes page 9**. .... Yes ○₁   No ○₂
53. As determined by a court in your state of legal residence, are you or were you an emancipated minor? **See Notes page 9**. Yes ○₁   No ○₂
54. As determined by a court in your state of legal residence, are you or were you in legal guardianship? **See Notes page 9**. .... Yes ○₁   No ○₂
55. At any time on or after July 1, 2012, did your high school or school district homeless liaison determine that you were an unaccompanied youth who was homeless? **See Notes page 9**. .... Yes ○₁   No ○₂
56. At any time on or after July 1, 2012, did the director of an emergency shelter or transitional housing program funded by the U.S. Department of Housing and Urban Development determine that you were an unaccompanied youth who was homeless? **See Notes page 9**. .... Yes ○₁   No ○₂
57. At any time on or after July 1, 2012, did the director of a runaway or homeless youth basic center or transitional living program determine that you were an unaccompanied youth who was homeless or were self-supporting and at risk of being homeless? **See Notes page 9**. .... Yes ○₁   No ○₂

If you (the student) answered "No" to every question in Step Three, go to Step Four.
If you answered "Yes" to any question in Step Three, skip Step Four and go to Step Five on page 8.
(Health professions students: Your college may require you to complete Step Four even if you answered "Yes" to any Step Three question.)
If you believe that you are unable to provide parental information, see Notes page 9.

Step Four (Parent): Complete this step if you (the student) answered "No" to all questions in Step Three.

Answer all the questions in Step Four even if you do not live with your parents. Grandparents, foster parents, legal guardians, aunts and uncles are not considered parents on this form unless they have legally adopted you. If your parents are living and married to each other, answer the questions about them. If your parent is single, widowed, divorced, separated or remarried, see the Notes on page 9 for additional instructions.

58. What is your parents' marital status as of today?
- Married or remarried ..... ◯ 1
- Single .... ◯ 2
- Divorced or separated ..... ◯ 3
- Widowed .... ◯ 4

59. Month and year they were married, remarried, separated, divorced or widowed.   MONTH   YEAR

What are the Social Security Numbers, names and dates of birth of the parents reporting information on this form?
If your parent does not have a Social Security Number, you must enter 000-00-0000. If the name includes a suffix, such as Jr. or III, include a space between the last name and suffix. Enter two digits for each day and month (e.g., for May 31, enter 05 31).

60. FATHER'S/STEPFATHER'S SOCIAL SECURITY NUMBER
61. FATHER'S/STEPFATHER'S LAST NAME, AND
62. FIRST INITIAL
63. FATHER'S/STEPFATHER'S DATE OF BIRTH   1 9

64. MOTHER'S/STEPMOTHER'S SOCIAL SECURITY NUMBER
65. MOTHER'S/STEPMOTHER'S LAST NAME, AND
66. FIRST INITIAL
67. MOTHER'S/STEPMOTHER'S DATE OF BIRTH   1 9

68. Your parents' e-mail address. If you provide your parents' e-mail address, we will let them know your FAFSA has been processed. This e-mail address will also be shared with your state and the colleges listed on your FAFSA to allow them to electronically communicate with your parents.

69. What is your parents' state of legal residence?   STATE

70. Did your parents become legal residents of this state before January 1, 2008?
- Yes ◯ 1
- No ◯ 2

71. If the answer to question 70 is "No," give the month and year legal residency began for the parent who has lived in the state the longest.   MONTH   YEAR

72. How many people are in your parents' household?
Include:
- yourself, even if you don't live with your parents,
- your parents,
- your parents' other children if (a) your parents will provide more than half of their support between July 1, 2013 and June 30, 2014, or (b) the children could answer "No" to every question in Step Three on page 5 of this form, and
- other people if they now live with your parents, your parents provide more than half of their support and your parents will continue to provide more than half of their support between July 1, 2013 and June 30, 2014.

73. How many people in your parents' household (from question 72) will be college students between July 1, 2013 and June 30, 2014?
Always count yourself as a college student. Do not include your parents. You may include others only if they will attend, at least half-time in 2013-2014, a program that leads to a college degree or certificate.

In 2011 or 2012, did you, your parents or anyone in your parents' household (from question 72) receive benefits from any of the federal programs listed? Mark all that apply. Answering these questions will not reduce eligibility for student aid or these programs. TANF may have a different name in your parents' state. Call 1-800-4-FED-AID to find out the name of the state's program.

74. Supplemental Security Income (SSI) ◯
75. Supplemental Nutrition Assistance Program (SNAP) ◯
76. Free or Reduced Price Lunch ◯
77. Temporary Assistance for Needy Families (TANF) ◯
78. Special Supplemental Nutrition Program for Women, Infants and Children (WIC) ◯

79. For 2012, have your parents completed their IRS income tax return or another tax return listed in question 80?
- My parents have already completed their return .... ◯ 1
- My parents will file but have not yet completed their return .... ◯ 2
- My parents are not going to file. **Skip to question 86.** .... ◯ 3

80. What income tax return did your parents file or will they file for 2012?
- IRS 1040 .... ◯ 1
- IRS 1040A or 1040EZ .... ◯ 2
- A foreign tax return. **See Notes page 2.** .... ◯ 3
- A tax return with Puerto Rico, another U.S. territory or Freely Associated State. **See Notes page 2.** .... ◯ 4

81. If your parents have filed or will file a 1040, were they eligible to file a 1040A or 1040EZ? **See Notes page 2.**
- Yes ◯ 1
- No ◯ 2
- Don't know ◯ 3

82. As of today, is either of your parents a dislocated worker? **See Notes page 9.**
- Yes ◯ 1
- No ◯ 2
- Don't know ◯ 3

Step Four CONTINUED from page 6

For questions 83–92, if the answer is zero or the question does not apply, enter 0. Report whole dollar amounts with no cents.

83. What was your parents' adjusted gross income for 2012? Adjusted gross income is on IRS Form 1040—line 37; 1040A—line 21; or 1040EZ—line 4. $

84. Enter your parents' income tax for 2012. Income tax amount is on IRS Form 1040—line 55; 1040A—line 35; or 1040EZ—line 10. $

85. Enter your parents' exemptions for 2012. Exemptions are on IRS Form 1040—line 6d or on Form 1040A—line 6d. For Form 1040EZ, **see Notes page 2**.

Questions 86 and 87 ask about earnings (wages, salaries, tips, etc.) in 2012. Answer the questions whether or not a tax return was filed. This information may be on the W-2 forms, or on IRS Form 1040—lines 7 + 12 + 18 + Box 14 (Code A) of IRS Schedule K-1 (Form 1065); on 1040A—line 7; or on 1040EZ—line 1. If any individual earning item is negative, do not include that item in your calculation.

86. How much did your father/stepfather earn from working in 2012? $

87. How much did your mother/stepmother earn from working in 2012? $

88. As of today, what is your parents' total current balance of cash, savings and checking accounts? $

89. As of today, what is the net worth of your parents' investments, including real estate? **Don't include** the home in which your parents live. Net worth means current value minus debt. **See Notes page 2.** $

90. As of today, what is the net worth of your parents' current businesses and/or investment farms? **Don't include** a family farm or family business with 100 or fewer full-time or full-time equivalent employees. **See Notes page 2.** $

91. Parents' 2012 Additional Financial Information (Enter the amounts for your parent[s].)

 a. Education credits (American Opportunity, Hope or Lifetime Learning tax credits) from IRS Form 1040—line 49 or 1040A—line 31. $

 b. Child support paid because of divorce or separation or as a result of a legal requirement. **Don't include** support for children in your parents' household, as reported in question 72. $

 c. Your parents' taxable earnings from need-based employment programs, such as Federal Work-Study and need-based employment portions of fellowships and assistantships. $

 d. Your parents' taxable student grant and scholarship aid **reported to the IRS in your parents' adjusted gross income**. Includes AmeriCorps benefits (awards, living allowances and interest accrual payments), as well as grant and scholarship portions of fellowships and assistantships. $

 e. Combat pay or special combat pay. Only enter the amount that was taxable and included in your parents' adjusted gross income. Do not enter untaxed combat pay. $

 f. Earnings from work under a cooperative education program offered by a college. $

92. Parents' 2012 Untaxed Income (Enter the amounts for your parent[s].)

 a. Payments to tax-deferred pension and savings plans (paid directly or withheld from earnings), including, but not limited to, amounts reported on the W-2 forms in Boxes 12a through 12d, codes D, E, F, G, H and S. $

 b. IRA deductions and payments to self-employed SEP, SIMPLE, Keogh and other qualified plans from IRS Form 1040—line 28 + line 32 or 1040A—line 17. $

 c. Child support received for any of your parents' children. **Don't include** foster care or adoption payments. $

 d. Tax exempt interest income from IRS Form 1040—line 8b or 1040A—line 8b. $

 e. Untaxed portions of IRA distributions from IRS Form 1040—lines (15a minus 15b) or 1040A—lines (11a minus 11b). Exclude rollovers. If negative, enter a zero here. $

 f. Untaxed portions of pensions from IRS Form 1040—lines (16a minus 16b) or 1040A—lines (12a minus 12b). Exclude rollovers. If negative, enter a zero here. $

 g. Housing, food and other living allowances paid to members of the military, clergy and others (including cash payments and cash value of benefits). **Don't include** the value of on-base military housing or the value of a basic military allowance for housing. $

 h. Veterans noneducation benefits, such as Disability, Death Pension, or Dependency & Indemnity Compensation (DIC) and/or VA Educational Work-Study allowances. $

 i. Other untaxed income not reported in items 92a through 92h, such as workers' compensation, disability, etc. Also include the first-time homebuyer tax credit from IRS Form 1040—line 67. **Don't include** student aid, earned income credit, additional child tax credit, welfare payments, untaxed Social Security benefits, Supplemental Security Income, Workforce Investment Act educational benefits, on-base military housing or a military housing allowance, combat pay, benefits from flexible spending arrangements (e.g., cafeteria plans), foreign income exclusion or credit for federal tax on special fuels. $

For Help — www.studentaid.gov/completefafsa

Step Five (Student): Complete this step only if you (the student) answered "Yes" to any questions in Step Three.

93. How many people are in your household?
Include:
- yourself (and your spouse),
- your children, if you will provide more than half of their support between July 1, 2013 and June 30, 2014, and
- other people if they now live with you, you provide more than half of their support and you will continue to provide more than half of their support between July 1, 2013 and June 30, 2014.

94. How many people in your (and your spouse's) household (from question 93) will be college students between July 1, 2013 and June 30, 2014? Always count yourself as a college student. Include others only if they will attend, at least half-time in 2013-2014, a program that leads to a college degree or certificate.

In 2011 or 2012, did you (or your spouse) or anyone in your household (from question 93) receive benefits from any of the federal programs listed? Mark all that apply. Answering these questions will not reduce eligibility for student aid or these programs. TANF may have a different name in your state. Call 1-800-4-FED-AID to find out the name of the state's program.

95. Supplemental Security Income (SSI) ○
96. Supplemental Nutrition Assistance Program (SNAP) ○
97. Free or Reduced Price Lunch ○
98. Temporary Assistance for Needy Families (TANF) ○
99. Special Supplemental Nutrition Program for Women, Infants and Children (WIC) ○

100. As of today, are you (or your spouse) a dislocated worker? **See Notes page 9.**   Yes ○ 1   No ○ 2   Don't know ○ 3

Step Six (Student): Indicate which colleges you want to receive your FAFSA information.

Enter the six-digit federal school code and your housing plans. You can find the school codes at **www.fafsa.gov** or by calling 1-800-4-FED-AID. If you cannot get the code, write in the complete name, address, city and state of the college. For state aid, you may wish to list your preferred college first. To find out how to have more colleges receive your FAFSA information, read **What is the FAFSA?** on page 10.

101.a 1ST FEDERAL SCHOOL CODE OR NAME OF COLLEGE / ADDRESS AND CITY   STATE   101.b on campus ○ 1 / with parent ○ 2 / off campus ○ 3

101.c 2ND FEDERAL SCHOOL CODE OR NAME OF COLLEGE / ADDRESS AND CITY   STATE   101.d on campus ○ 1 / with parent ○ 2 / off campus ○ 3

101.e 3RD FEDERAL SCHOOL CODE OR NAME OF COLLEGE / ADDRESS AND CITY   STATE   101.f on campus ○ 1 / with parent ○ 2 / off campus ○ 3

101.g 4TH FEDERAL SCHOOL CODE OR NAME OF COLLEGE / ADDRESS AND CITY   STATE   101.h on campus ○ 1 / with parent ○ 2 / off campus ○ 3

Step Seven (Student and Parent): Read, sign and date.

If you are the student, by signing this application you certify that you (1) will use federal and/or state student financial aid only to pay the cost of attending an institution of higher education, (2) are not in default on a federal student loan or have made satisfactory arrangements to repay it, (3) do not owe money back on a federal student grant or have made satisfactory arrangements to repay it, (4) will notify your college if you default on a federal student loan and (5) will not receive a Federal Pell Grant from more than one college for the same period of time.

If you are the parent or the student, by signing this application you certify that all of the information you provided is true and complete to the best of your knowledge and you agree, if asked, to provide information that will verify the accuracy of your completed form. This information may include U.S. or state income tax forms that you filed or are required to file. Also, you certify that you understand that **the Secretary of Education has the authority to verify information reported on this application with the Internal Revenue Service and other federal agencies.** If you sign any document related to the federal student aid programs electronically using a personal identification number (PIN), you certify that you are the person identified by the PIN and have not disclosed that PIN to anyone else. If you purposely give false or misleading information, you may be fined up to $20,000, sent to prison, or both.

102. Date this form was completed
MONTH DAY   2013 ○ or 2014 ○

103. Student (Sign below)
1

Parent (A parent from Step Four sign below.)
2

If you or your family paid a fee for someone to fill out this form or to advise you on how to fill it out, that person must complete this part.
Preparer's name, firm and address

104. Preparer's Social Security Number (or 105)

105. Employer ID number (or 104)

106. Preparer's signature and date
1

COLLEGE USE ONLY
D/O ○ 1   Homeless Youth Determination ○ 4
FAA Signature
1

FEDERAL SCHOOL CODE

DATA ENTRY USE ONLY: ○ P   ○ *   ○ L   ○ E

For Help — 1-800-433-3243

Notes for question 52 (page 5)

Answer "**Yes**" if at any time since you turned age 13:
- You had no living parent (biological or adoptive), even if you are now adopted; or
- You were in foster care, even if you are no longer in foster care today; or
- You were a dependent or ward of the court, even if you are no longer a dependent or ward of the court today. For federal student aid purposes, someone who is incarcerated is not considered a ward of the court.

The financial aid administrator at your school may require you to provide proof that you were in foster care or a dependent or ward of the court.

Notes for questions 53 and 54 (page 5)

The definition of legal guardianship does not include your parents, even if they were appointed by a court to be your guardians. You are also not considered a legal guardian of yourself.

Answer "**Yes**" if you can provide a copy of a court's decision that as of today you are an emancipated minor or are in legal guardianship. Also answer "**Yes**" if you can provide a copy of a court's decision that you were an emancipated minor or were in legal guardianship immediately before you reached the age of being an adult in your state. The court must be located in your state of legal residence at the time the court's decision was issued.

Answer "**No**" if you are still a minor and the court decision is no longer in effect or the court decision was not in effect at the time you became an adult.

The financial aid administrator at your college may require you to provide proof that you were an emancipated minor or in legal guardianship.

Notes for questions 55–57 (page 5)

Answer "**Yes**" if you received a determination at any time on or after July 1, 2012, that you were an unaccompanied youth who was homeless or, for question 57, at risk of being homeless.

- "**Homeless**" means lacking fixed, regular and adequate housing. You may be homeless if you are living in shelters, parks, motels or cars, or are temporarily living with other people because you have nowhere else to go. Also, if you are living in any of these situations and fleeing an abusive parent you may be considered homeless even if your parent would provide support and a place to live.
- "**Unaccompanied**" means you are not living in the physical custody of your parent or guardian.
- "**Youth**" means you are 21 years of age or younger or you are still enrolled in high school as of the day you sign this application.

Answer "**No**" if you are not homeless or at risk of being homeless, or do not have a determination. You should contact your financial aid office for assistance if you do not have a determination but believe you are an unaccompanied youth who is homeless or are an unaccompanied youth providing for your own living expenses who is at risk of being homeless.

The financial aid administrator at your college may require you to provide a copy of the determination if you answered "**Yes**" to any of these questions.

Notes for students unable to provide parental information on pages 6 and 7

Under very limited circumstances (for example, your parents are incarcerated; you have left home due to an abusive family environment; or you do not know where your parents are and are unable to contact them), you may be able to submit your FAFSA without parental information. **If you are unable to provide parental information**, skip Steps Four and Five, and go to Step Six. Once you submit your FAFSA without parental data, **you must follow up with the financial aid office at the college you plan to attend**, in order to complete your FAFSA.

Notes for Step Four, questions 58–92 (pages 6 and 7)

Additional instructions about who is considered a parent on this form:
- If your parent is widowed or single, answer the questions about that parent.
- If your widowed parent is remarried as of today, answer the questions about that parent and your stepparent.
- If your parents are divorced or separated, answer the questions about the parent you lived with more during the past 12 months. (If you did not live with one parent more than the other, give answers about the parent who provided more financial support during the past 12 months, or during the most recent year that you actually received support from a parent.) If this parent is remarried as of today, answer the questions about that parent and your stepparent.

Notes for questions 82 (page 6) and 100 (page 8)

In general, a person may be considered a dislocated worker if he or she:
- is receiving unemployment benefits due to being laid off or losing a job and is unlikely to return to a previous occupation;
- has been laid off or received a lay-off notice from a job;
- was self-employed but is now unemployed due to economic conditions or natural disaster; or
- is a displaced homemaker. A displaced homemaker is generally a person who previously provided unpaid services to the family (e.g., a stay-at-home mom or dad), is no longer supported by the husband or wife, is unemployed or underemployed, and is having trouble finding or upgrading employment.

If a person quits work, generally he or she is not considered a dislocated worker even if, for example, the person is receiving unemployment benefits.

Answer "**Yes**" to question 82 if your parent is a dislocated worker. Answer "**Yes**" to question 100 if you or your spouse is a dislocated worker.

Answer "**No**" to question 82 if your parent is not a dislocated worker. Answer "**No**" to question 100 if neither you nor your spouse is a dislocated worker.

Answer "**Don't know**" to question 82 if you are not sure whether your parent is a dislocated worker. Answer "**Don't know**" to question 100 if you are not sure whether you or your spouse is a dislocated worker. You can contact your financial aid office for assistance in answering these questions.

The financial aid administrator at your college may require you to provide proof that your parent is a dislocated worker, if you answered "**Yes**" to question 82, or that you or your spouse is a dislocated worker, if you answered "**Yes**" to question 100.

What is the FAFSA℠?

Why fill out a FAFSA?
The *Free Application for Federal Student Aid* (FAFSA) is the first step in the financial aid process. You use the FAFSA to apply for federal student aid, such as grants, loans and work-study. In addition, most states and colleges use information from the FAFSA to award nonfederal aid.

Why all the questions?
The questions on the FAFSA are required to calculate your Expected Family Contribution (EFC). The EFC measures your family's financial strength and is used to determine your eligibility for federal student aid. Your state and the colleges you list may also use some of your responses. They will determine if you may be eligible for school or state aid, in addition to federal aid.

How do I find out what my Expected Family Contribution (EFC) is?
Your EFC will be listed on your *Student Aid Report* (SAR). Your SAR summarizes the information you submitted on your FAFSA. It is important to review your SAR to make sure all of your information is correct and complete. Make corrections or provide additional information, as necessary.

How much aid will I receive?
Using the information on your FAFSA and your EFC, the financial aid office at your college will determine the amount of aid you will receive. The college will use your EFC to prepare a financial aid package to help you meet your financial need. Financial need is the difference between your EFC and your college's cost of attendance (which can include living expenses), as determined by the college. If you or your family have unusual circumstances that should be taken into account, contact your college's financial aid office. Some examples of unusual circumstances are: unusual medical or dental expenses or a large change in income from last year to this year.

When will I receive the aid?
Any financial aid you are eligible to receive will be paid to you through your college. Typically, your college will first use the aid to pay tuition, fees and room and board (if provided by the college). Any remaining aid is paid to you for your other educational expenses. If you are eligible for a Federal Pell Grant, you may receive it from only one college for the same period of enrollment.

How can I have more colleges receive my FAFSA information?
If you are completing a paper FAFSA, you can only list four colleges in the school code step. You may add more colleges by doing one of the following:
1. Use the Federal Student Aid PIN you will receive after your FAFSA has been processed and go to *FAFSA on the Web* at www.fafsa.gov. Click the "Login" button on the home page to log in to *FAFSA on the Web*, then click "Make FAFSA Corrections."
2. Use the *Student Aid Report* (SAR), which you will receive after your FAFSA is processed. Your Data Release Number (DRN) verifies your identity and will be listed on the first page of your SAR. You can call 1-800-4-FED-AID and provide your DRN to a customer service representative, who will add more school codes for you.
3. Provide your DRN to the financial aid administrator at the college you want added, and he or she can add their school code to your FAFSA.

Note: Your FAFSA record can only list up to ten school codes. If there are ten school codes on your record, any new school codes that you add will replace one or more of the school codes listed.

Where can I receive more information on student aid?
The best place for information about student financial aid is the financial aid office at the college you plan to attend. The financial aid administrator can tell you about student aid available from your state, the college itself and other sources.
- You can also visit our web site **StudentAid.gov**.
- For information by phone you can call our Federal Student Aid Information Center at 1-800-4-FED-AID (1-800-433-3243). TTY users (for the hearing impaired) may call 1-800-730-8913.
- You can also check with your high school counselor, your state aid agency or your local library's reference section.

Information about other nonfederal assistance may be available from foundations, religious organizations, community organizations and civic groups, as well as organizations related to your field of interest, such as the American Medical Association or American Bar Association. Check with your parents' employers or unions to see if they award scholarships or have tuition payment plans.

Information on the Privacy Act and use of your Social Security Number

We use the information that you provide on this form to determine if you are eligible to receive federal student financial aid and the amount that you are eligible to receive. Sections 483 and 484 of the Higher Education Act of 1965, as amended, give us the authority to ask you and your parents these questions, and to collect the Social Security Numbers of you and your parents. We use your Social Security Number to verify your identity and retrieve your records, and we may request your Social Security Number again for those purposes.

State and institutional student financial aid programs may also use the information that you provide on this form to determine if you are eligible to receive state and institutional aid and the need that you have for such aid. Therefore, we will disclose the information that you provide on this form to each institution you list in questions 101a - 101h, state agencies in your state of legal residence and the state agencies of the states in which the colleges that you list in questions 101a - 101h are located.

If you are applying solely for federal aid, you must answer all of the following questions that apply to you: 1-9, 14-16, 18, 21-23, 26, 28-29, 32-36, 38-58, 60-67, 69, 72-84, 86-100, 102-103. If you do not answer these questions, you will not receive federal aid.

Without your consent, we may disclose information that you provide to entities under a published "routine use." Under such a routine use, we may disclose information to third parties that we have authorized to assist us in administering the above programs; to other federal agencies under computer matching programs, such as those with the Internal Revenue Service, Social Security Administration, Selective Service System, Department of Homeland Security, Department of Justice and Veterans Affairs; to your parents or spouse; and to members of Congress if you ask them to help you with student aid questions.

If the federal government, the U.S. Department of Education, or an employee of the U.S. Department of Education is involved in litigation, we may send information to the Department of Justice, or a court or adjudicative body, if the disclosure is related to financial aid and certain conditions are met. In addition, we may send your information to a foreign, federal, state, or local law enforcement agency if the information that you submitted indicates a violation or potential violation of law, for which that agency has jurisdiction for investigation or prosecution. Finally, we may send information regarding a claim that is determined to be valid and overdue to a consumer reporting agency. This information includes identifiers from the record; the amount, status and history of the claim; and the program under which the claim arose.

State Certification

By submitting this application, you are giving your state financial aid agency permission to verify any statement on this form and to obtain income tax information for all persons required to report income on this form.

The Paperwork Reduction Act of 1995

According to the Paperwork Reduction Act of 1995, no persons are required to respond to a collection of information unless such collection displays a valid OMB control number, which for this form is 1845-0001. Public reporting burden for this collection of information is estimated to average three hours per response, including time for reviewing instructions, searching existing data sources, gathering and maintaining the data needed, and completing and reviewing the collection of information. The obligation to respond to this collection is voluntary. Send comments regarding the burden estimate or any other aspect of this collection of information, including suggestions for reducing this burden, to the Federal Student Aid Information Center, P.O. Box 84, Washington, D.C. 20044. Please do not return the completed FAFSA to this address.

We may request additional information from you to process your application more efficiently. We will collect this additional information only as needed and on a voluntary basis.

APPENDIX C: FAFSA Form—Spanish Version

FAFSA℠

Solicitud Gratuita de Ayuda Federal *para* Estudiantes

1 de julio de 2013 – 30 de junio de 2014

Federal Student Aid
An OFFICE of the U.S. DEPARTMENT of EDUCATION
PROUD SPONSOR of the AMERICAN MIND℠

Utilice este formulario, sin costo alguno, para solicitar las becas, puestos de estudio y trabajo, y préstamos educativos ofrecidos por el Gobierno federal y los estados.

O presente la solicitud gratis por Internet en www.fafsa.gov.

Plazos de solicitud

Para obtener ayuda federal, presente la solicitud lo antes posible, pero no antes del 1 de enero del 2013. Tenemos que recibir el formulario, a más tardar, el 30 de junio del 2014. La institución de educación superior en la que tiene previsto estudiar deberá tener los datos de la solicitud, correctos y completos, en una fecha no posterior al último día en que usted todavía se encuentre matriculado en la misma durante el curso 2013-2014.

El plazo para solicitar ayuda a los estados o instituciones educativas puede vencer tan pronto como en enero del 2013. En la lista a la derecha se presentan las fechas límite para solicitar ayuda estatal. En ocasiones hay que llenar otros formularios.

Para obtener información sobre los programas estatales e institucionales de ayuda estudiantil y los correspondientes plazos de solicitud, consulte al orientador de su escuela secundaria o al administrador de ayuda económica de su institución postsecundaria.

Si se acerca una fecha límite, conviene presentar la solicitud por Internet en, en **www.fafsa.gov**, ya que ésta es la forma más rápida y fácil de solicitar ayuda económica.

Usar la declaración de impuestos

Si usted o sus padres necesitan presentar una declaración de impuestos sobre los ingresos del 2012 al Servicio de Impuestos Internos (IRS), conviene hacerlo antes de llenar la FAFSA. Si aún no se ha presentado alguna de las declaraciones, usted puede entregar la FAFSA ahora con datos aproximados y luego corregir esa información después de presentada la declaración.

La manera más fácil de llenar o corregir la FAFSA es con la Herramienta de consulta y traspaso de datos del IRS, en **www.fafsa.gov**. En unos pasos sencillos, la información exacta de su declaración se puede consultar y transferir directamente a la FAFSA desde la base de datos del IRS.

Llenar la FAFSA℠

Si usted o su familia sufren alguna circunstancia excepcional que pudiera afectar su situación económica (p. ej., la pérdida de empleo), llene el formulario en lo que pueda, preséntelo según las indicaciones y luego consulte con la oficina de asistencia económica de la institución educativa en la que estudiará.

Para obtener más información, o si desea ayuda para llenar la FAFSA, acuda a nuestra página web **www.studentaid.gov/llenarfafsa** o llame al 1-800-433-3243. Ofrecemos atención en español. Los usuarios de teletipo (para personas con problemas de audición) pueden llamar al 1-800-730-8913.

Llene los campos directamente en la pantalla o imprima el formulario y llénelo a mano. Sus respuestas serán procesadas por computadora. Por lo tanto, si llena el formulario a mano:

- utilice tinta negra y rellene los círculos completamente: Correcto ● Incorrecto ⊗ ✓
- escriba con claridad en letra de molde (sólo MAYÚSCULAS), y deje un espacio entre cada palabra: `1 5   E L M   S T`
- anote las cantidades en dólares (por ejemplo, $12,356.41) así: `$ 1 2 3 5 6` sin centavos

La sección verde es para los datos del estudiante, y la morada es para los de los padres.

Enviar la FAFSA℠

Después de llenar la solicitud, conserve para su archivo una fotocopia de las páginas 3 a 8. Envíe las páginas originales a:

Federal Student Aid Programs, P.O. Box 7007, Mt. Vernon, IL 62864-0070

Una vez que se haya dado trámite a la solicitud, se le enviará el *Informe de Ayuda Estudiantil*, en el que se presentará un resumen de su información. Si usted proporciona una dirección electrónica, el informe le llegará por correo electrónico después de tres a cinco días. En caso de que no facilite una dirección electrónica, recibirá el informe por correo postal dentro de tres semanas. Si desea consultar el estado de su FAFSA, acuda a **www.fafsa.gov** o llame al 1-800-433-3243.

Empecemos

Pase a la página 3 del formulario de solicitud y comience a llenarlo.
Consulte las notas cuando se le indique.

El logotipo de Federal Student Aid y FAFSA son marcas de servicios o marcas registradas de servicios de la Oficina de Ayuda Federal para Estudiantes, Departamento de Educación de EE.UU.

PLAZOS DE SOLICITUD

Ayuda federal: 30 de junio del 2014
Ayuda estatal: ver abajo

Consulte con la oficina de asistencia económica para averiguar los plazos de los siguientes estados y territorios:
AL, AS *, AZ, CO, FM *, GA, GU *, HI *, MH *, MP *, NE, NM, NV *, PR, PW *, SD *, TX, UT, VA *, VI *, WI y WY *.

Preste atención a los símbolos que aparecen después de algunos de los plazos.

AK Beca de Estudios de Alaska y Beca de Rendimiento Académico *(Alaska Performance Scholarship)*: 30 de junio del 2013 *(fecha de recibo)*
AR Beca «Academic Challenge»: 1 de junio del 2013 *(fecha de recibo)*
    Beca de Formación de la Fuerza Laboral: consulte con la oficina de asistencia económica.
    Beca de Oportunidad de Estudios Superiores: 1 de junio del 2013 *(fecha de recibo)*
CA Concesiones iniciales: 2 de marzo del 2013 + *
    Concesiones complementarias en instituciones de dos años: 2 de septiembre del 2013 *(fecha de matasellos)* + *
CT 15 de febrero del 2013 #
DC 31 de mayo de 2013 *(fecha de recibo)* * Para consideración prioritaria, presente la solicitud antes del 30 de abril del 2013.
DE 15 de abril del 2013 *(fecha de recibo)*
FL 15 de mayo del 2013 *(fecha de tramitación)*
IA 1 de julio del 2013 *(fecha de recibo)*; los plazos de prioridad de algunos programas pueden terminar antes. *
ID Beca de Oportunidad: 1 de marzo del 2013 *(fecha de recibo)* # *
IL Lo antes posible a partir del 1 de enero del 2013.
    Se otorgará ayuda hasta agotar fondos.
IN 10 de marzo del 2013 *(fecha de recibo)*
KS 1 de abril del 2013 *(fecha de recibo)* *
KY Lo antes posible a partir del 1 de enero del 2013.
    Se otorgará ayuda hasta agotar fondos.
LA 30 de junio del 2014 (conviene mucho presentar la solicitud antes del 1 de julio del 2013)
MA 1 de mayo del 2013 *(fecha de recibo)* #
MD 1 de marzo del 2013 *(fecha de recibo)*
ME 1 de mayo del 2013 *(fecha de recibo)*
MI 1 de marzo del 2013 *(fecha de recibo)*
MN A 30 días de comenzar el período académico *(fecha de recibo)*
MO 1 de abril del 2013 *(fecha de recibo)*
MS Becas MTAG y MESG: 15 de septiembre del 2013 *(fecha de recibo)*
    Beca HELP: 31 de marzo del 2013 *(fecha de recibo)*
MT 1 de marzo del 2013 *(fecha de recibo)* #
NC Lo antes posible a partir del 1 de enero del 2013.
    Se otorgará ayuda hasta agotar fondos.
ND 15 de abril del 2013 *(fecha de recibo)* # Es posible que se adelanten los plazos establecidos para la consideración prioritaria en programas institucionales.
NH Nueva Hampshire no ofrecerá becas estatales este año.
NJ Becarios del Programa de Ayuda de Matrícula 2012-2013: 1 de junio del 2013 *(fecha de recibo)*
    Los demás solicitantes: 1 de octubre del 2013 (otoño y primavera) *(fecha de recibo)* 1 de marzo del 2013 (sólo la primavera) *(fecha de recibo)*
NY 30 de junio del 2014 *(fecha de recibo)*
OH 1 de octubre del 2013 *(fecha de recibo)*
OK 1 de marzo del 2013 *(fecha de recibo)* #
OR 1 de marzo del 2013 *(fecha de recibo)*
    Beca privada de OSAC: 1 de marzo del 2013 *(fecha de recibo)*
    Beca de Oportunidad de Oregón: 1 de febrero del 2013 *(fecha de recibo)*
PA Solicitantes nuevos que cursen estudios en un centro universitario de dos años, un centro de formación profesional o técnica, una escuela de enfermería de un hospital o en un programa de dos años cuyos créditos no se pueden convalidar: 1 de agosto del 2013.
    Los demás solicitantes: 1 de mayo del 2013 *(fecha de recibo)*
RI 1 de marzo del 2013 *(fecha de recibo)*
SC Beca de Matrícula: 30 de junio del 2013 *(fecha de recibo)*
    Comisión de Educación Superior de Carolina del Sur: lo antes posible a partir del 1 de enero del 2013. Se otorgará ayuda hasta agotar fondos.
TN Beca Estatal: lo antes posible a partir del 1 de enero del 2013. Se otorgará ayuda hasta agotar fondos.
    Lotería Estatal: 1 de septiembre del 2013 *(fecha de recibo)* #
VT Lo antes posible a partir del 1 de enero del 2013.
    Se otorgará ayuda hasta agotar fondos. *
WA Lo antes posible a partir del 1 de enero del 2013.
    Se otorgará ayuda hasta agotar fondos.
WV Beca Promesa *(Promise Scholarship)*: 1 de marzo del 2013 *(fecha de recibo)* # *
    Programa de Becas de Estudios Superiores de Virginia Occidental: 15 de abril del 2013 *(fecha de recibo)* #

\# Para consideración prioritaria, presente la solicitud para la fecha indicada.
+ Conviene obtener constancia del envío por correo.
* Es posible que se necesite otro formulario.

Notas sobre las preguntas 14 y 15 (página 3)
Si usted es extranjero con derecho a participar en los programas federales de ayuda estudiantil, escriba las ocho o nueve cifras de su número de registro de extranjeros (Alien Registration Number). Por lo general, se considera que uno es extranjero con derecho a participar si: (1) es residente permanente de EE.UU. y tiene la tarjeta de residencia permanente (I-551); (2) es residente permanente condicional y tiene la tarjeta de residencia condicional (I-551C); (3) tiene constancia (I-94) del registro de su llegada o salida (emitida por el Departamento de Seguridad Nacional) en la que se indique alguna de las siguientes categorías: «Refugiado», «Asilo otorgado», «Inmigrante cubano o haitiano», portador de visa tipo T (T-1, T-2, T-3, etc.) o «Admitido a prueba» (o «Parolee») (tratándose de esta última categoría, la I-94 es constancia de que la persona fue admitida a prueba por un año como mínimo y de que aún no ha vencido la correspondiente situación inmigratoria); o (4) tiene una certificación o constancia válida de cumplimiento de requisitos, emitida por el Departamento de Salud y Servicios Humanos, que indique la clasificación «Víctima del tráfico de seres humanos».
Si usted se encuentra en EE.UU. al amparo de la visa de estudiante tipo F1 o F2, de la visa de visitante por intercambio tipo J1 o J2, o de la visa serie G (relativa a organizaciones internacionales), seleccione «No, no soy ciudadano ni extranjero con derecho». No podrá recibir ayuda federal para los estudios superiores. Sin embargo, como es posible que reúna los requisitos para recibir ayuda del estado o de la institución educativa, conviene llenar la solicitud.

Notas sobre las preguntas 16 y 17 (página 3)
Indique el estado civil que tiene a la fecha de firmar la solicitud. Si cambia de estado civil después de firmar la FAFSA, consulte con la **oficina de asistencia económica de su institución educativa**. Según la Ley de Defensa del Matrimonio de 1996, «…la palabra "matrimonio" se refiere a la unión legal entre un hombre y una mujer como marido y mujer, y la palabra "cónyuge" se refiere a una persona del sexo opuesto que es el esposo o la esposa». Por lo anterior, la unión entre personas del mismo sexo no se considera matrimonio para efectos federales (incluido para efectos de la FAFSA).

Notas sobre la pregunta 22 (página 3)
El Sistema del Servicio Selectivo y la inscripción obligatoria de jóvenes varones ante el mismo aseguran la capacidad de satisfacer la necesidad de personal en las Fuerzas Armadas de EE.UU. (Ejército, Marina, Fuerza Aérea, Infantería de Marina o Guardacostas) durante emergencias. Casi todo varón de entre 18 y 25 años de edad deberá inscribirse. Para obtener más información sobre el Sistema del Servicio Selectivo, visite **www.sss.gov**.

Notas sobre las preguntas 33 (página 4) y 80 (página 6)
Si se presentó o se presentará alguna declaración de impuestos extranjera —o una correspondiente a Puerto Rico, a otro territorio de EE.UU. (p. ej., Guam, Samoa Estadounidense, las Islas Vírgenes Estadounidenses, las Islas de Swain o las Islas Marianas del Norte) o a alguno de los estados libres asociados (es decir, la República de Palaos, la República de las Islas Marshall o los Estados Federados de Micronesia)—, debe utilizarse la información contenida en la misma para llenar la presente solicitud. Si se presentó una declaración extranjera, todas las unidades monetarias deben convertirse a dólares estadounidenses utilizando el tipo de cambio vigente el día en que se llene la solicitud. El tipo de cambio de monedas extranjeras puede consultarse en la página web **www.federalreserve.gov/releases/h10/current**.

Notas sobre las preguntas 34 (página 4) y 81 (página 6)
En general, uno puede presentar el 1040A o 1040EZ si percibe ingresos inferiores a los $100,000 anuales, no detalla las deducciones, no obtiene ningún ingreso de su propio negocio o finca agrícola, ni recibe pensión alimenticia. No puede usar dichos formularios ninguna persona que: tenga un ingreso de $100,000 anuales o más; detalle las deducciones; perciba ingresos de su propio negocio o finca agrícola; trabaje por cuenta propia; reciba pensión alimenticia o deba presentar el Anexo D para declarar las ganancias de capital. Si se presentó el formulario 1040 sólo para reclamar los créditos tributarios American Opportunity, Hope o Lifetime Learning, y, en caso contrario, aún se habría podido utilizar el formulario 1040A o 1040EZ, hay que responder «Sí». Si se presentó el formulario 1040 aunque no era obligatorio presentar declaración, hay que contestar «Sí».

Notas sobre las preguntas 37 (página 4) y 85 (página 7): Notas para los usuarios del formulario 1040EZ
Si no se marcó ninguna de las casillas en el formulario 1040EZ, escriba 01 si la persona referida en el 1040EZ es soltera o 02 si es casada. En cambio, si se marcó «You» (Usted) o «Spouse» (Cónyuge) en el renglón 5, debe utilizarse el renglón F de la hoja de trabajo 1040EZ, para determinar el número de exenciones ($3,800 equivale a una exención).

Notas sobre las preguntas 41 y 42 (página 4) y las 89 y 90 (página 7)
«Valor neto» significa el valor económico actual menos las deudas. Si es negativo o cero, escriba «0».
Las inversiones incluyen los bienes raíces (salvo el domicilio habitual), fondos de fideicomiso, cuentas creadas al amparo de la Ley Uniforme de Donaciones a Menores (UGMA) y la Ley Uniforme de Transferencias a Menores (UTMA), fondos del mercado monetario, fondos comunes de inversión, certificados de depósito, acciones, opciones de compra de acciones, bonos, otros valores, contratos de venta a plazos y de venta de terrenos (incluidas las hipotecas), mercancías, etc.
Las inversiones también incluyen el valor de las cuentas autorizadas de beneficios educativos o de ahorro para la educación (p. ej., las cuentas de ahorro para la educación Coverdell, los planes de ahorro 529 para los estudios superiores y el valor de reembolso de planes de prepago de matrícula 529). Si el estudiante (o su cónyuge) es el titular y no está obligado a proporcionar los datos de sus padres, el valor de las cuentas deberá declararse en la pregunta 41 como una inversión propia. Si el estudiante tiene que proporcionar la información de sus padres, debe declarar como una inversión de ellos (en la pregunta 89) el valor de las cuentas de las que el estudiante sea el titular o de las que sus padres sean los titulares en beneficio de cualquier integrante del hogar.
Las inversiones no incluyen el domicilio habitual, ni el valor de las pólizas de seguro de vida, ni de los fondos de jubilación (planes 401(k), pensiones, rentas vitalicias o «anualidades», cuentas personales de jubilación que no sean para la educación, planes Keogh, etc.). Tampoco incluyen el dinero en efectivo, los ahorros y las cuentas corrientes que se hayan declarado en las preguntas 40 y 88.
Las inversiones tampoco incluyen las cuentas UGMA y UTMA que se tengan en custodia pero no en propiedad.
«Valor de inversión» consiste en el saldo actual o el valor actual de mercado de las inversiones. «Deuda de inversión» se refiere sólo a las deudas que guarden relación con las inversiones.
El valor de un negocio o una finca agrícola con fines de inversión incluye el valor de mercado de los terrenos, edificaciones, maquinaria, equipo, inventarios, etc. La deuda asociada con dicho negocio o finca se refiere sólo a las deudas contraídas como resultado de haber puesto el mismo negocio o finca en garantía.
El valor de una pequeña empresa no se debe incluir si su familia la posee y la controla con una participación de más del 50 por ciento, y la empresa no tiene más de 100 empleados a tiempo completo o equivalentes a tiempo completo. Para efectos del valor de pequeñas empresas, su familia incluye (1) personas con las que usted tenga parentesco por consanguinidad o adopción (como por ejemplo, su padre, hermano o primo) o (2) personas con las que tenga o haya tenido parentesco por afinidad (como por ejemplo, su cónyuge, padrastro o cuñado).
El valor de una finca agrícola con fines de inversión no incluye el valor de ninguna finca familiar en que habiten y trabajen usted, su cónyuge o sus padres.

Notas sobre la pregunta 48 (página 5)
Si presta servicio activo actualmente en las Fuerzas Armadas de EE.UU., o está alistado en la Guardia Nacional o las Reservas y presta servicio activo para fines ajenos al entrenamiento o al desempeño de funciones en el interior de EE.UU., conteste «Sí».
Responda «No» a esta pregunta si está alistado en la Guardia Nacional o las Reservas y presta servicio activo para fines de entrenamiento o de desempeño de funciones en el interior de EE.UU.

Notas sobre la pregunta 49 (página 5)
Responda «Sí» (que usted es veterano, o ex combatiente) si: (1) ha prestado servicio activo en las Fuerzas Armadas de EE.UU.; (2) está alistado en la Guardia Nacional o las Reservas, y fue llamado a filas para fines ajenos al entrenamiento o al desempeño de funciones en el interior de EE.UU. o fue cadete o guardiamarina en una de las academias militares, **y también** (3) fue dado de baja por motivos que no sean deshonrosos. También responda «Sí» si no es veterano, pero lo será para el 30 de junio de 2014.
Conteste «No» (que usted no es veterano) si: (1) nunca ha prestado servicio activo en las Fuerzas Armadas de EE.UU.; (2) actualmente es estudiante en el Programa de Formación de Oficiales de la Reserva (ROTC, por sus siglas en inglés), cadete o guardiamarina en una academia militar; (3) está alistado en la Guardia Nacional o las Reservas, y fue llamado a filas únicamente para fines de entrenamiento o del desempeño de funciones en el interior de EE.UU., o (4) ha prestado servicio activo en las Fuerzas Armadas de EE.UU. pero fue dado de baja por motivos deshonrosos.
También responda «No» si usted se encuentra actualmente alistado en las Fuerzas Armadas de EE.UU. y continuará estándolo hasta el 30 de junio del 2014.

FAFSA℠

Solicitud Gratuita de Ayuda Federal para Estudiantes

1 de julio de 2013 – 30 de junio de 2014

Federal Student Aid | PROUD SPONSOR of the AMERICAN MIND™
An OFFICE of the U.S. DEPARTMENT of EDUCATION

Primer paso (estudiante): En las preguntas 1-31, deje en blanco todas las que no correspondan a su situación (o sea, del estudiante). OMB # 1845-0001
Nombre completo (tal cual se escribe en su tarjeta de Seguro Social). Si hay algún sufijo (como Jr., hijo , padre, II o IV), deje un espacio entre el mismo y el apellido.

1. Apellido [ ]
2. Nombre [ ]
3. Inicial del 2.ᵈᵒ nombre [ ]

Dirección postal
4. Número y calle (incluya el número de apartamento) [ ]
5. Ciudad (y país, si no es EE.UU.) [ ]
6. Estado [ ]
7. Código postal [ ]

8. Número de Seguro Social [ ]-[ ]-[ ]
9. Fecha de nacimiento   MES [ ] DÍA [ ] AÑO [ ]
10. Número de teléfono habitual ([ ]) [ ]-[ ]

Licencia de conducir (si tiene alguna) y el estado que la expidió.
11. Número de licencia de conducir [ ]
12. Estado que expidió la licencia [ ]

13. Dirección de correo electrónico. Si proporciona su dirección de correo electrónico, nos comunicaremos con usted electrónicamente. Por ejemplo, una vez que se haya dado trámite a su FAFSA, se le informará por correo electrónico. Su dirección electrónica también se pondrá a disposición de su estado y de las instituciones educativas señaladas en la FAFSA, para que puedan comunicarse con usted. Si usted no tiene una dirección de correo electrónico, deje este campo en blanco.

[ ]@[ ]

14. ¿Es usted ciudadano de EE.UU.? (Rellene sólo uno de los círculos.) Vea la página 2.
 Sí, soy ciudadano (o persona nacional) de EE.UU. Pase a la pregunta 16..... ○ 1
 No, pero soy extranjero con derecho. Conteste la pregunta 15. .... ○ 2
 No, no soy ciudadano ni extranjero con derecho. Pase a la pregunta 16. .... ○ 3

15. Número de registro de extranjeros
A [ ]

16. A la fecha, ¿cuál es su estado civil? Vea la página 2.
 Soltero................ ○ 1   Separado............ ○ 3
 Casado en primeras o nuevas nupcias ○ 2   Divorciado o viudo ... ○ 4

17. Mes y año en que usted se casó, se separó, se divorció o enviudó Vea la página 2. MES [ ] AÑO [ ]

18. ¿En cuál estado del país tiene su residencia o domicilio habitual? ESTADO [ ]
19. ¿Se hizo residente de este estado antes del 1 de enero de 2008? SÍ ○ 1 No ○ 2
20. De haber respondido «No» a la pregunta 19, indique el mes y año en que se hizo residente del estado. MES [ ] AÑO [ ]

21. ¿Es usted hombre o mujer? Hombre ○ 1 Mujer ○ 2
22. **Si es mujer, pase a la pregunta 23.** Para poder obtener ayuda federal, la mayoría de los varones deberán inscribirse ante el Sistema del Servicio Selectivo. Si usted es varón, de entre 18 y 25 años de edad, y aún no está inscrito, rellene el círculo, y lo inscribiremos. **Vea la página 2.** Inscríbame ○ 1

23. ¿A usted se le ha declarado culpable de la posesión o la venta de drogas ilegales, a causa de una infracción cometida mientras recibía ayuda federal para los estudios superiores (becas, préstamos, o estudio y trabajo)?
Si nunca ha recibido ayuda federal para los estudios superiores o si nunca ha recibido condena por infracciones relacionadas con drogas y cometidas mientras recibía ayuda federal, conteste «No». Si tiene condena por alguna infracción relacionada con drogas que cometió mientras recibía ayuda federal para los estudios, conteste «Sí», y llene y presente la solicitud. Le enviaremos por correo una hoja de trabajo que le ayude a determinar si la infracción afectará su derecho a recibir ayuda económica. Para recibir orientación sobre cómo responder a esta pregunta, llame al 1-800-433-3243.
 No ○ 1
 Sí ○ 3

Algunos estados e instituciones de educación superior ofrecen ayuda económica según el nivel académico alcanzado por los padres del solicitante.
24. Nivel de estudios más alto completado por su padre   Medio/Intermedio (grados 6 a 8) ○ 1   Secundario (grados 9 a 12) ○ 2   Postsecundario ○ 3   Otro/desconocido ○ 4
25. Nivel de estudios más alto completado por su madre   Medio/Intermedio (grados 6 a 8) ○ 1   Secundario (grados 9 a 12) ○ 2   Postsecundario ○ 3   Otro/desconocido ○ 4

26. Al comenzar los estudios superiores en el curso académico 2013-2014, ¿cuál será su situación en cuanto al estado y modo de finalización de la escuela secundaria (grados 9 a 12)?
 Diploma de secundaria. Conteste la pregunta 27............. ○ 1   Programa de enseñanza secundaria en el hogar. Pase a la pregunta 28. ○ 3
 Certificado de equivalencia (GED). Pase a la pregunta 28.... ○ 2   Ninguno de los anteriores. Pase a la pregunta 28. .... ○ 4

Para mayor información: www.studentaid.gov/llenarfafsa   Página 3   El Primer paso CONTINÚA en la página 4.

CONTINUACIÓN del Primer paso (página 3)

27. ¿Cuál es el nombre de la escuela secundaria (grados 9 a 12) donde obtuvo u obtendrá su diploma de estudios secundarios? Escriba el nombre de la escuela y la ciudad y estado donde se ubica.

Escuela: _____
Ciudad: _____
Estado: _____

28. ¿Va a tener su primer título universitario de cuatro años (*bachelor's degree*) antes del 1 de julio del 2013?

Nota: Para los efectos prácticos, el equivalente más cercano en el mundo hispanohablante es la licenciatura (o «bachillerato» en Puerto Rico).

Sí ○ 1   No ○ 2

29. Al comienzo del curso 2013-2014, ¿cuál será su nivel de estudio?
(«Pregrado» se refiere a los estudios universitarios, profesionales y técnicos.)

1.er año de pregrado, sin estudios superiores anteriores. ○ 0
1.er año de pregrado, con estudios superiores anteriores. ○ 1
2.do año de pregrado. ○ 2
3.er año de pregrado. ○ 3
4.to año de pregrado. ○ 4
5.to año (o superior) de pregrado. ○ 5
1.er año de posgrado. ○ 6
2.do año (o superior) de posgrado. ○ 7

30. Al comienzo del curso 2013-2014, ¿a qué título o certificado conducirán sus estudios?

1.er título universitario de cuatro años. ○ 1
2.do título universitario de cuatro años. ○ 2
Grado asociado (dos años): formación profesional o técnica. ○ 3
Grado asociado (dos años): estudios generales o de convalidación. ○ 4
Diploma o certificado: programa de formación profesional, técnica o académica que dura menos de dos años. ○ 5
Diploma o certificado: programa de formación profesional, técnica o académica que dura dos años o más. ○ 6
Certificación docente (programa no conducente a título). ○ 7
Título de posgrado. ○ 8
Otro / indeciso. ○ 9

31. ¿Le interesa ser considerado para el programa de estudio y trabajo?   Sí ○ 1   No ○ 2   No sé ○ 3

Segundo paso (estudiante): Conteste las preguntas 32-57 dando información sobre sí mismo (o sea, el estudiante). En caso de estar soltero, separado, divorciado o viudo actualmente, sólo proporcione información sobre sí mismo. Si está casado actualmente, incluya la información sobre su cónyuge (o sea, su esposo o su esposa).

32. ¿Ha preparado usted (el estudiante) alguna planilla de declaración de impuestos sobre los ingresos del 2012 emitida por el IRS, u otro tipo de declaración indicado en la pregunta 33?

Ya preparé mi declaración. ○ 1
La presentaré pero aún no la he preparado. ○ 2
No la voy a presentar. **Pase a la pregunta 38.** ○ 3

33. ¿Qué tipo de declaración de impuestos del 2012 presentó o presentará?

IRS 1040. ○ 1
IRS 1040A o 1040EZ. ○ 2
Declaración extranjera. **Vea la página 2.** ○ 3
Declaración de impuestos de Puerto Rico o de otro territorio de EE.UU., o de alguno de los estados libres asociados. **Vea la página 2.** ○ 4

34. Si presentó (o presentará) el formulario 1040, ¿también reuniá (o reúne) los requisitos para presentar el 1040A o 1040EZ? **Vea la página 2.**   Sí ○ 1   No ○ 2   No sé ○ 3

En las preguntas 35-44, si la respuesta es cero o la pregunta no corresponde a su situación, escriba «0». Redondee los valores al dólar entero más cercano (sin centavos).

35. ¿Cuál fue su ingreso bruto ajustado (y el de su cónyuge) en el 2012? Esta cantidad se encuentra en los siguientes formularios del IRS: 1040 (renglón 37); 1040A (renglón 21) o 1040EZ (renglón 4). $ ☐☐☐☐☐☐

36. Escriba la cantidad del impuesto sobre sus ingresos del 2012 (y sobre los de su cónyuge). Esta cantidad se encuentra en los siguientes formularios del IRS: 1040 (renglón 55); 1040A (renglón 35) o 1040EZ (renglón 10). $ ☐☐☐☐☐☐

37. Escriba el número de exenciones que usted (y su cónyuge) indicó en la declaración del 2012. Las exenciones se encuentran en el formulario del IRS 1040 (renglón 6d) o en el 1040A (renglón 6d). Si se utilizó el 1040EZ, **vea la página 2.**   ☐☐

Las preguntas 38 y 39 piden información sobre los ingresos obtenidos por el trabajo (salarios, sueldos, propinas, etc.) en el 2012. Conteste las preguntas si se ha presentado o no declaración de impuestos. Este dato puede encontrarse en los formularios W-2 o en los siguientes del IRS: 1040 (suma de los renglones 7, 12 y 18 y la casilla 14 [código A] del Anexo K-1 [Formulario 1065]); 1040A (renglón 7) o 1040EZ (renglón 1). Si alguna de las partidas es negativa, no la incluya en el cálculo.

38. ¿Cuánto ganó usted por su trabajo en el 2012? $ ☐☐☐☐☐☐

39. ¿Cuánto ganó su cónyuge por su trabajo en el 2012? $ ☐☐☐☐☐☐

40. A la fecha, ¿cuál es el saldo de efectivo, ahorros y cuentas corrientes que tiene usted (y su cónyuge)? **No incluya** la ayuda estudiantil. $ ☐☐☐☐☐☐

41. A la fecha, ¿cuál es el valor neto de las inversiones que tiene usted (y su cónyuge)? Incluya los bienes raíces. **No incluya** su domicilio habitual. «Valor neto» significa el valor económico actual menos las deudas. **Vea la página 2.** $ ☐☐☐☐☐☐

42. A la fecha, ¿cuál es el valor neto de los negocios o fincas agrícolas con fines de inversión que tiene usted (y su cónyuge)? **No incluya** el valor de ninguna finca o empresa familiar con no más de 100 empleados a tiempo completo o equivalentes a tiempo completo. **Vea la página 2.** $ ☐☐☐☐☐☐

Para mayor información: 1-800-433-3243   Página 4   El Segundo paso CONTINÚA en la página 5.

CONTINUACIÓN del Segundo paso (página 4)

43. Otra información económica del 2012: estudiante (Escriba la suma total que corresponda a usted y su cónyuge.)

a. Créditos tributarios por gastos educativos (*American Opportunity*, *Hope* y *Lifetime Learning*), según el formulario del IRS 1040 (renglón 49) o el 1040A (renglón 31). $ ☐☐☐,☐☐☐

b. Manutención pagada a favor de los hijos menores, a causa de separación, divorcio u orden legal. **No incluya** el sustento para los hijos que integren el hogar de usted, según indicados en la pregunta 93. $ ☐☐☐,☐☐☐

c. Ingresos sujetos a impuesto que se obtienen de programas que otorgan empleos según la necesidad económica del beneficiario (p. ej., el Programa Federal de Estudio y Trabajo, y aquellos ingresos obtenidos de programas de ayudantías y de becas de investigación que también se calculen según la necesidad económica). $ ☐☐☐,☐☐☐

d. Parte tributable de subvenciones o becas de estudios **declaradas al IRS como parte de su ingreso bruto ajustado**. Se incluyen los subsidios de AmeriCorps (concesiones monetarias, asignaciones para cubrir los gastos de manutención y el pago de intereses acumulados), así como las partes no reembolsables de becas de investigación y de ayudantías. $ ☐☐☐,☐☐☐

e. Paga por combate o paga extraordinaria por combate. Sólo escriba la cantidad tributable que haya formado parte de su ingreso bruto ajustado. **No incluya** la paga por combate no tributable. $ ☐☐☐,☐☐☐

f. Ingresos por el trabajo en programas de educación cooperativa brindados por instituciones educativas. $ ☐☐☐,☐☐☐

44. Ingresos no tributables del 2012: estudiante (Escriba la suma total que corresponda a usted y su cónyuge.)

a. Aportaciones a planes de pensión y de ahorro con impuestos diferidos (ya sean efectuadas directamente por el titular o retenidas de sus ingresos), incluidas, sin carácter limitativo, las cantidades indicadas en el formulario W-2 (casillas 12a a la 12d, códigos D, E, F, G, H y S). $ ☐☐☐,☐☐☐

b. Aportaciones deducibles hechas a cuentas personales de jubilación y a planes de jubilación para personas empleadas por cuenta propia (SEP, SIMPLE, Keogh y otros planes aprobados), según el formulario del IRS 1040 (suma de los renglones 28 y 32) o el 1040A (renglón 17). $ ☐☐☐,☐☐☐

c. Manutención recibida a favor de cualquiera de los hijos menores. **No incluya** los pagos por cuidado de crianza temporal ni los pagos de asistencia por adopción. $ ☐☐☐,☐☐☐

d. Ingreso por intereses exento de impuestos, según el formulario del IRS 1040 (renglón 8b) o el 1040A (renglón 8b). $ ☐☐☐,☐☐☐

e. Parte no tributable de distribuciones de cuentas personales de jubilación, según el formulario del IRS 1040 (renglón 15a menos 15b) o el 1040A (renglón 11a menos 11b). Excluya las reinversiones. Si la cantidad es negativa, escriba un cero. $ ☐☐☐,☐☐☐

f. Parte no tributable de distribuciones de pensiones de jubilación, según el formulario del IRS 1040 (renglón 16a menos 16b) o el 1040A (renglón 12a menos 12b). Excluya las reinversiones. Si la cantidad es negativa, escriba un cero. $ ☐☐☐,☐☐☐

g. Asignaciones para alojamiento, comida y otros gastos de manutención, pagadas a militares, clérigos y otros (incluidos los pagos en efectivo y el valor monetario de las prestaciones). **No incluya** el valor de alojamiento en la base militar ni el valor de asignaciones básicas para el alojamiento de militares. $ ☐☐☐,☐☐☐

h. Asistencia no educativa para veteranos, como Discapacidad, Pensión por Fallecimiento o Compensación de Dependencia e Indemnización (DIC), o los subsidios educativos del Programa de Estudio y Trabajo del Departamento de Asuntos de Veteranos. $ ☐☐☐,☐☐☐

i. Otros ingresos no tributables que no se hayan declarado en las partidas 44a a 44h, como la compensación del seguro obrero, la indemnización por discapacidad, etc. También incluya el crédito tributario para quienes compran viviendas por primera vez, según el formulario del IRS 1040 (renglón 67). **No incluya** la ayuda estudiantil, ni el crédito por ingreso del trabajo, ni el crédito tributario adicional por hijos, ni la asistencia social, ni los beneficios no tributables del Seguro Social, ni el Ingreso Suplementario de Seguridad, ni la asistencia educativa recibida al amparo de la Ley de Inversión en la Fuerza Laboral (*Workforce Investment Act*), ni el alojamiento en la base militar o asignaciones para el alojamiento de militares, ni la paga por combate, ni los beneficios de arreglos especiales para gastos (p. ej., los planes tipo «cafetería»), ni la exclusión de ingresos obtenidos en el extranjero ni el crédito por impuesto federal a los combustibles especiales. $ ☐☐☐,☐☐☐

j. Dinero en efectivo recibido, o dinero pagado en su nombre (p. ej., las cuentas de servicios públicos), que no se haya declarado en ninguna otra parte del presente formulario. $ ☐☐☐,☐☐☐

Tercer paso (estudiante): Conteste todas las preguntas de este paso para determinar si necesita proporcionar la información de sus padres. Si responde «Sí» a cualquiera de las preguntas del Tercer paso, omita el Cuarto paso y pase al Quinto, en la página 8.

45. ¿Nació antes del 1 de enero de 1990? .... Sí ○ No ○

46. ¿Está casado actualmente? (En caso de estar separado pero no divorciado, hay que contestar «Sí».) .... Sí ○ No ○

47. Al comienzo del curso 2013-2014, ¿estará cursando un programa de maestría o de doctorado (p. ej., MA, MBA, MD, JD, PhD, EdD, certificado de posgrado, etc.)? .... Sí ○ No ○

48. ¿Presta servicio activo actualmente en las Fuerzas Armadas de EE.UU., para fines ajenos al entrenamiento? **Vea la página 2**. .... Sí ○ No ○

49. ¿Es veterano de las Fuerzas Armadas de EE.UU.? **Vea la página 2**. .... Sí ○ No ○

50. ¿Tiene hijos a los que proporcionará más de la mitad del sustento, entre el 1 de julio del 2013 y el 30 de junio del 2014? .... Sí ○ No ○

51. ¿Tiene a su cargo personas (aparte de sus hijos y su cónyuge) que viven con usted y a las que proporcionará más de la mitad del sustento, entre hoy y el 30 de junio del 2014? .... Sí ○ No ○

52. En cualquier momento desde que cumplió 13 años de edad, ¿era huérfano de ambos padres, o estaba bajo cuidado de crianza temporal o bajo la tutela de los Tribunales? **Vea la página 9.** .... Sí ○ No ○

53. Según la determinación de un tribunal ubicado en el estado de donde es residente, ¿es o era menor de edad emancipado? **Vea la página 9**. .... Sí ○ No ○

54. Según la determinación de un tribunal ubicado en el estado de donde es residente, ¿se encuentra o se encontraba bajo tutela legal? **Vea la página 9**. .... Sí ○ No ○

55. En cualquier momento a partir del 1 de julio del 2012, ¿determinó su escuela secundaria (*high school*), o la persona de enlace entre el distrito escolar y los que carecen de hogar, que usted era un joven no acompañado sin hogar? **Vea la página 9**. .... Sí ○ No ○

56. En cualquier momento a partir del 1 de julio del 2012, ¿determinó el director de un programa de refugios de emergencia o de viviendas de transición financiado por el Departamento de Vivienda y Desarrollo Urbano de EE.UU. que usted era un joven no acompañado sin hogar? **Vea la página 9**. .... Sí ○ No ○

57. En cualquier momento a partir del 1 de julio del 2012, ¿determinó el director de un programa de viviendas de transición, o de un centro básico de acogida para jóvenes sin hogar o que huyen del hogar, que usted era un joven no acompañado sin hogar o que se mantenía con recursos propios y estaba en riesgo de quedarse sin hogar? **Vea la página 9**. .... Sí ○ No ○

Para mayor información: www.studentaid.gov/llenarfafsa

Si usted (el estudiante) respondió «No» a cada pregunta del Tercer paso, pase al Cuarto.
Si respondió «Sí» a cualquiera de las preguntas del Tercer paso, omita el Cuarto paso y pase al Quinto, en la página 8.
(Atención estudiantes de ciencias de la salud: Es posible que su institución educativa le pida que conteste las preguntas del Cuarto paso, aunque usted haya contestado «Sí» a alguna de las preguntas del Tercer paso.)
Si considera que no puede proporcionar la información de sus padres, vea la página 9.

Cuarto paso (padres): Llene esta sección si usted (el estudiante) respondió «No» a todas las preguntas del Tercer paso.
En el Cuarto paso, conteste todas las preguntas, aunque usted no viva con sus padres. A los abuelos, a los padres de crianza temporal, a los tutores legales y a los tíos no se les considera padres para efectos del presente formulario, a menos que lo hayan adoptado legalmente. Si sus padres viven y siguen casados el uno con el otro, conteste las preguntas dando información sobre los dos. Si su padre o su madre está soltero, viudo, divorciado, separado o casado en nuevas nupcias, consulte las indicaciones en la página 9.

58. A la fecha, ¿cuál es el estado civil de sus padres?
Casados en primeras o nuevas nupcias... ○₁   Divorciados o separados..... ○₃
Soltero.. ○₂   Viudo........................ ○₄

59. Mes y año en que sus padres se casaron, se separaron, se divorciaron o enviudaron.   MES   AÑO

¿Cuáles son el número de Seguro Social, nombre y fecha de nacimiento de los padres cuya información se incluye en el presente formulario?
Si alguno de sus padres no tiene número de Seguro Social, escriba «000-00-0000». Si se incluye algún sufijo en la tarjeta de Seguro Social (como Jr., hijo, padre, II o IV), deje un espacio entre el mismo y el apellido. Utilice dos dígitos para indicar tanto el día como el mes (p. ej., para el 31 de mayo, use 05 31).

60. NÚMERO DE SEGURO SOCIAL DEL PADRE/PADRASTRO   61. APELLIDO DEL PADRE/PADRASTRO   62. INICIAL DEL NOMBRE   63. FECHA DE NACIMIENTO DEL PADRE/PADRASTRO   1 9

64. NÚMERO DE SEGURO SOCIAL DE LA MADRE/MADRASTRA   65. APELLIDO DE LA MADRE/MADRASTRA   66. INICIAL DEL NOMBRE   67. FECHA DE NACIMIENTO DE LA MADRE/MADRASTRA   1 9

68. **Dirección de correo electrónico de sus padres.** Si proporciona la dirección electrónica de sus padres, les informaremos de la tramitación de la FAFSA. La dirección se enviará al estado de donde usted es residente y a las instituciones educativas señaladas en la FAFSA, para que puedan comunicarse con sus padres.

@

69. ¿En cuál estado del país tienen sus padres su residencia o domicilio habitual?   ESTADO

70. ¿Se hicieron sus padres residentes del estado antes del 1 de enero del 2008?   Sí ○₁   No ○₂

71. De haber respondido «No» a la pregunta 70, escriba el mes y el año en que se hizo residente la persona (padre o madre) que haya vivido más tiempo en ese estado.   MES   AÑO

72. ¿Cuántas personas integran el hogar de sus padres? Incluya en la respuesta las siguientes personas:
 • usted, aun cuando no viva con sus padres;
 • sus padres;
 • los otros hijos de sus padres, si (a) éstos se les darán más de la mitad del sustento entre el 1 de julio del 2013 y el 30 de junio del 2014, o si (b) esos hijos podrían responder «No» a cada pregunta del Tercer paso, en la página 5, y también
 • otras personas que vivan actualmente con los padres de usted, si éstos les dan más de la mitad del sustento y seguirán haciéndolo entre el 1 de julio del 2013 y el 30 de junio del 2014.

73. De todas las personas que integran el hogar de sus padres (según se calculó en la pregunta 72), ¿cuántas cursarán estudios superiores entre el 1 de julio del 2013 y el 30 de junio del 2014? Usted siempre debe incluirse a sí mismo como estudiante de educación superior. No incluya a sus padres. Puede incluir otras personas sólo si cursarán estudios, con una dedicación mínima de medio tiempo, durante el curso 2013-2014, en un programa conducente a un certificado o título de educación superior.

En el 2011 o el 2012, ¿recibieron usted, sus padres u otras personas del hogar de ellos (según se calculó en la pregunta 72) asistencia de alguno de los programas federales indicados a continuación? Marque todos los programas que correspondan. El contestar estas preguntas no afectará su derecho a recibir ayuda estudiantil o estos otros tipos de asistencia. En algunos estados se les conoce por otro nombre al Programa TANF. Si desea confirmar el nombre de este programa, llame al 1-800-433-3243.

74. Programa de Ingreso Suplementario de Seguridad (SSI) ○
75. Programa de Asistencia de Nutrición Suplementaria (SNAP) ○
76. Programa de Almuerzos Escolares Gratuitos o de Precio Reducido ○
77. Programa de Ayuda Temporal para Familias Necesitadas (TANF) ○
78. Programa Especial de Nutrición Suplementaria para Mujeres, Bebés y Niños (WIC) ○

79. ¿Han preparado sus padres alguna planilla de declaración de impuestos sobre los ingresos del 2012 emitida por el IRS, u otro tipo de declaración indicado en la pregunta 80?
Ya prepararon su declaración .... ○₁
La presentarán pero aún no la han preparado. .... ○₂
No la van a presentar. Pase a la pregunta 86. .... ○₃

80. ¿Qué tipo de declaración de impuestos del 2012 han presentado o presentarán sus padres?
IRS 1040.. ○₁
IRS 1040A o 1040EZ .... ○₂
Declaración extranjera. Vea la página 2. .... ○₃
Declaración de impuestos de Puerto Rico o de otro territorio de los EE.UU., o de alguno de los estados libres asociados. Vea la página 2. .... ○₄

81. Si sus padres presentaron (o presentarán) el formulario 1040, ¿también reunían (o reúnen) los requisitos para presentar el 1040A o 1040EZ? Vea la página 2.
Sí ○₁   No ○₂   No sé ○₃

82. A la fecha, ¿es alguno de sus padres trabajador desplazado? Vea la página 9.
Sí ○₁   No ○₂   No sé ○₃

CONTINUACIÓN del Cuarto paso (página 6)

En las preguntas 83-92, si la respuesta es cero o la pregunta no corresponde a la situación de sus padres, escriba «0».
Redondee los valores al dólar entero más cercano (sin centavos).

83. ¿Cuál fue el ingreso bruto ajustado de sus padres en el 2012? Esta cantidad se encuentra en los siguientes formularios del IRS: 1040 (renglón 37); 1040A (renglón 21) o 1040EZ (renglón 4). $ ☐☐☐☐☐☐☐

84. Escriba la cantidad del impuesto sobre los ingresos obtenidos por sus padres en el 2012. Esta cantidad se encuentra en los siguientes formularios del IRS: 1040 (renglón 55); 1040A (renglón 35) o 1040EZ (renglón 10). $ ☐☐☐☐☐☐☐

85. Escriba el número de exenciones que sus padres indicaron en la declaración del 2012. Las exenciones se encuentran en el formulario del IRS 1040 (renglón 6d) o en el 1040A (renglón 6d). Si se utilizó el 1040EZ, **vea la página 2**. ☐☐

Las preguntas 86 y 87 piden información sobre los ingresos obtenidos por el trabajo (salarios, sueldos, propinas, etc.) en el 2012. Conteste las preguntas si se ha presentado o no declaración de impuestos. Este dato puede encontrarse en los formularios W-2 o en los siguientes del IRS: 1040 (suma de los renglones 7, 12 y 18 y la casilla 14 [código A] del Anexo K-1 [Formulario 1065]); 1040A (renglón 7) o 1040EZ (renglón 1). Si alguna de las partidas es negativa, no la incluya en el cálculo.

86. ¿Cuánto ganó su padre (o padrastro) por su trabajo en el 2012? $ ☐☐☐☐☐☐☐

87. ¿Cuánto ganó su madre (o madrastra) por su trabajo en el 2012? $ ☐☐☐☐☐☐☐

88. A la fecha, ¿cuál es el saldo de efectivo, ahorros y cuentas corrientes que tienen sus padres? $ ☐☐☐☐☐☐☐

89. A la fecha, ¿cuál es el valor neto de las inversiones de sus padres? Incluya los bienes raíces. **No incluya** el domicilio habitual de sus padres. «Valor neto» significa el valor económico actual menos las deudas. **Vea la página 2**. $ ☐☐☐☐☐☐☐

90. A la fecha, ¿cuál es el valor neto de los negocios o fincas agrícolas con fines de inversión que tienen sus padres? **No incluya** el valor de ninguna finca o empresa familiar con no más de 100 empleados a tiempo completo o equivalentes a tiempo completo. **Vea la página 2.** $ ☐☐☐☐☐☐☐

91. Otra información económica del 2012: padres (Escriba la suma total que corresponda a sus padres.)
a. Créditos tributarios por gastos educativos (*American Opportunity, Hope y Lifetime Learning*), según el formulario del IRS 1040 (renglón 49) o el 1040A (renglón 31). $ ☐☐☐☐☐☐☐

b. Manutención pagada a favor de los hijos menores, a causa de separación, divorcio u orden legal. **No incluya** el sustento para los hijos que integran el hogar de sus padres, según indicados en la pregunta 72. $ ☐☐☐☐☐☐☐

c. Ingresos sujetos a impuesto que sus padres obtuvieron de programas que otorgan empleos según la necesidad económica del beneficiario (p. ej., el Programa Federal de Estudio y Trabajo, y aquellos ingresos obtenidos de programas de ayudantías y de becas de investigación que también se calculen según la necesidad económica). $ ☐☐☐☐☐☐☐

d. Parte tributable de subvenciones o becas de estudios **declaradas al IRS como parte del ingreso bruto ajustado de sus padres**. Se incluyen los subsidios de AmeriCorps (concesiones monetarias, asignaciones para cubrir los gastos de manutención y el pago de intereses acumulados), así como las partes no reembolsables de becas de investigación y de ayudantías. $ ☐☐☐☐☐☐☐

e. Paga por combate o paga extraordinaria por combate. Sólo escriba la cantidad tributable que haya formado parte del ingreso bruto ajustado de sus padres. **No incluya** la paga por combate no tributable. $ ☐☐☐☐☐☐☐

f. Ingresos por el trabajo en programas de educación cooperativa brindados por instituciones educativas. $ ☐☐☐☐☐☐☐

92. Ingresos no tributables del 2012: padres (Escriba la suma total que corresponda a sus padres.)
a. Aportaciones a planes de pensión y de ahorro con impuestos diferidos (ya sean efectuadas directamente por el titular o retenidas de sus ingresos), incluidas, sin carácter limitativo, las cantidades indicadas en el formulario W-2 (casillas 12a a la 12d, códigos D, E, F, G, H y S). $ ☐☐☐☐☐☐☐

b. Aportaciones deducibles hechas a cuentas personales de jubilación y a planes de jubilación para personas empleadas por cuenta propia (SEP, SIMPLE, Keogh y otros planes aprobados), según el formulario del IRS 1040 (suma de los renglones 28 y 32) o el 1040A (renglón 17). $ ☐☐☐☐☐☐☐

c. Manutención recibida a favor de cualquiera de los hijos menores de sus padres. **No incluya** los pagos por cuidado de crianza temporal ni los pagos de asistencia por adopción. $ ☐☐☐☐☐☐☐

d. Ingreso por intereses exento de impuestos, según el formulario del IRS 1040 (renglón 8b) o el 1040A (renglón 8b). $ ☐☐☐☐☐☐☐

e. Parte no tributable de distribuciones de cuentas personales de jubilación, según el formulario del IRS 1040 (renglón 15a menos 15b) o el 1040A (renglón 11a menos 11b). Excluya las reinversiones. Si la cantidad es negativa, escriba un cero. $ ☐☐☐☐☐☐☐

f. Parte no tributable de distribuciones de pensiones de jubilación, según el formulario del IRS 1040 (renglón 16a menos 16b) o el 1040A (renglón 12a menos 12b). Excluya las reinversiones. Si la cantidad es negativa, escriba un cero. $ ☐☐☐☐☐☐☐

g. Asignaciones para alojamiento, comida y otros gastos de manutención, militares, clérigos y otros (incluidos los pagos en efectivo y el valor monetario de las prestaciones). **No incluya** el valor de alojamiento en la base militar ni el valor de asignaciones básicas para el alojamiento de militares. $ ☐☐☐☐☐☐☐

h. Asistencia no educativa para veteranos, como Discapacidad, Pensión por Fallecimiento o Compensación de Dependencia e Indemnización (DIC), o los subsidios educativos del Programa de Estudio y Trabajo del Departamento de Asuntos de Veteranos. $ ☐☐☐☐☐☐☐

i. Otros ingresos no tributables que no se hayan declarado en las partidas 92a a 92h, como la compensación del seguro obrero, la indemnización por discapacidad, etc. También incluya el crédito tributario para quienes compran viviendas por primera vez, según el formulario del IRS 1040 (renglón 67). **No incluya** la ayuda estudiantil, ni el crédito por ingreso del trabajo, ni el crédito tributario adicional por hijos, ni la asistencia social, ni los beneficios no tributables del Seguro Social, ni el Ingreso Suplementario de Seguridad, ni la asistencia educativa recibida al amparo de la Ley de Inversión en la Fuerza Laboral (*Workforce Investment Act*), ni el alojamiento en la base militar o asignaciones para el alojamiento de militares, ni la paga por combate, ni los beneficios de arreglos especiales para gastos (p. ej., los planes tipo «cafetería»), ni la exclusión de ingresos obtenidos en el extranjero ni el crédito por impuesto federal a los combustibles especiales. $ ☐☐☐☐☐☐☐

Para mayor información: www.studentaid.gov/llenarfafsa   Página 7

Quinto paso (estudiante): Llene esta sección sólo si usted (el estudiante) respondió «Sí» a alguna de las preguntas del Tercer paso.

93. ¿Cuántas personas integran su hogar?
Incluya en la respuesta las siguientes personas:
- usted (y su cónyuge);
- sus hijos, si les dará más de la mitad del sustento entre el 1 de julio del 2013 y el 30 de junio del 2014, y también
- otras personas que actualmente vivan con usted, si les da más de la mitad del sustento y seguirá haciéndolo entre el 1 de julio del 2013 y el 30 de junio del 2014.

94. De todas las personas que integran el hogar de usted (y su cónyuge) (según se calculó en la pregunta 93), ¿cuántas cursarán estudios superiores entre el 1 de julio del 2013 y el 30 de junio del 2014? Debe incluirse a sí mismo como estudiante de educación superior. Incluya a otras personas sólo si cursarán estudios, con una dedicación mínima de medio tiempo, durante el curso 2013-2014, en un programa conducente a un certificado o título de educación superior.

En el 2011 o el 2012, ¿recibieron usted, su cónyuge o cualquier otra persona de su hogar (según se calculó en la pregunta 93) asistencia de alguno de los programas federales indicados a continuación? Marque todos los programas que correspondan. El contestar estas preguntas no afectará su derecho a recibir ayuda estudiantil o estos otros tipos de asistencia. En algunos estados se les conoce por otro nombre al Programa TANF. Si desea confirmar el nombre de este programa, llame al 1-800-433-3243.

95. Programa de Ingreso Suplementario de Seguridad (SSI) ○
96. Programa de Asistencia de Nutrición Suplemementaria (SNAP) ○
97. Programa de Almuerzos Escolares Gratuitos o de Precio Reducido ○
98. Programa de Ayuda Temporal para Familias Necesitadas (TANF) ○
99. Programa Especial de Nutrición Suplementaria para Mujeres, Bebés y Niños (WIC) ○

100. A la fecha, ¿es usted (o su cónyuge) trabajador desplazado? **Vea la página 9.** Sí ○ 1   No ○ 2   No sé ○ 3

Sexto paso (estudiante): Indique las instituciones de educación superior que deben recibir los datos de la solicitud.

Escriba el código federal de seis cifras que corresponda a cada institución e indique el modo previsto de alojamiento durante su estancia en las mismas. Puede obtener los códigos en www.fafsa.gov o llamando al 1-800-433-3243. Si no puede obtener el código, escriba el nombre completo de la institución, así como la dirección, ciudad y estado donde se ubica. Para efectos del otorgamiento de asistencia estatal, conviene poner a la cabeza de la lista la institución preferida. Si desea que más instituciones reciban los datos de la FAFSA, lea *¿Qué es la FAFSA?*, en la página 10.

MODO DE ALOJAMIENTO

101.a 1.er CÓDIGO FEDERAL   INSTITUCIÓN EDUCATIVA / DIRECCIÓN Y CIUDAD   ESTADO   101.b en el recinto ○ 1 / con los padres ○ 2 / fuera del recinto ○ 3

101.c 2.do CÓDIGO FEDERAL   INSTITUCIÓN EDUCATIVA / DIRECCIÓN Y CIUDAD   ESTADO   101.d en el recinto ○ 1 / con los padres ○ 2 / fuera del recinto ○ 3

101.e 3.er CÓDIGO FEDERAL   INSTITUCIÓN EDUCATIVA / DIRECCIÓN Y CIUDAD   ESTADO   101.f en el recinto ○ 1 / con los padres ○ 2 / fuera del recinto ○ 3

101.g 4.to CÓDIGO FEDERAL   INSTITUCIÓN EDUCATIVA / DIRECCIÓN Y CIUDAD   ESTADO   101.h en el recinto ○ 1 / con los padres ○ 2 / fuera del recinto ○ 3

Séptimo paso (estudiante y padres): Después de leer lo siguiente, firme en la casilla correspondiente e indique la fecha.

Si usted es el alumno, al firmar la presente solicitud, certifica lo siguiente: (1) que utilizará la ayuda económica estudiantil, ya sea federal o estatal, sólo para pagar el costo de estudiar en una institución de enseñanza superior; (2) que no se encuentra en incumplimiento de pago de ningún préstamo educativo federal o, de estarlo, que ha convenido en pagar dicha obligación de manera satisfactoria; (3) que no adeuda dinero por el pago en exceso de una beca de estudios federal o, de hacerlo, que ha convenido en pagarlo de manera satisfactoria; (4) que le informará a su institución educativa en caso de incurrir en incumplimiento de pago de un préstamo educativo federal y (5) que no recibirá más de una Beca Federal Pell para pagar el costo de estudiar en más de una institución durante un mismo período.

Si usted es el padre, la madre o el estudiante, al firmar esta solicitud, certifica que toda la información proporcionada es verdadera y completa a su leal saber y entender y, si se le solicita, acepta proporcionar documentación que acredite la exactitud de los datos del presente formulario. Esta documentación puede incluir las planillas de declaración de impuestos federales o estatales que los firmantes hayan presentado o deberán presentar. Asimismo, usted entiende y acepta que **el secretario de Educación tiene la autoridad para comprobar que los datos contenidos en este formulario coincidan con los registros del Servicio de Impuestos Internos (IRS) y de otros organismos federales.** Si usted utiliza un número de identificación personal (PIN) para firmar algún documento relacionado con los programas federales de ayuda económica para estudiantes, afirma ser la persona identificada por el PIN y que no ha revelado el mismo a terceros. Si intencionalmente proporciona información falsa o engañosa, puede quedar sujeto a una multa de hasta $20,000, al encarcelamiento o ambas penas.

102. Fecha en que se llenó el presente formulario.
MES   DÍA   2013 ○   ó   2014 ○

103. Firma del estudiante (Firme en la casilla.)

Firma del padre o de la madre (cuyos datos se hayan proporcionado en el Cuarto paso) (Firme en la casilla.)

Si otra persona llenó el formulario o le asesoró sobre cómo llenarlo, y usted o su familia pagaron una comisión por el servicio, esa persona («preparador») debe llenar esta sección.
Nombre, empresa y dirección del preparador.

104. Número de Seguro Social del preparador (o 105)

105. Número de identificación patronal (o 104)

106. Firma del preparador y fecha

PARA USO EXCLUSIVO DE LA INSTITUCIÓN EDUCATIVA   CÓDIGO FEDERAL
D/O ○   Clasificación como joven sin hogar ○
Firma del administrador de ayuda económica

PARA USO EXCLUSIVO DEL PERSONAL DE ENTRADA DE DATOS   ○ P   ○ *   ○ L   ○ E

Para mayor información: 1-800-433-3243

Notas sobre la pregunta 52 (página 5)
Conteste «Sí» si hubo un momento, desde que usted cumplió 13 años de edad, en que:
- no estaba vivo ninguno de sus padres (ya sean éstos biológicos o adoptivos), incluso si ahora usted tiene padres adoptivos;
- estaba bajo cuidado de crianza temporal, incluso si no lo está actualmente, o
- estaba bajo la tutela de los Tribunales, incluso si no lo está actualmente.

Para efectos de la solicitud de ayuda estudiantil federal, a los encarcelados no se les considera bajo tutela de los Tribunales.

La oficina de asistencia económica de la institución educativa puede pedirle que aporte pruebas de que usted estaba bajo cuidado de crianza temporal o bajo la tutela de los Tribunales.

Notas sobre las preguntas 53 y 54 (página 5)
La definición de tutela legal no incluye a sus padres, aun cuando un tribunal les haya otorgado la tutela. Tampoco se considera que usted pueda ser su propio tutor.

Si puede aportar copia del dictamen judicial por el que se le considera a usted, a la fecha, menor de edad emancipado o bajo tutela legal, conteste «Sí». Si puede aportar copia del dictamen judicial por el que se le consideraba menor de edad emancipado o bajo tutela legal justo antes de cumplir la mayoría de edad según determinada por el estado de donde es residente, también debe contestar «Sí». El tribunal emisor del dictamen debe estar ubicado en el estado donde usted era residente a la fecha de emisión.

En cambio, si todavía es menor de edad y el dictamen del tribunal ya no tiene vigencia o no tenía vigencia cuando usted cumplió la mayoría de edad, conteste «No».

La oficina de asistencia económica de la institución educativa puede pedirle que aporte pruebas de que usted era menor de edad emancipado o que estaba bajo tutela legal.

Notas sobre las preguntas 55-57 (página 5)
Si, a partir del 1 de julio del 2012, se determinó que usted era un joven no acompañado sin hogar o, para efectos de la pregunta 57, estaba en riesgo de quedarse sin hogar, conteste «Sí».
- «Sin hogar» significa no tener vivienda fija, habitual ni adecuada, lo cual puede incluir vivir en refugios, parques, hoteles o automóviles, o vivir temporalmente con otras personas por no tener a dónde ir. También, si usted se encuentra en cualquiera de estas situaciones y está huyendo de sus padres debido al maltrato por parte de uno de ellos, se le puede considerar una persona sin hogar, incluso si ese padre o madre, en otras circunstancias, lo mantendría y le daría dónde vivir.
- «No acompañado» significa que ninguno de los padres o tutores tiene la guarda y custodia del estudiante.
- «Joven» significa tener 21 o menos años de edad o cursar todavía los estudios secundarios (*high school*) a la fecha en que se firme la solicitud.

Si no se encuentra sin hogar ni en riesgo de estarlo, o si no ha recibido una determinación a tal efecto, conteste «No». Si no ha recibido una determinación pero se considera a sí mismo un joven no acompañado que carece de hogar, o bien un joven no acompañado que se mantiene con recursos propios y está en riesgo de quedarse sin hogar, debe comunicarse con la oficina de asistencia económica para obtener ayuda con esta pregunta.

Si usted contesta «Sí» a cualquiera de estas preguntas, el administrador de asistencia económica de su institución educativa posiblemente le pedirá que aporte copia de la determinación correspondiente.

Notas para los que no pueden proporcionar los datos de sus padres en las páginas 6 y 7.
En circunstancias muy determinadas (como por ejemplo, sus padres están encarcelados; se ha ido de la casa de ellos a causa de una situación de maltrato, o desconoce el paradero de sus padres y no puede comunicarse con ellos), usted quizás pueda presentar la FAFSA sin los datos de sus padres. **Si usted no puede proporcionar los datos de sus padres**, omita el Cuarto y Quinto paso, y pase al Sexto. Una vez que haya presentado la FAFSA sin los datos de sus padres, **deberá acudir a la oficina de asistencia económica de su institución educativa** para completar la solicitud.

Notas sobre el Cuarto paso, preguntas 58-92 (páginas 6 y 7)
Más indicaciones sobre cómo determinar quién es considerado el padre o la madre del estudiante para efectos del presente formulario:
- Si alguno de sus padres es viudo o soltero, responda a las preguntas dando información sobre él o ella en particular.
- Si su padre o madre viudo está actualmente casado en nuevas nupcias, responda a las preguntas dando información sobre él o ella y también sobre su padrastro o madrastra.
- Si sus padres están separados o divorciados, responda a las preguntas dando información sobre aquél con el que usted haya vivido más tiempo durante los últimos doce meses. (De no haber vivido más tiempo ni con el uno ni con el otro, proporcione información sobre el que le haya dado más ayuda económica durante los últimos doce meses, o durante el último año en que haya recibido sustento de parte de alguno de ellos.) Si esta persona está actualmente casada en nuevas nupcias, responda a las preguntas dando información sobre él o ella y también sobre su padrastro o madrastra.

Notas sobre las preguntas 82 (página 6) y 100 (página 8)
En general, a un trabajador se le podría considerar desplazado si:
- recibe compensación por desempleo a causa del despido temporal o definitivo o de la pérdida de su puesto de trabajo, y tiene pocas probabilidades de volver a trabajar en una profesión u oficio anterior;
- ha sido despedido, ya sea de forma temporal o definitiva, o ha recibido aviso de despido;
- trabajaba por cuenta propia pero actualmente se encuentra desempleado a causa de condiciones económicas desfavorables o de un desastre natural, o
- es ama o amo de casa desplazado. En general, tal persona anteriormente prestaba servicios no remunerados a su familia (p. ej., una madre o un padre que se queda en casa), ya no cuenta con los ingresos del cónyuge para su mantenimiento, se encuentra desempleada o subempleada y tiene dificultades para encontrar empleo o para mejorar la calidad de su empleo.

En general, a las personas que renuncien a su empleo no se les considera trabajadores desplazados, aunque, por ejemplo, reciban compensación por desempleo.

Si su padre o su madre son trabajadores desplazados, responda «Sí» a la pregunta 82. Si usted o su cónyuge son trabajadores desplazados, responda «Sí» a la pregunta 100.

Si ni su padre ni su madre son trabajadores desplazados, responda «No» a la pregunta 82. Si ni usted ni su cónyuge son trabajadores desplazados, responda «No» a la pregunta 100.

Si no sabe con certeza si su padre o su madre son trabajadores desplazados, responda «No sé» a la pregunta 82. Si no sabe con certeza si usted o su cónyuge son trabajadores desplazados, responda «No sé» a la pregunta 100. Si necesita ayuda para contestar estas preguntas, puede comunicarse con la oficina de asistencia económica de su institución educativa.

Si usted respondió «Sí» a la pregunta 82 o a la 100, la oficina de asistencia económica de la institución educativa puede pedirle que aporte pruebas de que las personas en referencia son trabajadores desplazados.

¿Qué es la FAFSA℠?

¿Por qué hay que llenar la FAFSA?
El primer paso para obtener ayuda económica para los estudios superiores es llenar la *Solicitud Gratuita de Ayuda Federal para Estudiantes* (FAFSA, por sus siglas en inglés). Este formulario se utiliza para solicitar ayuda federal, que incluye las becas (subvenciones), los préstamos educativos y los puestos de estudio y trabajo. La mayoría de los estados e instituciones de educación superior también hacen uso de la información reunida en la FAFSA para otorgar asistencia de fuentes no federales.

¿Por qué hay tantas preguntas?
Las preguntas de la FAFSA son necesarias para el cálculo del aporte familiar previsto (EFC). Este número sirve como indicador de la capacidad económica del estudiante y su familia, y se emplea para determinar el otorgamiento de ayuda federal. Algunas de las respuestas las utilizan también el estado y las instituciones educativas incluidas en la solicitud. El estado y las instituciones se encargarán de determinar si usted puede recibir, además de la ayuda otorgada por el Gobierno federal, la asistencia que ellos mismos conceden.

¿Cómo puedo saber cuál es mi aporte familiar previsto?
Usted podrá encontrar su aporte familiar previsto en el *Informe de Ayuda Estudiantil* (SAR). En este documento se presentará un resumen de los datos que usted proporcionó en la FAFSA. Es importante revisar el informe para asegurarse de que todos los datos están correctos y completos. Debe corregir los errores o proporcionar los datos que faltan, según sea necesario.

¿Cuánta ayuda me van a dar?
Con la información de la FAFSA y el aporte familiar previsto, la oficina de asistencia económica de su institución educativa calculará la cantidad de ayuda que se le otorgará. Estas instituciones utilizarán el aporte familiar previsto para preparar un paquete de ayuda que contribuya a satisfacer la necesidad económica que usted demuestre. La necesidad económica es la diferencia entre el aporte familiar previsto y el costo de estudiar en la institución educativa (incluidos los gastos de manutención), según lo determine la institución. Si usted o su familia sufren circunstancias excepcionales que deben tenerse en cuenta, comuníquese con la oficina de asistencia económica de su institución. Entre las circunstancias que se pueden tener en cuenta están los gastos médicos u odontológicos extraordinarios, o una variación importante en los ingresos entre el año pasado y el presente.

¿Cuándo me van a entregar la ayuda?
Su institución educativa se encargará de entregarle la ayuda otorgada. En general, la institución primero usará los fondos para pagar los derechos de matrícula y otras cuotas, y el alojamiento y comida (si corresponde). Cualquier ayuda restante se le pagará directamente a usted, para que pueda cubrir sus otros gastos educativos. Si reúne los requisitos de la Beca Federal Pell, la puede utilizar para pagar sus gastos en una misma institución educativa durante un mismo período de estudios.

¿Cómo hago para que más instituciones reciban los resultados de mi FAFSA?
Si utiliza la versión impresa de la FAFSA, puede incluir sólo cuatro instituciones educativas en la correspondiente sección. Puede añadir más instituciones a su expediente usando cualquiera de los siguientes métodos:

1. Acudir al sitio *FAFSA on the Web* (www.fafsa.gov) y usar el número de identificación personal (PIN) que le enviará la Oficina de Ayuda Federal para Estudiantes después de dar trámite a su FAFSA. Pulse el botón «Regresar a la FAFSA» en la página de inicio de *FAFSA on the Web*, y luego haga clic en «Corregir la FAFSA».
2. Usar el *Informe de Ayuda Estudiantil*, que le llegará después de que se haya dado trámite a la FAFSA. En la primera página del informe, estará impresa la clave de autorización, que permite verificar su identidad. Al llamar al 1-800-433-3243 y proporcionar la clave al representante, se podrán añadir a su expediente los códigos de otras instituciones.
3. Proporcionar la clave de autorización al administrador de asistencia económica de la institución educativa que le interesa. Esta persona podrá agregar el código de la institución a su expediente de FAFSA.

Nota: El expediente de su FAFSA puede tener los códigos de diez instituciones. Si se excede ese límite, los códigos de las nuevas instituciones reemplazarán un número igual de los originales.

¿Dónde puedo obtener más información sobre la ayuda estudiantil?
El mejor lugar es la oficina de asistencia económica de la institución en la que tiene previsto estudiar. El administrador de ayuda económica podrá informarle sobre la asistencia ofrecida por la misma institución, el estado u otras entidades.

- Visite nuestro sitio web StudentAid.gov.
- Si desea obtener información por teléfono, puede llamar al Centro de Información sobre Ayuda Federal para Estudiantes al 1-800-433-3243. Los usuarios de teletipo (para personas con problemas de audición) pueden llamar al 1-800-730-8913.
- También conviene hablar con el orientador de su escuela secundaria, con la agencia encargada de los programas estatales de ayuda económica y con el personal de la sección de referencia de su biblioteca local.

En ocasiones se ofrece información sobre la ayuda no federal mediante fundaciones, asociaciones religiosas o comunitarias, grupos cívicos y organizaciones afines a ciertos campos de estudio, como por ejemplo, la Asociación de Médicos de Estados Unidos (*American Medical Association*) o el Colegio de Abogados de Estados Unidos (*American Bar Association*). También conviene consultar al empleador o sindicato de sus padres para averiguar si ofrecen becas o planes de pago de matrícula.

La Ley de Confidencialidad de Información y el uso del número de Seguro Social

La información que se proporcione en el presente formulario se usará para determinar si usted tiene derecho a recibir ayuda estudiantil de los programas federales, así como para calcular la cantidad de ayuda que se le pueda otorgar. Las secciones 483 y 484 de la Ley de Educación Superior de 1965 (según enmendada) nos autorizan a pedirles esta información a usted y a sus padres y a solicitar el número de Seguro Social de ustedes. Utilizaremos dicho número para verificar la identidad de ustedes y para tener acceso a sus datos; nos reservamos el derecho a pedirles otra vez el número para los mismos fines.

Los encargados de programas institucionales y estatales de ayuda estudiantil también pueden servirse de la información proporcionada en el formulario, para determinar si usted reúne los correspondientes requisitos de participación y para calcular el grado de necesidad que usted tenga con respecto a dicha ayuda. Por lo tanto, pondremos esta información a disposición de todas las instituciones educativas que usted señale en las preguntas 101a a la 101h y también de los pertinentes organismos estatales, tanto los del estado de donde usted es residente como los del estado donde se encuentran las instituciones señaladas en las preguntas 101a a la 101h.

Si usted solicita ayuda federal solamente, deberá responder a todas las preguntas, indicadas a continuación, que correspondan a su situación: 1-9, 14-16, 18, 21-23, 26, 28-29, 32-36, 38-58, 60-67, 69, 72-84, 86-100, 102-103. Si no responde a estas preguntas, no recibirá ayuda federal.

Asimismo, sin necesidad de previo consentimiento, el Departamento puede, al amparo de una cláusula debidamente publicada relativa al «uso normal», poner a disposición de otras entidades cualquier información que usted haya proporcionado. En virtud de esta cláusula podemos dar información a terceras partes que hayamos autorizado a ayudarnos a administrar los programas ya mencionados. También podemos ceder cualquiera de los datos a otros organismos federales que participan en los programas de cotejo electrónico de registros oficiales. Entre estos organismos figuran el Servicio de Impuestos Internos (IRS), la Administración del Seguro Social, el Sistema del Servicio Selectivo, el Departamento de Seguridad Nacional, el Departamento de Justicia y el Departamento de Asuntos de Veteranos. La información también puede darse a sus padres o cónyuge, o a congresistas, si usted solicita los servicios de éstos últimos para resolver dudas sobre la ayuda estudiantil.

En caso de que sean partes en un litigio algún organismo federal, el Departamento de Educación de EE.UU. o algún empleado del Departamento, podemos ceder la información pertinente al Departamento de Justicia, a los Tribunales o a cualquier otro organismo jurídico, siempre que dicha cesión de datos guarde relación con la ayuda económica y se cumplan ciertas condiciones. Asimismo, podemos revelar sus datos a cualquier agencia del orden público, ya sea extranjera, federal, estatal o local, si los datos que usted proporcione indican una posible o efectiva violación de la ley, sobre la cual dicha agencia tiene competencia para iniciar una investigación o para entablar una acción judicial. Finalmente, les podemos dar a las agencias de informes crediticios cualquier información sobre las demandas de pago que determinemos ser legítimas y vencidas. Esta información incluye los datos identificativos de los correspondientes registros; la cantidad, estado e historial de la demanda, y el programa según el cual dicha demanda se originó.

Certificación estatal
Al presentar este formulario de solicitud, usted autoriza al organismo encargado de la concesión de ayuda económica en su estado a verificar cualquier dato incluido en el mismo y a obtener la información tributaria de toda persona a la que corresponda declarar información sobre los ingresos en el formulario.

Ley de Reducción de Trámites de 1995
Según lo dispuesto en la Ley de Reducción de Trámites de 1995, ninguna persona estará en la obligación de responder a un instrumento de recolección de datos que no exhiba un número de control vigente emitido por la Oficina de Administración y Presupuesto (OMB). Para efectos del presente formulario, dicho número es 1845-0001. Se calcula que una persona del público en general necesitará un promedio de tres horas para llenar el presente instrumento de recolección de datos, o sea, para leer las instrucciones, buscar la información en los documentos correspondientes, reunir y mantener los datos necesarios, consignarlos en el instrumento y revisar todo el conjunto. La obligación de responder a este instrumento es voluntaria. Si usted tiene algún comentario sobre el cálculo del tiempo necesario para llenar este instrumento o sobre cualquier otro aspecto del instrumento, o si tiene alguna sugerencia sobre cómo reducir el tiempo necesario para llenarlo, escriba a la siguiente dirección: Federal Student Aid Information Center, P.O. Box 84, Washington, D.C. 20044. No devuelva a esta dirección la FAFSA con los datos completos.

Es posible que le pidamos más información para agilizar la tramitación de su solicitud. Reuniremos más información sólo cuando sea necesario hacerlo y mediante participación voluntaria.

APPENDIX D: Private Education Loan Applicant Self-Certification Form

Private Education Loan Applicant Self-Certification

This space for lender use only

OMB No. 1845-0101
Form Approved
Exp. Date 05-31-2016

Important: Pursuant to Section 155 of the Higher Education Act of 1965, as amended, (HEA) and to satisfy the requirements of Section 128(e)(3) of the Truth in Lending Act, a lender must obtain a self-certification signed by the applicant before disbursing a private education loan. The school is required on request to provide this form or the required information only for students admitted or enrolled at the school. Throughout this Applicant Self-Certification, "you" and "your" refer to the applicant who is applying for the loan. The applicant and the student may be the same person.

Instructions: Before signing, carefully read the entire form, including the definitions and other information on the following page. Submit the signed form to your lender.

SECTION 1: NOTICES TO APPLICANT

- Free or lower-cost Title IV federal, state, or school student financial aid may be available in place of, or in addition to, a private education loan. To apply for Title IV federal grants, loans and work-study, submit a Free Application for Federal Student Aid (FAFSA) available at www.fafsa.ed.gov, or by calling 1-800-4-FED-AID, or from the school's financial aid office.
- A private education loan may reduce eligibility for free or lower-cost federal, state, or school student financial aid.
- You are strongly encouraged to pursue the availability of free or lower-cost financial aid with the school's financial aid office.
- The financial information required to complete this form can be obtained from the school's financial aid office. If the lender has provided this information, you should contact your school's financial aid office to verify this information and to discuss your financing options.

SECTION 2: COST OF ATTENDANCE AND ESTIMATED FINANCIAL ASSISTANCE

If information is not already entered below, obtain the needed information from the school's financial aid office and enter it on the appropriate line. Sign and date where indicated. See Section 5 for definitions of financial aid terms.

A. Student's cost of attendance for the period of enrollment covered by the loan $ _____
B. Estimated financial assistance for the period of enrollment covered by the loan $ _____
C. Difference between amounts A and B $ _____

WARNING: If you borrow more than the amount on line C, you risk reducing your eligibility for free or lower-cost federal, state, or school financial aid.

SECTION 3: APPLICANT INFORMATION

Enter or correct the information below.

Full Name and Address of School _____

Applicant Name (last, first, MI) _____   Date of Birth (mm/dd/yyyy) ____/____/____

Permanent Street Address _____

City, State, Zip Code _____

Area Code / Telephone Number Home ( ) _____   Other ( ) _____
E-mail Address _____
Period of Enrollment Covered by the Loan (mm/dd/yyyy)   From ___/___/___   to ___/___/___

If the student is not the applicant, provide the student's name and date of birth.

Student Name (last, first, MI) _____   Student Date of Birth (mm/dd/yyyy) ____/____/____

SECTION 4: APPLICANT SIGNATURE

I certify that I have read and understood the notices in Section 1 and, that to the best of my knowledge, the information provided on this form is true and correct.

Signature of Applicant _____   Date (mm/dd/yyyy) _____

SECTION 5: DEFINITIONS

Cost of attendance is an estimate of tuition and fees, room and board, transportation, and other costs for the period of enrollment covered by the loan, as determined by the school. A student's cost of attendance may be obtained from the school's financial aid office.

Estimated financial assistance is all federal, state, institutional (school), private, and other sources of assistance used in determining eligibility for most Title IV student financial aid, including amounts of financial assistance used to replace the expected family contribution. The student's estimated financial assistance is determined by the school and may be obtained from the school's financial aid office.

A **lender** is a private education lender as defined in Section 140 of the Truth in Lending Act and any other person engaged in the business of securing, making, or extending private education loans on behalf of the lender.

A **period of enrollment** is the academic year, academic term (such as semester, trimester, or quarter), or the number of weeks of instructional time for which the applicant is requesting the loan.

A **private education loan** is a loan provided by a private education lender that is not a Title IV loan and that is issued expressly for postsecondary education expenses, regardless of whether the loan is provided through the school that the student attends or directly to the borrower from the private education lender. A private education loan does not include (1) An extension of credit under an open-end consumer credit plan, a reverse mortgage transaction, a residential mortgage transaction, or any other loan that is secured by real property or a dwelling; or (2) An extension of credit in which the school is the lender if the term of the extension of credit is 90 days or less or an interest rate will not be applied to the credit balance and the term of the extension of credit is one year or less, even if the credit is payable in more than four installments.

Title IV student financial aid includes the Federal Pell Grant Program, the Federal Supplemental Educational Opportunity Grant (FSEOG) Program, the Federal Work-Study (FWS) Program, the William D. Ford Federal Direct Loan (Direct Loan) Program, the Federal Perkins Loan Program, and the Teacher Education Assistance for College and Higher Education (TEACH) Grant Program. To apply for Title IV federal grants, loans, and work-study, submit a Free Application for Federal Student Aid (FAFSA), which is available at www.fafsa.gov, by calling 1-800-4-FED-AID, or from the school's financial aid office.

SECTION 6: PAPERWORK REDUCTION NOTICE

Paperwork Reduction Notice: According to the Paperwork Reduction Act of 1995, no persons are required to respond to a collection of information unless it displays a currently valid OMB control number. The valid OMB control number for this information collection is 1845-0101. The time required to complete this information collection is estimated to average 0.25 hours (15 minutes) per response, including the time to review instructions, search existing data resources, gather and maintain the data needed and complete and review the information collection.

If you have any comments concerning the accuracy of the time estimate(s) or suggestions for improving this form, please write to: U.S. Department of Education, Washington, DC 20202-4651

If you have any comments or concerns regarding the status of your individual submission of this form, contact your lender.

Glossary

Academic progress Includes a school's standards for satisfactory academic progress toward a degree or certificate offered by the institution.

Accreditation Confirms that the college or career school meets certain minimum academic standards, as defined by an accrediting body recognized by the U.S. Department of Education.

Adjusted gross income (AGI) The total of wages, salaries, interest, and dividends minus certain deductions from income as reported on a federal income tax return.

Adverse credit history Can include bankruptcy, repossession of collateral (both voluntary and involuntary), foreclosure, deed in lieu of foreclosure, accounts 90 days or more delinquent, unpaid collection accounts, charge-offs, write-offs, wage garnishment, defaulting on a loan, lease or contract termination, and county, state, and federal tax liens. To qualify for a PLUS loan, applicants cannot have an adverse credit history.

Associate degree An undergraduate academic degree granted after completion of two years of study. Community colleges and career colleges award associate degrees.

Award letter An official letter or notification from a school where students have been accepted outlining their financial aid package. It can include loans, scholarships, work-study, and grants.

Bachelor's degree An undergraduate academic degree awarded for a course of study that generally lasts four years. Colleges and universities generally award bachelor's degrees.

Cancellation The release of the borrower's obligation to repay all or a designated portion of principal and interest on a student loan that may be taxed as income in the year the debt was canceled. Cancellation is also called *discharge* or *forgiveness* of a loan.

Capitalization The addition of unpaid interest to the principal balance of a loan. When the interest is not paid as it accrues during periods of in-school status, the grace period, deferment, or forbearance, a lender may capitalize the interest, and this increases the outstanding principal amount due on the loan. It causes monthly payment amounts to increase.

CLEP (College-Level Examination Program) CLEP exams test mastery of college-level material acquired in a variety of ways through general academic instructions, significant independent study, or extracurricular work. CLEP exam takers include adults just entering or returning to school, military service members, and traditional college students.

COA (cost of attendance) A college's estimated student budget of tuition and fees, housing, books and supplies, and personal and miscellaneous costs.

Collection costs Expenses charged on defaulted loans that are added to the outstanding principal balance of the loan.

Consolidation The process of combining one or more loans into a single new loan.

Cosigner The signer of a loan accepting full financial responsibility to pay a debt, regardless of whether or not the other cosigner fails to do so.

Credit bureau An agency that tracks and reports an individual's credit history of paying bills and calculates the ability to repay future loans. It researches and collects individual credit information and sells it for a fee to creditors so they can make a decision on granting loans. The three national credit bureau agencies are Equifax, Experian, and TransUnion.

Credit report An individual's credit history. It includes information on where a person lives, how they pay their bills, and whether they have been sued or have filed for bankruptcy. Nationwide credit reporting companies sell the information in a credit report to creditors, insurers, employers, and other businesses that use it to evaluate applications for credit, insurance, employment, or renting a home.

Credit score A credit score is included on a credit report that is used by lenders to determine credit risk. An individual's credit score can range from 300 to 850. Higher credit scores typically mean lower credit risks.

Creditworthy Having a satisfactory credit rating.

Data Release Number (DRN) A four-digit number assigned to an individual's FAFSA that allows the release of FAFSA data to schools not listed on the original FAFSA. The number is also used when making corrections to a mailing address.

Default Failure to repay a loan according to the terms agreed to in the promissory note. For most federal student loans, borrowers will be considered in default when a payment has not been paid for over 270 days. See *promissory note*.

Deferment A postponement on a loan that is allowed under certain conditions. Any unpaid interest that accrues during a deferment period may be added to the principal balance (capitalized).

Delinquent A loan is delinquent when loan payments are not received by the due dates.

Department of Education The department of the U.S. federal government that administers federal programs dealing with education. It was created in 1979, largely by transfer from part of the former Department of Health, Education and Welfare.

Dependent student A student who does not meet any of the criteria for an independent student. See *independent student*.

Direct Consolidation Loan Allows students to consolidate (combine) multiple federal student loans into one loan. The result is a single monthly payment instead of multiple payments.

Direct Loan A federal student loan, made through the William D. Ford Federal Direct Loan Program, for which eligible students and parents borrow directly from the U.S. Department of Education at participating schools. Direct Subsidized Loans, Direct Unsubsidized Loans, Direct PLUS Loans, and Direct Consolidation Loans are types of Direct Loans.

Direct PLUS Loan A loan made by the U.S. Department of Education to graduate or professional students and parents of dependent undergraduate students for which the borrower is fully responsible for paying.

Disbursement Payment of the loan funds to the borrower by the school. Students generally receive their federal student loan in two or more disbursements.

Discharge The release of a borrower from the obligation to repay their loan (which may result in taxable income).

Entrance counseling A mandatory information session that takes place before students receive their first federal student loan that explains loan responsibilities and rights as a borrower.

Exit counseling An information session that takes place when college students graduate or attend school less than half-time that explains loan repayment responsibilities when repayment begins.

Expected Family Contribution (EFC) The number used to determine a student's eligibility for federal student financial aid. It is the amount of money that a student's family is expected to contribute to a student's college education. The EFC results from the financial information that students and families provide on the FAFSA, the application for federal student aid. The EFC is reported to students on the Student Aid Report (SAR).

Extended repayment plan A federal student loan repayment plan where monthly principal and interest payments may be fixed or graduated for up to 20 years.

FAFSA (Free Application for Federal Student Aid) A form that can be prepared annually by current and prospective college students (undergraduate and graduate) in the United States to determine their eligibility for student financial aid (including the Pell Grant, federal student loans, and Federal Work-Study). The FAFSA is used to apply for federal student aid, such as federal grants, loans, and work-study. College students and parents of dependent college students are required to complete the FAFSA for any federal financial aid. Some states and colleges also require completion of the FAFSA for their aid programs.

FAFSA4caster An online tool that provides an early estimate of federal student aid eligibility to help students and their families financially plan for college.

Federal Family Education Loan (FFEL) Program Under this program, private lenders provided loans to students that were guaranteed by the federal government. These loans included Subsidized Federal Stafford Loans, Unsubsidized Federal Stafford Loans, FFEL PLUS Loans, and FFEL Consolidation Loans. Federal student loans under the FFEL Program are no longer made by private lenders. Instead, all new federal student loans come directly from the U.S. Department of Education under the Direct Loan Program.

Federal Pell Grant A federal grant for undergraduate students with financial need.

Federal Perkins Loan A federal student loan, made by the recipient's school, for undergraduate and graduate students who demonstrate financial need.

Federal School Code An identifier that the U.S. Department of Education assigns to each college or career school that participates in the federal student aid programs. In order to send FAFSA information to a particular school, the student must list the Federal School Code.

Federal Student Aid PIN An electronic personal identification number that serves the student or parents as an identifier to allow access to personal information in various U.S. Department of Education systems and acts as a digital signature on some online forms. A PIN can be requested online at http://www.pin.ed.gov.

Federal student loans Loans funded by the government to help pay a student's education. A federal student loan is borrowed money that must be repaid with interest.

Federal Work-Study A federal student aid program that provides part-time employment while a student is enrolled in school to help pay education expenses.

FICO A type of credit score that makes up a substantial portion of the credit report that lenders use to assess an applicant's credit risk and whether to extend a loan. FICO is an acronym for the Fair Isaac Corporation, the creator of the FICO score.

Financial Aid Certification College financial aid offices are required to certify that all financial aid does not exceed a college's cost of attendance (COA).

Financial aid office The office at a college or career school that is responsible for preparing and communicating information on financial aid. The office helps students apply for and receive student loans, grants, scholarships, and other types of financial aid.

Financial aid package The total amount of financial aid (federal and nonfederal) that a student is offered by a college or career school. A school's financial aid staff combines various forms of aid into a "package" to help meet a student's education costs. Loans are included as a form of financial aid.

Financial need The difference between the cost of attendance (COA) at a school and the Expected Family Contribution (EFC).

Fixed interest rate The interest rate is fixed and remains the same for the term of the loan.

Forbearance Allows borrowers to temporarily suspend or reduce monthly loan payments. During forbearance, principal payments are postponed but interest continues to accrue. Unpaid interest that accrues during the forbearance will be added to the principal balance (capitalized) on the loan, increasing the total amount owed.

Free Application for Federal Student Aid See *FAFSA*.

Grace period A period of time after borrowers graduate, leave school, or drop below half-time enrollment where they are not required to make payments on certain federal student loans. Some loans will accrue interest during the grace period, and if the interest is unpaid, it will be added to the principal balance (capitalized) of the loan.

Graduated Repayment Plan A federal student loan repayment plan where monthly principal and interest payments are lower at first and then increase, usually every two years. The maturity is up to 10 years.

Grant Financial aid, often based on financial need, that does not need to be repaid unless, for example, a student withdraws from school and owes a refund.

Guaranteed Student Loans (GSL) GSL is the name of the Federal Family Education Loan (FFEL) Program loans that were made prior to 1992.

Guaranty agency A state agency or a private, nonprofit organization that administers Federal Family Education Loan (FFEL) Program loans.

Income-Based Repayment Plan A federal student loan repayment plan for students having a partial financial hardship. Payments change as income changes. The maturity is up to 25 years. Any forgiven amount may be taxed as income.

Income-Contingent Repayment Plan A federal student loan repayment plan where payments are calculated each year and based on adjusted gross income, family size, and the total amount of Direct federal student loans. Payments change as income changes. The maturity is up to 25 years. If students do not repay this loan in full after making the equivalent of 25 years of qualifying monthly payments, the unpaid portion will be forgiven under the current rules. The forgiven amount may be taxed as income.

Income-Sensitive Repayment Plan This is a federal student loan repayment plan where monthly payment amounts are determined from the borrower's income. Payments change as income changes. The maturity is up to 10 years.

Independent student One of the following: at least 24 years old, married, a graduate or professional student, a veteran, a member of the armed forces, an orphan, a ward of the court, someone with legal dependents other than a spouse, an emancipated minor, or someone who is homeless or at risk of becoming homeless.

Interest A loan expense charged for the use of borrowed money. Interest is paid by a borrower to a lender. The expense is calculated as a percentage of the unpaid principal amount of the loan.

ISIR (Institutional Student Information Record) The electronic version of the Student Aid Report (SAR).

Lender The organization that made the loan initially; the lender could be the borrower's school; a bank, credit union, or other lending institution; or the U.S. Department of Education.

Light bulb moment A sudden realization about something, like the light bulbs used to indicate an idea in cartoons.

Loan forgiveness The cancellation of all or some portion of a loan balance. If a loan is forgiven, it will be reported and could be taxed as income.

Loan servicer A company that collects payments on a loan, responds to customer service inquiries, and performs other administrative tasks associated with maintaining a loan on behalf of a lender. Federal student loan servicers can be found online at http://www.nslds.ed.gov.

Need-based award Based on an applicant's financial need. It could be a loan or a grant based on an applicant's low income.

Net Price Calculator A tool that allows current and prospective students, families, and other consumers to estimate the net price of attending a particular college or career school.

New borrower An applicant is a new borrower if they have no outstanding balance on a Direct Loan Program Loan or a Federal Family Education Loan on or after October 1, 2007.

Out-of-state student A student who is attending a college or career school outside of their state of legal residence.

Parent PLUS Loan An unsubsidized loan made to parents of dependent undergraduate students.

Partial financial hardship An eligibility requirement for the income-based repayment requirement for the Income-Based Repayment (IBR) and Pay As You Earn plans.

Pay As You Earn repayment plan A federal student loan repayment plan where the maximum monthly payment is 10 percent of discretionary income. Payments change as income changes. The maturity is up to 20 years.

Pell Grant A federal grant for undergraduate students with financial need.

Perkins Loan A Federal Perkins Loan, or Perkins Loan, is a need-based student loan offered by the U.S. Department of Education to assist American college students in funding their post-secondary education. The program is named after Carl D. Perkins, a former member of the U.S. House of Representatives from Kentucky. Perkins Loans carry a fixed interest rate of 5 percent for the duration of the 10-year repayment period. The Perkins Loan Program has a nine-month grace period.

PLUS loan A loan available to graduate students and parents of dependent undergraduate students for which the borrower is fully responsible for paying the principal and interest.

Principal The total sum of money borrowed plus any interest that has been capitalized.

Private loan A nonfederal loan made by a private lender such as a bank, credit union, state agency, or school.

Promissory note A binding legal document that borrowers sign for a loan. It lists the terms and conditions of the loan and explains the borrower's rights and responsibilities.

Room and board An allowance for the cost of housing and food while the student attends college or career school.

Scholarship Money awarded based on academic or other achievements to help pay for education expenses. Scholarships generally do not have to be repaid.

Self-certification Required of a borrower to list their college cost of attendance (COA) and all other financial aid awarded to them to confirm loan eligibility. It is used to raise borrower awareness about their financial aid and to prevent borrowers from overborrowing. An applicant's combined financial aid cannot exceed their college's COA during this process.

SLATE Act Student Lending, Accountability, Transparency and Enforcement Act. Initiated by New York State Attorney General Andrew M. Cuomo, the SLATE Act of 2007 was passed to protect college students and their families from conflicts of interest regarding student lending.

Stafford Loan A federal student loan offered to eligible students enrolled in accredited American institutions of higher education to help finance their education.

Standard Repayment Plan A federal student loan repayment plan where monthly principal and interest payments are a fixed amount of at least $50 per month and for up to 10 years.

State aid Financial aid from a student's state of legal residence.

Student Aid Report (SAR) A paper or electronic document that gives students some basic information about their eligibility for federal student aid as well as listing the answers to the questions on the FAFSA.

Subsidized loan A federal loan based on financial need for which the federal government pays the interest that accrues while the borrower has an in-school, grace, or deferment status. For Direct Subsidized Loans first disbursed between July 1, 2012, and July 1, 2014, the borrower will be responsible for paying any interest that accrues during the grace period. If the interest is not paid during the grace period, the interest will be added to the loan's principal balance.

Title IV debt Student financial aid authorized by the Higher Education Act of 1965 (later amended) and administered by the U.S. Department of Education. It includes the federal Perkins Loan, federal Parent PLUS Loan, federal Stafford Loan, and federal Graduate PLUS Loan.

Undergraduate Postsecondary education up to the level of a bachelor's degree.

Unsubsidized loan A federal loan for which the borrower is fully responsible for paying the interest regardless of the loan status. Interest on unsubsidized loans accrues from the date of disbursement and continues throughout the life of the loan.

Variable interest rate An interest rate that fluctuates according to changes in an index rate. A variable interest rate may or may not have a cap on how high the interest rate can increase or a floor on how low the interest rate can decrease. Beginning July 1, 2013, federal student loans have variable interest rates, with the exception of the fixed-rate federal Perkins Loan.

Verification The verification process is completed by college financial aid counselors and confirms data that applicants report on the FAFSA. The school has the authority to contact applicants for documentation to support income and other information that was reported.

Wage garnishment Withholding a portion of earnings to collect on unpaid debts.

William D. Ford Federal Direct Loan Program A federal program that provides loans to eligible student and parent borrowers under Title IV of the Higher Education Act. Funds are provided by the federal government to eligible borrowers through participating schools.

Work-Study The Federal Work-Study program is a federally funded student aid program in the United States that assists students with the costs of postsecondary education. It helps enrolled students earn financial funding through a part-time work program.

Select Bibliography

ACT Research. 2013. *The Reality of College Readiness 2013 National.* http://www.act.org/readinessreality/13/pdf/Reality-of-College-Readiness-2013.pdf. Accessed August 23, 2013.

Agrawal, Tanya. 2013. "Sallie Mae to split into two companies, names new CEO." (May 29.) http://www.reuters.com/article/2013/05/29/us-salliemae-ceo-idUSBRE94S13Y20130529. Accessed November 9, 2013.

American Student Assistance. n.d. "Student Loan Debt Statistics." http://www.asa.org/policy/resources/stats/. Accessed June 11, 2013.

AnnualCreditReport.com. n.d. Free Credit Report. http://www.annualcreditreport.com. Accessed August 30, 2013.

Armstrong, Elizabeth A., and Laura T. Hamilton. 2013. *Paying for the Party—How College Maintains Inequality.* Cambridge, MA: Harvard University Press.

Baker, Jeff. 2013. "Update on Direct Loan Interest Rates Effective July 1, 2013." IFAP. (August 9.) http://ifap.ed.gov/eannouncements/ 080913DirectLoanInterestRate2013t2014Eff070113.html. Accessed August 16, 2013.

Benjamin, Michael A. 2007. *The Student Lending, Accountability, Transparency and Enforcement Act.* New York State Assembly. http://assembly.state.ny.us/member_files/079/20080226/. Accessed June 8, 2013.

Bennett, William J., and David Wilezol. 2013. *Is College Worth It?* Nashville, TN: Thomas Nelson.

The Best Colleges. 2013. "The 50 Most Amazing College Campuses for 2013." (September 30.) http://www.thebestcolleges.org/most-beautiful-campuses/. Accessed October 20, 2013.

Bissonnette, Zac. 2010. *Debt Free U*. New York: Penguin.

Blackburn, Virginia. 2007. "Cautionary Tales of the Student Debt Crisis." http://www.bvu.edu/admissions/financial-assistance/credit-management.dot. Accessed August 18, 2013.

BookRenter. n.d. http://www.bookrenter.com. Accessed November 7, 2013.

Buena Vista University. n.d. "Credit Management." http://www.bvu.edu/admissions/financial-assistance/credit-management.dot. Accessed August 18, 2013.

Burd, Stephen. 2006. "As the volume of private loans soars, students feel the pinch." (September 22.) http://www.chronicle.com/article/As-the-Volume-of-Private-Loans/33814. Accessed July 27, 2013.

Career Solvers. 2013. "Average Starting Salary for New College Grads Increases 5.3 Percent." http://www.careersolvers.com/blog/2013/04/19/average-starting-salary-for-new-college-grads-increases-5-3-percent/. Accessed September 6, 2013.

CFPB Web Team. 2013. "Proposed Clarifications of the Ability to Repay/QM and Mortgage Servicing Rules." (April 19.) Consumer Financial Protection Bureau. http://www.consumerfinance.gov/blog/proposed-clarifications-of-the-ability-to-repayqm-and-mortgage-servicing-rules/. Accessed August 28, 2013.

Charter One Private Student Loans. n.d. http://charterone.com/student-services/. Accessed August 30, 2013.

Chegg. n.d. http://www.chegg.com/. Accessed November 7, 2013.

Chopra, Rohit. 2013a. "Explainer: Scoring student loan servicers." Consumer Financial Protection Bureau. (September 23.) http://www.consumerfinance.gov/blog/scoring-student-loan-servicers. Accessed September 26, 2013.

Chopra, Rohit. 2013b. "Student Debt Swells, Federal Loans Now Top a Trillion." Consumer Financial Protection Bureau. (July 17.) http://www.consumerfinance.gov/speeches/student-debt-swells-federal-loans-now-top-a-trillion/. Accessed August 27, 2013.

Chronicle of Higher Education. 2011. "Faculty: Median Earnings by Major and Subject Area." (May 23.) http://chronicle.com/article/Median-Earnings-by-Major-and/127604/. Accessed September 2, 2013.

Citizens Bank. n.d. Citizens Bank Private Student Loans. http://www.citizens bank.com/student-services/. Accessed August 30, 2013.

College Affordability and Transparency Center. n.d. http://collegecost.ed.gov. Accessed September 5, 2013.

College Board Advocacy & Policy Center. 2007. "Trends in Student Aid 2007." http://www.collegeboard.com/prod_downloads/about/news_info/trends/trends_aid_07.pdf. Accessed June 2, 2013.

College Board Advocacy & Policy Center. 2009. "Trend in Student Aid 2009." http://advocacy.collegeboard.org/sites/default/files/2009_Trends_Student_Aid_report_0.pdf. Accessed October 28, 2013.

College Board Advocacy & Policy Center. 2012. "Trends in Student Aid 2012." http://trends.collegeboard.org/sites/default/files/student-aid-2012-full-report.pdf. Accessed June 4, 2013.

College Board Advocacy & Policy Center. n.d.-a. "Trends in Higher Education." http://trends.collegeboard.org. Accessed June 23, 2013.

College Board Advocacy & Policy Center. n.d.-b. "Tuition and Fee and Room and Board Charges Over Time in Current Dollars and in 2012 Dollars." http://trends.collegeboard.org/college-pricing/figures-tables/tuition-and-fee-and-room-and-board-charges-over-time. Accessed August 31, 2013.

Condon, Stephanie. 2013. "Student loan saga over after Obama signs bill." CBS News. (August 9.) http://www.cbsnews.com/8301-250_162-57597826/student-loan-saga-over-after-obama-signs-bill/. Accessed August 13, 2013.

Congress.gov. 2013. "S546—Smarter Borrowing Act." (Introduced March 13.) http://beta.congress.gov/bill/113th-congress/senate-bill/546. Accessed August 1, 2013.

Congressional Budget Office. 2013. H.R. 1911, Bipartisan Student Loan Certainty Act of 2013. http://www.cbo.gov/publication/44442. Accessed August 16, 2013.

Congressman Tom Petri. 2012. "Student Loan Bill." (April 16.) http://petri.house.gov/studentloans. Accessed July 10, 2013.

Consumer Financial Protection Bureau. 2011. "Know Before You Owe: Student Loans Project." http://www.consumerfinance.gov/students/knowbeforeyouowe/. Accessed July 31, 2013.

Consumer Financial Protection Bureau. 2012. *Private Student Loans Report*. (July 19.) http://www.consumerfinance.gov/reports/private-student-loans-report/. Accessed July 31, 2013.

Consumer Financial Protection Bureau. 2013. *Student Loan Affordability: Analysis of Public Input on Impact and Solutions*. (May 8.) http://files.consumer finance.gov/f/201305_cfpb_rfi-report_student-loans.pdf. Accessed August 1, 2013.

Consumer Financial Protection Bureau. n.d. "Paying for College." http://www.consumerfinance.gov/paying-for-college/repay-student-debt/#Question-1. Accessed September 26, 2013.

Consumer Reports. 2013. "Student Loan Borrowers Shouldn't Get a Degree in Debt." (March.) http://www.consumerreports.org/cro/2013/03/student-loan-borrowers-shouldn-t-get-a-degree-in-debt/index.htm. Accessed June 4, 2013.

Cornett, Brandon. 2013. "Borrowers with Debt-to-Income Ratios Above 43% Squeezed Out of Mortgage Market." Home-Buying Institute. (January 14.) http://www.homebuyinginstitute.com/news/fha-debt-to-income-296/. Accessed July 9, 2013.

Couch, Christina. 2011. "College Debt: How Much Is Too Much?" Fox Business. (April 27.) http://www.foxbusiness.com/personal-finance/2011/04/21/college-debt-1576872568/. Accessed August 31, 2013.

Couch, Christina. n.d. "Facing student loan debt and retirement." Bankrate. http://www.bankrate.com/finance/student-loans/student-loan-debt-retirement.aspx. Accessed August 31, 2013.

Coy, Peter. 2012. "The Needless Tragedy of Student Loan Defaults." *Bloomberg Businessweek*. (November 28.) http://www.businessweek.com/articles/2012-11-28/the-needless-tragedy-of-student-loan-defaults. Accessed September 13, 2013.

Day, Jennifer Cheeseman, and Eric C. Newburger. 2002. *The Big Payoff: Educational Attainment and Synthetic Estimates of Work-Life Earnings*. U.S. Census Bureau. (July.) http://www.census.gov/prod/2002pubs/p23-210.pdf. Accessed September 6, 2013.

Debt.org. n.d. "Pell Grants." http://www.debt.org/students/pell-grants/. Accessed July 27, 2013.

DefendYourDollars.org. 2013. "New legislation looks to strengthen student loan counseling standards." (March 13.) http://defendyourdollars.org/press_release/new-legislation-looks-to-strengthen-student-loan-counseling-standards. Accessed August 15, 2013.

Denhart, Chris. 2013. "How the $1.2 Trillion College Debt Crisis Is Crippling Students, Parents and the Economy." *Forbes*. (August 7.) http://forbes.com/

sites/specialfeatures/2013/08/07/how-the-college-debt-is-crippling-students-parents-and-the-economy/. Accessed September 28, 2013.

Discover Student Loans. n.d. Private Student Loans for College. CFA10.docx http://www.discover.com/student-loans/. Accessed June 13, 2013.

ED Pubs. n.d. "Order Free U.S. Department of Education Publications." http://www.edpubs.gov/default.aspx. Accessed October 20, 2013.

Ellis, Blake. 2012. "Parents to college kids: Live at home, get a job." CNN Money. (August 29.) http://money.cnn.com/2012/08/29/pf/college/parents-college-debt/index.html. Accessed August 24, 2013.

Ellis, Blake. 2013. "Class of 2013 grads average $35,200 in total debt." CNN Money. (May 17.) http://money.cnn.com/2013/05/17/pf/college/student-debt/index.html. Accessed June 30, 2013.

English, Cynthia. 2011. "Most Americans See College as Essential to Getting a Good Job." Gallup. (August 18.) http://www.gallup.com/poll/149045/Americans-College-Essential-Getting-Good-Job.aspx. Accessed July 31, 2013.

Equifax Credit Bureau. n.d. www.equifax.com. Accessed August 30, 2013.

Experian Credit Bureau. n.d. www.experian.com. Accessed August 30, 2013.

FAFSA. 2013. Application for Federal Student Aid, 2013–2014. http://www.fafsa.ed.gov/fotw1314/pdf/PdfFafsa13-14.pdf. Accessed July 31, 2013.

FAFSA. n.d.-a. "Expected Family Contribution." http://www.fafsa.ed.gov/help/fftoc01g.htm. Accessed September 2, 2013.

FAFSA. n.d.-b. Free Application for Federal Student Aid. http://www.fafsa.ed.gov/. Accessed July 31, 2013.

FAFSA4caster. n.d. http://studentaid.ed.gov/fafsa/estimate. Accessed August 23, 2013.

Fairbanks, Amanda M. 2011. "College Grads Moving Home, Saddled with Historic Levels of Student Loan Debt." *Huffington Post*. (May 24.) http://www.huffingtonpost.com/2011/05/13/college-graduates-moving-home-debt_n_861849.html. Accessed July 1, 2013.

Fairchild, Caroline, and Tom Keene. 2012. "Student Loan Debt Tied to U.S. Home Sales Lag, Soss Says." *Bloomberg*. (July 24.) http://www.bloomberg.com/news/2012-07-24/student-loan-debt-tied-to-u-s-home-sales-lag-soss-says.html. Accessed August 28, 2013.

Federal Reserve. 2012. "Regulation Z—Truth in Lending." (June.) http://www.federalreserve.gov/boarddocs/supmanual/cch/til.pdf. Accessed July 16, 2013.

Federal Reserve. 2013. *Federal Reserve Statistical Release.* (September 3.) http://www.federalreserve.gov/releases/H15/current/h15.pdf. Accessed September 6, 2013.

Federal Student Aid. 1997a. "Entrance Counseling Guide for Counselors." (July.) http://ifap.ed.gov/dlpamphlets/doc0003_bodyoftext.htm. Accessed September 13, 2013.

Federal Student Aid. 1997b. "Exit Counseling Guide for Counselors." (July). http://www.ifap.ed.gov/dlpamphlets/doc0005_bodyoftext.htm. Accessed September 13, 2013.

Federal Student Aid. 1997c. "Information and Counseling for Borrowers," 1997–1998. http://ifap.ed.gov/dlsguides/doc0043_bodyoftext.htm. Accessed September 13, 2013.

Federal Student Aid. n.d.-a. "About Us." http://studentaid.ed.gov/about. Accessed September 2, 2013.

Federal Student Aid. n.d.-b. "Adverse Credit History." http://studentaid.ed.gov/glossary#Adverse_Credit_History. Accessed August 31, 2013.

Federal Student Aid. n.d.-c. "Aid for Military Families." http://studentaid.ed.gov/types/grants-scholarships/military. Accessed August 31, 2013.

Federal Student Aid. n.d.-d. "Current Consolidation Interest Rate." http://loanconsolidation.ed.gov/help/rate.html. Accessed August 31, 2013.

Federal Student Aid. n.d.-e. "Direct Loans." http://www.direct.ed.gov. Accessed June 23, 2013.

Federal Student Aid. n.d.-f. "Basic Eligibility Criteria." http://studentaid.ed.gov/eligibility/basic-criteria. Accessed October 20, 2013.

Federal Student Aid. n.d.-g. "Federal Direct Consolidation Loans." https://loanconsolidation.ed.gov. Accessed June 23, 2013.

Federal Student Aid. n.d.-h. Federal Student Aid. http://studentaid.ed.gov. Accessed January 16, 2013.

Federal Student Aid. n.d.-i. "Forgiveness, Cancellation, and Discharge." http://studentaid.ed.gov/repay-loans/forgiveness-cancellation. Accessed June 23, 2013.

Federal Student Aid. n.d.-j. "Subsidized and Unsubsidized Loans." http://www.studentaid.ed.gov/types/loans/subsidized-unsubsidized. Accessed January 14, 2013.

Federal Student Aid n.d.-k. "PIN Web site." http://www.pin.ed.gov/PINWebApp/pinindex.jsp. Accessed October 20, 2013.

Federal Student Aid. n.d.-l. "Repay Your Loans." http://studentaid.ed.gov/repay-loans. Accessed August 27, 2013.

FedPrimeRate.com. n.d. "Prime Interest Rate History." http://www.fedprimerate.com/wall_street_journal_prime_rate_history.htm. Accessed August 16, 2013.

FinAid. n.d.-a. "Credit Scores." http://www.finaid.org/loans/creditscores.phtml. Accessed July 7, 2013.

FinAid. n.d.-b. "Direct Loans vs. the FFEL Program." http://www.finaid.org/loans/dl-vs-ffel.phtml. Accessed July 9, 2013.

FinAid. n.d.-c. "Guide to Financial Aid Award Letters." http://www.finaid.org/fafsa/awardletters.phtml. Accessed August 21, 2012.

FinAid. n.d.-d. "History of Student Financial Aid." http://www.finaid.org/educators/history.phtml. Accessed July 15, 2013.

FinAid. n.d.-e. "Loan Calculator." http://www.finaid.org/calculators/loanpayments.phtml. Accessed October 20, 2013.

FinAid. n.d.-f. "Parent Loans." http://www.finaid.org/loans/parentloan.phtml. Accessed August 31, 2013.

FinAid. n.d.-g. "Private Student Loan Consolidation." http://www.finaid.org/loans/privateconsolidation.phtml. Accessed July 18, 2013.

FinAid. n.d.-h. "Private Student Loans." http://www.finaid.org/loans/privatestudentloans.phtml. Accessed January 15, 2013.

FinAid. n.d.-i. "Public Service Loan Forgiveness." http://www.finaid.org/loans/publicservice.phtml. Accessed August 31, 2013.

FinAid. n.d.-j. "Single Holder Rule Loopholes." http://www.finaid.org/loans/singleholderrule.phtml. Accessed October 28, 2013.

FinAid. n.d.-k. "Student Loan Discounts." http://www.finaid.org/loans/studentloandiscounts.phtml. Accessed August 15, 2013.

FinAid. n.d.-l. "Student Loans." http://www.finaid.org/loans. Accessed June 23, 2013.

FinAid. n.d.-m. "Taxability of Student Loan Forgiveness." http://www.finaid.org/loans/forgivenesstaxability.phtml. Accessed July 10, 2013.

FinAid. n.d.-n. "What can you do if your parents refuse to help?" http://www.finaid.org/otheraid/parentsrefuse.phtml. Accessed August 12, 2013.

Financial Aid Guide. 2012. Iowa College Access Network, 2012–2013. http://www.icansucceed.org. Accessed August 30, 2013.

FindLaw. n.d. "Consequences of a Student Loan Default." http://bankruptcy.findlaw.com/debt-relief/consequences-of-a-student-loan-default.html. Accessed June 17, 2013.

FindTheData. n.d. American Community Survey—Average Rent in the United States. http://acs-housing-state.findthedata.org/app-question/2351/What-is-the-average-rent-in-the-United-States. Accessed August 2, 2013.

Franken, Senator Al. 2013. "Sens. Franken, Harkin, Mikulski Introduce Legislation to Improve Student Loan Counseling." (March 13.) http://www.franken.senate.gov/?p=press_release&id=2324. Accessed August 1, 2013.

Fry, Richard. 2013. "A Rising Share of Young Adults Live in Their Parents' Home." Pew Research Social & Demographic Trends. (August 1.) http://pewsocialtrends.org/2013/08/01/a-rising-share-of-young-adults-live-in-their-parents-home/. Accessed August 22, 2013.

Golden, Alana. 2013. Student Debt Movie: Face the Red with SALTmoney.org. California Financial Literacy Month Blog. (October 24). http://caflm.blogs.ca.gov/2013/10/24/student-debt-movie-face-the-red-with-salt/. Accessed October 25, 2013.

Gongloff, Mark. 2013. "Student Loan Debt Tenacious as U.S. Households Shed Other Debt: Study." *Huffington Post*. (May 14.) http://www.huffingtonpost.com/2013/05/14/student-loan-debt_n_3274377.html. Accessed August 1, 2013.

Goodman, Leah McGrath. 2008. "The Billionaire's Black Sheep." *Marie Claire*. (December 11.) http://www.marieclaire.com/world-reports/news/warren-buffett-granddaughter-nicole-buffett. Accessed July 29, 2013.

GovTrack.us. 2012. S. 3244 (112th): Understanding the True Cost of College Act of 2012. http://www.govtrack.us/congress/bills/112/s3244/text. Accessed July 31, 2013

Gray, Michael. 2012. "A record $1 trillion of student-loan debt is being carried by college and grad school alums: NY Fed." *New York Post*. (December 10.) http://www.nypost.com/p/news/business/in_school_loans_EGQu18uJk1w1VTHLayRcLK. Accessed July 17, 2013.

Groux, Catherine. 2012. "Employers more accepting of online degrees." *U.S. News and World Report* University Directory. (July 10.) http://www.usnewsuniversitydirectory.com/articles/employers-more-accepting-of-online-degrees_12500.aspx. Accessed September 2, 2013.

Hacker, Andrew, and Claudia Dreifus. 2011. *Higher Education? How Colleges Are Wasting Our Money and Failing Our Kids—and What We Can Do About It.* New York: St. Martin's Press.

HCM Strategists. 2012. *The American Dream 2.0: How Financial Aid Can Help Improve College Access, Affordability, and Completion.* http://www.hcmstrategists.com/americandream2-0/report/HCM_Gates_Report_1_17_web.pdf, http://americandream2-0.com. Accessed August 27, 2013.

Hechinger, John, and Janet Lorin. 2012. "Student-Loan Default Rates Rise as Federal Scrutiny Grows." *Bloomberg.* (September 28.) http://www.bloomberg.com/news/2012-09-28/student-loan-defaults-soar-as-government-scrutiny-grow.html. Accessed July 20, 2013.

Hechinger, John, and Janet Lorin. 2013. "Sallie Mae Split Marks Bet on Abused Private Student Loans." *Bloomberg.* (May 31.) http://www.bloomberg.com/news/2013-05-31/sallie-mae-split-marks-bet-on-much-abused-private-student-loans.html. Accessed August 30, 2013.

Higuera, Valencia. n.d. "Do You Need Your Parents to Cosign on a Federal School Loan?" eHow. http://www.ehow.com/info_12085558_need-parents-cosign-federal-school-loan.html. Accessed August 31, 2013.

Holland, Kelley. 2013. "The most expensive colleges in America—really." CNBC. (July 11.) http://www.cnbc.com/id/100880127. Accessed July 12, 2013.

HometownSource.com. 2013. "Sen. Franken introduces legislation to improve student loan counseling." (March 13.) www.hometownsource.com/2013/03/13/sen-franken-introduces-legislation-to-improve-student-loan-counseling/. Accessed August 1, 2013.

Huffington, Arianna. 2011. "Back to school and deeper in debt." *Huffington Post.* (September 6.) http://www.huffingtonpost.com/arianna-huffington/back-to-school-and-deeper-in-debt_b_951205.html. Accessed September 6, 2013.

Huffington Post. 2012. "Cost of College Degree in U.S. Has Increased 1,120 Percent in 30 Years, Report Says." (August 15.) http://www.huffingtonpost.com/2012/08/15/cost-of-college-degree-increase-12-fold-1120-percent-bloomberg_n_1783700.html. Accessed August 30, 2013.

Jaschik, Scott. 2007. "Bucking the Tide on Private Loans." Inside Higher Ed. (July 16.) http://www.insidehighered.com/news/2007/07/16/barnard. Accessed July 7, 2013.

Jaschik, Scott. 2013. "Obama's Ratings for Higher Ed." Inside Higher Ed. (August 22.) http://www.insidehighered.com/news/2013/08/22/president-obama-proposes-link-student-aid-new-ratings-colleges. Accessed August 22, 2013.

Jensen, Carol. 2008. *Private Loan Counseling for Undergraduate Students: The Role of College Financial Aid Counselors.* PhD dissertation, University of Nebraska. http://www.eric.ed.gov/ERICWebPortal/search/detailmini.jsp?_nfpb=true& _&ERICExtSearch_SearchValue_0=ED503771&ERICExtSearch_SearchType _0=no&accno=ED503771. CFA10.docxAccessed May 15, 2013.

Jensen, Carol. 2010. "Private Loan Counseling for Undergraduate Students: The Role of College Financial Aid Counselors." *Enrollment Management Journal.* (Summer.) http://www.tgslc.org/pdf/emj-s10-counseling.pdf. Accessed July 31, 2013.

Jerousek, Madelaine. 2003. "Loans, Easy Credit Fuel Student Debt." *Des Moines Register.* (February 24.) http://www.bus.iastate.edu/news/2003/022403.asp. Accessed June 8, 2013.

Kingkade, Tyler. 2012. "Pell Grants Cover Smallest Portion of College Costs in History as GOP Calls for Cuts." *Huffington Post.* (August 29.) http://www .huffingtonpost.com/2012/08/27/pell-grants-college-costs_n_1835081.html. Accessed August 30, 2013.

Kingkade, Tyler. 2013. "Student Loan Debt: New Reports Find 'Unsustainable' Trend Dragging Economy." *Huffington Post.* (January 31.) http://www .huffingtonpost.com/2013/01/31/student-loan-debt-unsustainable_n _2593303.html. Accessed July 31, 2013.

Lederman, Doug. 2006. "Private Lender Accused of Misleading Students." Inside Higher Ed. (September 28.) http://www.insidehighered.com/news/2006/09 /28/loans. Accessed July 31, 2013.

Lewin, Tamar. 2011. "College Graduation Rates Are Stagnant Even as Enrollment Rises, a Study Finds." *New York Times.* (September 27.) http://dl.drop boxusercontent.com/u/28697036/The%20New%20York%20Times%20%20 -%20College%20Graduation%20Rates%20Are%20Stagnant%2C%20Even% 20as%20Enrollment%20Rises%2C%209.27.11.pdf. Accessed October 20, 2013.

Lexington. 2013. "The American Dream, RIP?" *Economist.* (September 21–27.) http://www.economist.com/news/united-states/21586581-economist-asks -provocative-questions-about-future-social-mobility-american. Accessed October 20, 2013.

Longley, Robert. 2010. "Lifetime Earnings Soar with Education." About.com— U.S. Government Info. (February 13; updated August 17, 2013.) http:// usgovinfo.about.com/od/moneymatters/a/edandearnings.htm. Accessed September 6, 2013.

Lorin, Janet. 2012. "Forty Percent of Student Loan Borrowers Don't Get Advice." *BusinessWeek*. (October 11.) http://www.businessweek.com/news/2012-10-11/forty-percent-of-student-loan-borrowers-dont-get-advice. Accessed August 28, 2013.

Ma, Jennifer, and Sandy Baum. 2012. "Trends in Tuition and Fees, Enrollment, and State Appropriations for Higher Education by State." College Board Advocacy & Policy Center—Analysis Brief. (July.) http://advocacy.collegeboard.org/sites/default/files/12b_5761_TrendsByState_AnalysisBrief_WEB_120719.pdf. Accessed September 2, 2013.

Meacham, Jon, Eliza Gray, Maya Rhodan. 2013. "The Class of 2025: How They'll Learn and What They'll Pay." *Time* 182, no. 15 (October 7).

Meyerowitz, Steven. 2011. "Elizabeth Warren Announces Initiative to Combine Mortgage Loan Disclosures." Financial Fraud Law. (May 18.) http://www.financialfraudlaw.com/lawblog/elizabeth-warren-announces-initiative-combine-mortgage-loan-disclosures/2306. Accessed June 4, 2013.

Mui, Ylan Q. 2012. "Durbin targets private student loan defaults." *Washington Post*. (March 20.) http://articles.washingtonpost.com/2012-03-20/business/35447206_1_student-loans-private-student-loan-debt-student-loan-interest-rates. Accessed July 31, 2013.

National Association of Colleges and Employers (NACE). 2013. *NACE Salary Survey: Starting Salaries for New College Graduates*. (April.) http://www.naceweb.org/uploadedFiles/NACEWeb/Research/Salary_Survey/Reports/salary-survey-april-2013-executive-summary.pdf. Accessed September 2, 2013.

National Association of State Student Grant & Aid Programs. n.d. http://www.nassgap.org/links.aspx. Accessed July 18, 2013.

National Center for Education Statistics (NCES). 2012. "Income of young adults." U.S. Department of Education. http://nces.ed.gov/fastfacts/display.asp?id=77. Accessed July 12, 2013.

National Center for Education Statistics. n.d.-a. "College Navigator." http://nces.ed.gov/collegenavigator/. Accessed September 6, 2013.

National Center for Education Statistics. n.d.-b. "Digest of Education Statistics." http://nces.ed.gov/programs/digest/d11/tables/dt11_349.asp. Accessed September 2, 2013.

National Center for Education Statistics. n.d.-c. "Fast Facts." http://nces.ed.gov/FastFacts/display.asp?id=76. Accessed July 1, 2013.

Nawaguna, Elvina. 2013. "Senate approves deal to reverse spike in student loan rates." Reuters. (July 24.) http://www.reuters.com/article/2013/07/24/us-usa-studentloans-deal-idUSBRE96N1J920130724. Accessed July 31, 2013.

Nelson, Libby. 2013. "Federal Student Loan Debt Tops $1 Trillion." *Politico*. (July 17.) http://www.politico.com/story/2013/07/student-loan-debt-tops-1-trillion-94316.html. Accessed September 27, 2013.

New York State Assembly. 2008. "The Student Lending, Accountability, Transparency and Enforcement (SLATE) Act." http://assembly.state.ny.us/member_files/079/20080226/. Accessed July 10, 2013.

New York State Office of Higher Education. 2008. "New York State Participation in the 2008 National Postsecondary Student Aid Study." (March.) http://www.highered.nysed.gov/memos/memo032008.html. Accessed June 8, 2013.

Noss, Amanda. 2012. Household Income for States: 2010 and 2011. U.S. Census Bureau. (September.) http://www.census.gov. Accessed August 24, 2013.

OptOutPrescreen.com. n.d. "OptOutPrescreen." https://www.optoutprescreen.com/?rf=t. Accessed October 20, 2013.

O'Shaughnessy, Lynn. 2013. "Student loans reach another troubling milestone." CBS MoneyWatch. (July 18.) http://www.cbsnews.com/8301-500395_162-57594250/student-loans-reach-another-troubling-milestone/. Accessed August 31, 2013.

Owens, Eric. 2012. "Survey shows 40 percent of college students don't receive required loan counseling." *Daily Caller*. (October 23.) http://dailycaller.com/2012/10/23/survey-shows-40-percent-of-college-students-dont-receive-required-loan-counseling/. Accessed August 28, 2013.

ParentPLUSLoan.com. n.d.-a. "PLUS Loan Deferment." http://www.parentplusloan.com/repayment/deferment.php. Accessed August 27, 2013.

ParentPLUSLoans.com. n.d.-b. "PLUS Loans: Federal Loan for Parents Introduction." http://www.parentplusloan.com/plus-loans/. Accessed August 24, 2013.

Petri, Rep. Tom. 2012. The Earnings Contingent Education Loans (ExCEL) Act. http://petri.house.gov/sites/petri.house.gov/files/documents/ExCELAct-SummaryAndFAQ-12-17-2012%20%282%29.pdf. Accessed July 23, 2013.

PNC Education Loan Center. n.d. Private Loans for Undergraduates. http://www.pnconcampus.com/studentloanguide/privateloans/undergraduates/index.html. Accessed June 13, 2013.

Post, Tim. 2010. "Students Rely More on Grandparents to Help Pay for College." Minnesota Public Radio News. (August 23.) http://minnesota.publicradio.org/display/web/2010/08/22/families-paying-for-college. Accessed July 15, 2013.

The Project on Student Debt. 2008. *Student Debt and the Class of 2007*. (October.) http://www.projectonstudentdebt.org/files/pub/classof2007.pdf. Accessed July 10, 2013.

The Project on Student Debt. 2009. *Student Debt and the Class of 2008*. (December.) http://www.projectonstudentdebt.org/files/pub/classof2008.pdf. Accessed July 10, 2013.

The Project on Student Debt. 2010a. *Bankruptcy and The Private Student Loan Market*. Institute for College Access & Success. CFA10.docx http://projectonstudentdebt.org/files/pub/Bankruptcy_the_Private_Student_Loan_Market_April_2010.pdf. Accessed July 10, 2013.

The Project on Student Debt. 2010b. *Student Debt and the Class of 2009*. (October.) http://www.projectonstudentdebt.org/files/pub/classof2009.pdf. Accessed July 10, 2013.

The Project on Student Debt. 2011a. *Private Loans: Facts and Trends*. (July.) http://projectonstudentdebt.org/files/pub/private_loan_facts_trends_09.pdf. Accessed July 10, 2013.

The Project on Student Debt. 2011b. *Student Debt and the Class of 2010*. (November.) http://www.projectonstudentdebt.org/files/pub/classof2010.pdf. Accessed July 10, 2013.

The Project on Student Debt. 2012. *Student Debt and the Class of 2011*. Institute for College Access & Success. http://www.projectonstudentdebt.org/files/pub/classof2011.pdf. Accessed July 10, 2013.

Reed, Matthew, Lauren Asher, Seth Frotman, Debbie Cochrane. 2011. *Critical Choices: How Colleges Can Help Students and Families Make Better Decisions about Private Loans*. The Project on Student Debt. (July.) http://projectonstudentdebt.org/files/pub/critical_choices.pdf. Accessed June 11, 2013.

Reif, L. Rafael. 2013. "Online Learning Will Make College Cheaper. It Will Also Make It Better." *Time* 182, no. 15 (October 7).

Ritt, Adam. n.d. "Can You Still Help Pay for College?" Grandparents.com. http://www.grandparents.com/money-and-work/family%20finance/you-can-still-help-pay-for-college. Accessed July 15, 2013.

Sallie Mae. n.d. Private Student Loans for Undergraduates. https://www.salliemae.com/student-loans/. Accessed August 30, 2013.

SBA.gov. n.d. "Pre-Employment Background Checks." U.S. Small Business Administration. http://www.sba.gov/content/performing-pre-employment-background-checks. Accessed October 19, 2013.

Scheer, Marc. 2008. *No Sucker Left Behind: Avoiding the Great College Rip-Off.* Monroe, ME: Common Courage Press.

Schoof, Renee. 2013. "New App Calculates the True Costs of College." McClatchy DC. (October 10.) http://www.mcclatchydc.com/2013/10/10/204989/lifting-the-veil-off-the-true.html. Accessed October 12, 2013.

Selingo, Jeffrey J. 2013. *College Unbound: The Future of Higher Education and What It Means for Students.* New York: Houghton Mufflin Harcourt Publishing Co.

Silver, Assembly Speaker Sheldon. 2007. "Announcing Introduction of 'The Student Lending Accountability, Transparency and Enforcement (SLATE) Act.'" Press conference. (April 16.) http://assembly.state.ny.us/Press/20070416/. Accessed June 8, 2013.

Simon, Ruth, Rachel Louise Ensign, Al Yoon. 2013. "Student-Loan Securities Stay Hot." *Wall Street Journal.* (March 4.) http://online.wsj.com/news/articles/SB10001424127887323293704578334542910674174.

Sourmaidis, Demetrios. 2013. "Shifting Trends between Private and Federal Loans." Student Debt Relief. http://www.studentdebtrelief.us/news/shifting-trends-between-private-and-federal-loans/. Accessed August 28, 2013.

Stratford, Michael. 2012. "Default Rate on Federal Student Loans Rises Again." *Chronicle of Higher Education.* (September 30.) http://chronicle.com/article/Default-Rate-on-Federal/134786/. Accessed June 8, 2013.

StudentAds.com. 2012. "Private Student Loans for College." Student Loan Information. http://loans.studentads.com/l/Personal-Student-Loans. Accessed January 15, 2013.

Student Lending Analytics. 2012. "Private Loan Options." http://studentlendinganalytics.com/alternative_loan_options.html. Accessed August 29, 2013.

Student Loan Borrower Assistance. n.d. "License Revocations." http://www.studentloanborrowerassistance.org/collections/government-collection-tools/license-revocations/. Accessed June 24, 2013.

SunTrust. n.d. Education Loans. https://www.suntrust.com/personalbanking/loans/educationloans. Accessed June 13, 2013.

Supiano, Beckie. 2011. "What Are You Going to Do With That?" *Chronicle of Higher Education.* (May 24.) http://chronicle.com/article/Whats-a-Degree-Worth-Report/127612/. Accessed July 12, 2013.

SwitchYard Media. n.d. "Ten incredibly pricey college dorms." MSN Money. http://money.msn.com/family-money/10-incredibly-pricey-college-dorms. Accessed August 14, 2013.

Texas Guaranteed Student Loan Corporation. n.d.-a. "Council for Student Financial Success in Higher Education: Student Loan Counseling Resources." http://www.tgslc.org/council/counseling-resources.cfm. Accessed July 25, 2013.

Texas Guaranteed Student Loan Corporation. n.d.-b. "Private Education Loan Applicant Self-Certification Form." http://www.tgslc.org/forms/self-certification.cfm. Accessed July 18, 2013.

TransUnion Credit Bureau. n.d. http://www.transunion.com. Accessed August 30, 2013.

U.S. Department of Education. 2008. "Higher Education Opportunity Act—2008." http://www2.ed.gov/policy/highered/leg/hea08/index.html. Accessed August 31, 2013.

U.S. Department of Education. 2010. *Funding Education Beyond High School: The Guide to Federal Student Aid 2010–11.* http://www.edpubs.gov/document/EN0913P.pdf. Accessed January 14, 2013.

Vedder, Richard. 2010. "Why Did 17 Million People Go to College?" (October 20.) *Chronicle of Higher Education.* http://chronicle.com/blogs/innovations/why-did-17-million-students-go-to-college/27634. Accessed August 31, 2013.

Wang, Marian, Beckie Supiano, Andrea Fuller. 2012. "Student loans, backed by government, crush many families." NBC News Business. (October 7.) http://www.nbcnews.com/business/student-loans-backed-government-crush-many-families-1C6323932. Accessed August 24, 2013.

Warren, Elizabeth, and Amelia Warren Tyagi. 2003. *The Two-Income Trap: Why Middle-Class Parents Are Going Broke.* New York: Basic Books.

Wegmann, Catherine A., Alisa F. Cunningham, and Jamie P. Merisotis. 2003. *Private Loans and Choice in Financing Higher Education.* ERIC. http://www.eric.ed.gov/ERICWebPortal/search/detailmini.jsp?ERICExtSearch_SearchValue_0=ED478298&ERICExtSearch_SearchType_0=no&accno=ED478298. Accessed July 31, 2013.

Weise, Karen. 2013. "Why Your Student Loan Interest Rate Is So High." *Bloomberg Businessweek.* (April 4.) http://www.businessweek.com/articles/2013-04-04/why-your-student-loan-interest-rate-is-so-high.

Wells Fargo. n.d. "Student Loans for College." https://wellsfargo.com/student/index. Accessed June 13, 2013.

Weston, Liz. 2012. "The Growing Student-Loan Crisis." MSN Money. (September 12). http://money.msn.com/debt-management/the-growing-student-loan-crisis. Accessed September 19, 2012.

Whitsett, Healey C. 2012. *High Debt, Low Information: A Survey of Student Loan Borrowers*. NERA Economic Consulting. (March 21.) http://www.nera.com/nera-files/PUB_Student_Loans_0312.pdf. Accessed June 4, 2013.

Whitsett, Healey C., and Rory O'Sullivan. 2012. *Lost Without a Map: A Survey about Students' Experiences Navigating the Financial Aid Process*. NERA Economic Consulting. (October 11.) http://www.nera.com/nera-files/PUB_Student_Loan_Borrowers_1012.pdf. Accessed June 4, 2013.

Yee, Christopher. 2011. "Middle-class families make sacrifices to afford UC Berkeley education." *Daily Californian*. (November 6.) http://www.dailycal.org/2011/11/06/middle-class-families-make-sacrifices-to-afford-uc-berkeley-education/. Accessed August 24, 2013.

About the Author

CAROL JENSEN holds a PhD in educational leadership and has a master's degree in business administration. Since the early 1980s, her primary career has been in banking. While living in Iowa her entire life, Dr. Jensen has also taught numerous college courses via traditional classroom and online deliveries. She experienced her own decade of "kids, cars, and college" from 1995 to 2005. Carol Jensen can be reached at caroljensen2013@gmail.com.